In Search of the Hermaphrodite

The Hermaphrodite, 1978. Ink and crayons. Cyleste Collins, age 5.

In Search of the Hermaphrodite
A MEMOIR
RICHARD COLLINS

TOUGH POETS PRESS
ARLINGTON, MASSACHUSETTS

Copyright © 2024 by Richard Collins.

All rights reserved.

Part of Chapter 8, "That Was the Kif Talking," previously appeared in *Exquisite Corpse* (Feb/Mar 2000) as "Four Roses for Paul Bowles."

Front cover photo: *Sleeping Hermaphroditus* (detail), 2nd century. The Louvre, Paris. Public domain image.

Back cover photo of the author by David Andrews.

The Timid Proud One, by Asger Jorn (1957) © 2024 Donation Jorn, Silkeborg / Artists Rights Society (ARS), New York / VISDA

ISBN 979-8-218-44527-0

Tough Poets Press
Arlington, Massachusetts 02476
U.S.A.

www.toughpoets.com

To the true loves of my life,
my wife Leigh,
and my daughters
Cyleste and Isabel

Hermaphrodite is an example of *pure myth*, conceived in the mind of man as he groped to find his place in the world and devised the figure best able both to sum up his origins and to symbolise certain of his aspirations.

—Marie Delcourt, *Hermaphrodite*

Chapters

1 / My Sexual Prehistory 11
2 / A Toy of Double Shape. 19
3 / Americans in Ashley Gardens 27
4 / An Obsession Is a Hypothesis 39
5 / Mnemosyne and Mary Poppins 49
6 / London with its Foolscap Crown. 59
7 / Visiting Velázquez in London and Madrid 75
8 / That Was the Kif Talking 95
9 / Mencius of Hyde Park Corner 109
10 / The Dark Night of the Spring 127
11 / The Ex-Beauty Queen's Daughter 143
12 / The Garden of Edinburgh 161
13 / Decadent Interludes 181
14 / *Lysglimt*. 205
15 / Life Is as a Tribe of Birds .219
16 / The Timid Proud One 233
17 / Retrospective 243
18 / Postscript: Epipsychidion 261

Illustrations

The Hermaphrodite, Cyleste Collins . . . . Frontispiece
Hermaphroditus, Anonymous 18
Lady with a Fan, Diego Velázquez.. 74
The Stone Operation (Extracting the Stone of Madness),
    Hieronymus Bosch 94
Sleeping Hermaphroditus, Anonymous 108
Salome with the Head of John the Baptist, Caravaggio. 126
Lamentations Around the Remains of Christ, Anonymous . . . 160
Hylas and the Water Nymphs (detail),
    John William Waterhouse 180
Bacchanal of Satyrs and Cupids, Gerard van Opstal. 203
Maria Magdalene, Carlo Crivelli. 204
The Timid Proud One, Asger Jorn 232

1 / My Sexual Prehistory

> The members of them mingled were and fastned both togither,
> They were not any lenger two: but (as it were) a toy
> Of double shape. Ye could not say it was a perfect boy,
> Nor perfect wench; it seemed both and none of both to beene.
> —Ovid, *Metamorphoses* (IV 367–70)
> Arthur Golding translation (1567)

My brother was a mythographical liar. I never knew when he was serious. When he returned from Vietnam in 1966 he was full of tales, some taller than others. This scar, for which he received a medal, was the result of a firefight on the edge of the jungle (false: it was actually earned dancing Zorba the Greek style in the back of a truck, which hit a bump and bounced him onto the dark road, drunk). If you stare into the sun, you will go blind (true). The correct spelling of *airplane*, he said, is *aeroplane* (false: in the U.S.; true: in Britain) or *arrowplane* (true: in DC Comics). His cure for crablice involved a razor, a cigarette lighter, and an icepick (I will spare you the unpleasant details, but I suspect this was false). And if you have sex with a girl underwater, he said, you will stick together like dogs in the yard, and surgeons will have to separate you.

The last lie lodged somewhere in my mind deep enough that when I discovered Ovid's myth of Hermaphroditus I was hooked without ever consciously connecting it to my brother's mythmaking. I'm sure Ernie had never read how the pubescent son of Hermes and Aphrodite was traveling one day when he stopped to cool himself in an Anatolian spring, where the nymph Salmacis saw him, wanted him, and had him against his will—underwater. She enjoyed the experience so much that she asked the gods to keep them joined together in this way forever, inseparable, and thus—thanks to the gods' mercurial and venereal sense of humor—the figure of double sex came to be. Anyway, that is one origin story of many.

Ernie no doubt was just mining his own insecurities in his memorable tale of penis captivus, or just passing along some suburban sex myth. But it is indicative of the reproductive power of the overendowed figure that it could take root and blossom in such disparate eras and locales as Ancient Rome, Elizabethan England, and 1960s San Fernando Valley.

My preoccupation with the image goes even further back (and also forward) in my sexual prehistory to a whole nexus of experiences that together formed what some might consider an obsession. At six years old, for example, I can point to two formative experiences with females that left me astonished for different reasons and, in each case, making my way bewildered down the middle of the road, first in an ecstasy of infatuation, then in an ecstasy of fear.

My first "sexual" dalliance was with Maria in the first grade in Upland, California. I was devastated by Maria's wild flurry of black curls and dark and sparkling eyes like .45s. After school and her Mexican mother's spicy cookies and chocolate milk in the kitchen, we would disappear into the bushes to practice what passed for "making out" to six-year-olds. Afterwards, I fairly danced home down the painted centerline of Campus Avenue, like Gene Kelly singing in the rain. Someone in the role of perplexed patrolman reported to my mother this exhibition of twitterpated bravura, which I never managed to live down.

At about the same period, I found myself in the middle of the street again, this time not out of newly whetted desire but out of abject "sexual" fear. I had just fled the matinee showing of *The Attack of the 50-foot Woman* at the Grove Theatre. When the spurned and cheated-on wife started to grow taller than the buildings and to go on her first rampage, towering over the now Lilliputian men, I slumped out of my seat and escaped the darkened cinema. Although I was now protected by the full light of the sun, I was still petrified. How, I wondered, had She managed not to grow out of her clothes to reveal all that was hidden and forbidden in the shadows of her expanding magnificence? All the way home I was fearful that She would appear over the little frame houses crouched along that sunny street in Southern California. How easily She might stoop over the trees and scoop me up like a mouse! So I ran until I passed the Stone Funeral Home catty-corner to the movie theater, then strode defiantly down the middle of the street, glancing at the treetops, the cars slowing and honking as they steered around me, unable to dislodge me from my middle path.

Those two formative experiences of fear and desire were followed by others still stranger and mysterious.

Perhaps a year later, I was passing Doctor Dight's office, a few doors from the Grove Theatre, when I saw on the ground just outside the threshold what appeared to be a detached fleshy sac, a scrotum in fact. A terrifying sight. Why didn't I examine it further? It might have turned out to be nothing, a dead baby bird, for example, still naked and unfledged, its bald head, rib cage, and subcutaneous blue veins mistaken for detached testicles. If only I had investigated further and discovered it to be some unfortunate newborn bird, I might have filed that nightmare image away in the no-longer-a-mystery drawer. Instead, the specter of castration haunted my preadolescent imagination.

At about thirteen I dreamed of the current sex symbol, curvaceous Ann-Margret, seducing me in a hayloft, kneeling over me and, with that bright and generous Scandinavian smile, offering me first one magnificent breast lifted out of her white shirt tied at the waist, then the other just-as-magnificent breast, and then, finally, from the V of the zipper dentata of her cut-off jeans, an equally magnificent and pendulous member. Of that more later.

At fifteen, childish fun and fears in the past, my adolescent dreams and cultural icons were made flesh in the form of a real woman. Seven years older than me, she was a close friend of the family, so close in fact that what happened could almost be considered incest. One summer she taught me how to swim in the clear blue water of a swimming pool at the apartment she shared with her husband. Buoyed up by her outstretched arms, I paddled and kicked, feeling the nearness of her freckled breasts, water pooling in the warm cleavage. Her long-lashed eyes, laden with mascara, were bright with laughter and her lips were even brighter with luminous orange lipstick. The swimming lesson morphed into something more erotic. I wasn't able to discover, however, whether my brother's mythical fears of penis captivus were true or not since only the subtle half-promises of an unacknowledged foreplay occurred in the water that day. It was months later, in the darkness of a bedroom in my parents' house that she appeared, soft and succulent succubus, and ravished me, as Salmacis ravished Hermaphroditus in Ovid's telling of the myth.[1] The dawning darkness of adolescence exploded into a luminous orange awakening, a blinding sunrise. Lit up by a transformative experience more powerful than anything I could ever have imagined, I was never the same after this initiation. I was as captivated as a dog in the yard: no surgeon (or therapist) could have separated me from my experience of ecstasy.

At sixteen, I had a dream that remains the most vivid of my life. I was an eighteenth-century court jester, performing for a roomful of bosomy, beauty-spotted, and bewigged ladies-in-waiting. Preparing for my chef d'oeuvre, the pièce de résistance of my act, I asked these women not to make any sudden moves or to come nearer to me than they already were. Then, with little more fanfare, I removed

---

[1] This euphemism, "ravishment," used so often by translators of Ovid to soften and romanticize and even excuse the notion of rape, has recently been corrected in the Stephanie McCarter translation of the *Metamorphoses* (New York: Penguin, 2022), which states plainly in the subtitle to the episode in Book IV, "Salmacis Rapes Hermaphroditus." This interpretation of the Latin *vis* (violent force or power) suggests a violation which, in my case, while accurate legally, does not quite capture the psychological ambivalence of this willing victim.

my head, to their titters and more-than-polite applause, and tucked it under my arm.[2] One of the women, disobeying the protocol, came up behind me, looked down inside my neck and, seeing the abyss that gaped there, screamed and fainted. Alarmed, I tried to get my head back on straight and snap it into place but failed, dropping it on the floor. I could feel it bounce on the carpet and roll under a table. As my helpless body groped to find its crown, I watched my arms and legs struggle but I had no control over those detached and flailing appendages. I could not tell the torso where its head was because, of course, while my head still had a mouth and could moan if not better articulate my pain and fear, my estranged body had no ears to hear me with, nor brain to process what I had to say.[3] Slowly, the carpet went in and out of focus, the darkness pulsing deep red into black until I lost consciousness altogether.

No doubt relevant too is the year I worked in the adult bookstore in Hollywood, when every form of sexuality was at my fingertips in the form of erotic words and pictures, from autogynephilia to teratophilia.[4] It was 1974, and I was twenty-one, the year I finally decided to go to college. I spent much of my time behind the counter reading great literature like *Ulysses* and writing bad novels of my own.

---

[2] I had begun to shave around this time. The first aftershave lotion I bought was Jade East in a plastic bottle in the form of a dark green Buddha in zazen, like the famous bronze monument at Kamakura, but whose head screwed on and off to dispense its floral fragrance of bergamot tea and incense. My own head in the dream, however, popped off like a doll's with a wet, suggestive sound but no scent.

[3] While it would be dangerous to overinterpret these admittedly formative events, the obvious motif of castration associated with beheading appears to be related to an interest I later developed in depictions of the beheading of John the Baptist by Salome and of Holofernes by Judith. Was I also aware at that time of how Orpheus was torn to pieces by the Thracian women, his severed head and lyre carried off in the streams and borne to the shore of Lesbos, of all places?

[4] The first of several bookstores where I worked was on Hollywood Boulevard. It was called Woody's, a puerile pun it took me decades to decode; I always expected the owner to show up one day, but "Woody" never did. Woody's was owned by the faceless parent company, probably mob-connected, and headquartered in the San Fernando Valley, Erotic Words and Pictures (EWAP).

But I recall fondly some of the customers. For example, the timid man who acquired first a succession of dildos and artificial vaginas and then, at my repeated suggestion, reluctantly ("Oh no, no, my wife would not approve of *that!*") upgraded to a lifesize blow-up doll, Cindy, with the surprised expression on her ever-inviting, ever-red and ever-ready, open lips. There were also the proud transsexuals who lived in the hotel next door and made their living modeling for the he/she magazines by day and hustling the johns with that acquired taste by night. Sometimes they came in, first thing in the morning (I opened the doors at 10:00 a.m.), to show their new friends their less-than-artistic postures and poses, so like the gesture of *anasyrma* one often sees in depictions of the hermaphrodite, a gesture at once inviting and forbidding.[5]

All of these moments together form a direct narrative of my sexual prehistory, a syzygy of near perfect alignment. It has taken me four decades, however, to connect the dots to see how they inform one another, how they culminated in my fascination with the myth of the hermaphrodite, and how my year in London conducting research for my dissertation on the hermaphrodite in art and literature was even more personal than professional. This is the story of that parallel research.[6]

It would take me first to the museums and libraries of London and then to its pubs and clubs, bars and bedrooms, where this awkward and inexperienced body tried to catch up with the nimble and inquiring mind that was its traveling companion. But what I was always after was the reality of the real, the special weight and pres-

---

[5] "The revealing of the sexual organs had a double purpose, both positive, to stimulate the powers of life, and prophylactic, to ward off evil forces." Marie Delcourt, *Hermaphrodite: Myths and Rites of the Bisexual Figure in Classical Antiquity*, Trans. Jennifer Nicholson (London: Studio Books, 1961), 63.

[6] I should note that *hermaphrodite* has recently become controversial, with *intersex* being the preferred term for people on the physical spectrum between male and female. Indeed, hermaphrodite has always been a more or less derogatory term when applied to human beings, although it is still used for various animals which maintain the organs and some of the functions of both sexes. It has been used for

ence of the world now, the kind of thing the previous generation of London painters wanted to depict, what the tragic and erotic Pauline Boty called the "nostalgia for now." While my search began as intellectual, iconographical and literary, it traveled through the tactile textures of flesh and blood and paint, so that the slick sexualizations of Allen Jones became just as important as the screams of Francis Bacon. Above all, though, the naked portraiture of Lucian Freud became a constant model, the visual equivalent for my own writing of this book, with its unflinching focus on the intimate details of what is—or was—real. In Europe, though, I found artists like Dubuffet and Asger Jorn, whose enlightening humor cleansed a jaded palate and cleared the way for new tastes and temptations to evolve. Eventually, this would lead, directly or indirectly, to a life devoted to Zen practice, in which the way things are is all that matters, not as we might wish them to be. But that is another story.

Let me begin with Concha, because with Concha it all begins.

---

centuries as a euphemism for males who were effeminate or suspected of homosexuality, although I can recall my father speaking of "morphodites," a dialectical garbling of hermaphrodite that memorably appears in *To Kill a Mockingbird* to describe the snowman that Jem and Scout say resembles both Mr. Avery and Miss Maudie. I remember my father using morphodite to refer to homosexuals, although I'm sure he would have considered the term not derogatory but merely descriptive. When my cousin, his nephew, Patrick, transitioned to become Linda in the 1970s, he never referred to them in this way. As an Okie who had migrated to California during the Dust Bowl, he knew something about the effects of name-calling.

18   *In Search of the Hermaphrodite*

Hermaphroditus. Herm, in the gesture of *anasyrma*.
National Gallery, Stockholm.

". . . the gesture of *anasyrma* one often sees in depictions of the hermaphrodite, a gesture at once inviting and forbidding." (p. 16)

2 / A Toy of Double Shape

> And whosoever hath seen thee, being so fair,
> Two things turn all his life and blood to fire;
> A strong desire begot on great despair,
> A great despair cast out by strong desire.
> —Swinburne, "Hermaphroditus"
> Au Musée du Louvre, Mars 1863

The blast from the horn woke me in the middle of the street. I had not been paying attention to my new surroundings, allowing myself as I often did in those days to become immersed in a daydream about my life so far, coming up in the vast anonymous suburbs of Los Angeles and arriving here in the very different metropolis of London, that palimpsest of historic and picturesque names, where the ghosts of literary figures were more real to me than the flesh-and-blood people around me, where the L.A. smog was replaced by a legendary but long-gone London fog, and where freeways of white concrete had given way to these haunted imaginary cobblestones and the clatter of horse-drawn carriages ...

I shook my head and looked up. I'd almost been run over by a very real lorry which had ground to a stop in front of me, its wheezing exposed greasy motor clattering right in my face. It took a moment to get it into focus. The driver was leaning out the window, lashing at me with his free arm, blaring some indecipherable cockney curse.

My first thought was, why was he driving on the wrong side of the road? For all the seeming familiarity of British culture and language, I was still caught off guard by moments like this, where a slip of the tongue, or the failure to look both ways, could have dire consequences.

It was my second week in London, and the last day to register at the Immigration Office, Lamb's Conduit Street, Holborn.

The young woman in front of me in the queue had sleek black hair that fell to the collar of her button-down oxford shirt and cardigan sweater of British racing car green. As she paused fidgeting with her papers, she held her delicate hands crossed behind her back for a moment. Her nails were clipped short, clean, and bore no trace of polish. Above the trim hips clad in tobacco colored corduroy trousers, I could see the embossed gold leaf letters of her blood-red leatherette passport: "ESPAÑA."

"You're from Spain," I observed, seizing on the obvious. One had to start somewhere.

She turned to me, her smile open, polite, unselfconscious. Unlike mine, which I could feel was tentative, guarded, perhaps appearing more furtive than shy. She was proud; I was timid. Or maybe she disguised her timidity with pride, while I hid pride behind my timidity. Her teeth were perfect, lined up like tiny immaculate tombstones. Her lips, delicious. Her forehead high, with a widow's peak. Other than her smile, a kind of assent, she didn't deign to respond to my observation of the obvious. And since I had no followup, she turned away again with a confident, knowing smile. Her hair was sleek, dark, modest and (I was standing that close to her) fragrant and clean.

"Where in Spain do you come from?" I pursued, somewhat belatedly, feeling that we already had something in common as foreigners trapped together in a bureaucratic queue. It wasn't as though I had accosted her on the street.

"Salamanca," she stated over her shoulder, with a breathy, almost husky hauteur, it seemed to me.

What made me expect Madrid or Valencia, Cádiz or Valladolid,

Barcelona or Seville? Perhaps it was because she seemed so modern, and Salamanca so insular and medieval. In my unworldly ignorance, Salamanca evoked only art history slide images of ornate Gothic cathedrals dripping wax and gilded woodwork, and one of the oldest universities in the world. Yes, she said, she had gone to that university and had come to London to perfect her command of English. Someday she would teach my language, "not American English, of course," she added for clarity, which she did not consider "pure." She would live in a city not too distant, perhaps, from Salamanca. She loved London, though. More than Paris? More than Paris. More than Madrid or any other Spanish city? More than Salamanca? No, not more than Salamanca.

"You are American," she said, with only a slightly mocking smile. Her eyes were playfully slanted and yet serious too.

I held up my blue passport with its one-eyed gold eagle embossed on the cover. It was brand new, with only two stamps: my exit from the U.S. and my entry into the U.K. An amateur traveler, green, barely out of the gate. A callow youth. Yet not so young.

"California," I said, still tongue-tied, suddenly conscious of its Spanish origins.

"Why do you come *here*?" Her accent was almost British.

"It's required," I said, thinking at first she meant the Immigration Office. "Oh, here to London, you mean. Like you, to study."

"What do you study?"

"Like you, English."

She found that amusing.

"But you already speak English! It's funny."

"Only American English," I quipped.

"Still," she said, with a half-smile, measuring my ironic rebuke. "It's funny."

"Yes, I guess it is funny," I conceded. "English literature," I specified and wondered whether I should try to explain my research topic. It seemed like a lot to try to get across, and I couldn't think of a single hermaphrodite in Spanish literature, other than the hermaphrodite Priestess of Zafra, Don Juan Díaz Donoso, who was persecuted by the Spanish Inquisition. Bringing up the Inquisition hardly seemed like a smart opening gambit for seduction. Maybe I would drop the idea of trying to pick her up altogether. English was beginning to feel like a foreign language. And I felt like a rube.

She must have been tired of the exchange, too, in spite of our commonalities, because she turned and faced the counter. Now and then, though, she would sigh and turn her head to see if I was still there and bestow a polite if not exactly friendly smile. We were almost back where we started.

Her eyes were large and clear, all black surrounded on three sides by white, set off by the confidence of her cheekbones and the intelligent thumbprints at her temples, from which her sleek black hair was combed back behind alert ears.

The queue had been long, but it was dwindling now. A long row of desks received each alien in turn, processed us, and then punched us out the door and into the wrong-way London streets, one by one.

Should I tell her about my flight from Los Angeles? Ask her how her trip from Spain had been? Had she flown? Taken the train and ferry? Where was she living? I didn't want to pry. Would she like a cigarette? Smoking was not permitted. Who were her favorite English writers? But before I could speak she was being called to a desk by a broad Pakistani woman who might once have been in our shoes.

I was called to another desk by a young man whose eyes were weak, whose complexion was pasty, whose teeth were bad, whose chest was caving in, and whose manner was superior. A true Englishman, born and bred.

"Yes," he said, confirming some observation to himself as he took my passport. "I could tell from across the room that you were American. Either that or Australian."

I had spent the last weeks of summer on the beaches of Laguna and Corona del Mar. I was still tan, and toned from swimming in the sea, hair still radiant with highlights bleached by Pacific salt and California sun. I guess I stuck out, in other words, like a healthy American—or Australian—thumb. "Thank you," I said.

Or maybe it was my less-than-fashionable attire.

"It was not *necessarily* a compliment," he replied, more to himself than to me, the "necessarily" just flat enough to save his remark from becoming an insult.

"Not Canadian?"

"Canadian *is* American, you see," he hmmphed. "You don't own the whole continent. But no, not Canadian."

I glanced over at my Spanish acquaintance. I should have asked her name. Wouldn't that have been a natural and unthreatening opening gambit, especially if I had offered my name first? Why had I fixated on her city? What a clumsy amateur Don Juan I was! She glanced in my direction, and my smile met hers. At this distance, I felt somehow very close to her, more than acquaintances, compatriots in a way, two outsiders knocking at the city gate. Sign language seemed sufficient to communicate with, almost preferable.

In a moment she threw up her arms and said something, quite loud, in Spanish to her clerk. Her little explosion was amplified by the fluorescent low-ceilinged bureaucratic box, which was elevated to the status of a stage by her vivid presence. She drew stares from the officials behind the desks and nervous grins from those of us on the other side, our solidarity instinctive if tentative.

"Miss Sanchez," said the official, matching her decibels before lowering them a bit. "I do not understand Spanish. I hope what you have said is not offensive. Would you like for me to call an interpreter?"

Several possible Spaniards waiting in line laughed quietly.

"Not necessarily," said my new Salamancan friend. It was almost an echo of my conversation with my Pale Bureaucrat, which she could not have heard. I suppose she meant that an interpreter would not be necessary.

"Ahem, so." My own official was in favor of speeding up the process of getting rid of me. "With what university will you be affiliated during your stay?"

"The University of Reading, officially." I wanted to add something clever, like *Oscar Wilde's alma mater—no, not Magdalen Col-*

lege at Oxford but Reading—Gaol, that is.

"Then you'll be enrolled at the University of Reading."

"Not exactly."

"No? In what capacity then will you be affiliated at the University? Not teaching?" The mere possibility seemed incredible to him, whether because of my age or my nationality, I couldn't say.

He had not deigned to read carefully the documents I had given him, so I nudged them a little closer under his nose to let him know that he could find the answers to all his questions *therein.*

"Independent research," I said. "Mostly in London. But I will be consulting with Professor Ian Fletcher at Reading. He's my advisor."

While he glanced down at the documents from the Fulbright Commission, I glanced over at Ms. Sanchez. She was sitting very erect in her chair, hands on her hips, which accentuated the slight profile of her chest. I had not noticed before but she had breasts. Subtle but firm, small but assertive. Slim and boyish in her collegiate costume of pleated corduroy trousers, polished oxblood penny loafers, and button-down shirt, she had seemed simply well-groomed and modest. With breasts, she seemed to be traveling incognito, like Mademoiselle de Maupin.

"And what is it that you will be researching—independently?"

"Hermaphrodites."

"Her*máph*rodites . . ." His high-pitched emphasis on the second syllable seemed excessive, matching the high pitch of one eyebrow, the left. This jaded bureaucrat had come to work this morning thinking he had heard it all, but perhaps he was wrong.

"English hermaphrodites mostly, but also European," I specified. "In art and literature," I added. "Mostly the late nineteenth century, fin de siècle, the Decadence." I lathered additional details less to enlighten him than to delay my exit to coincide with that of Srta. Sanchez a few desks away. "Pre-Raphaelites. Also the Romantics."

"And there are several?"

"Hermaphrodites? You'd be surprised. They're all over the place."

"Very well," he said conclusively, convinced but not content with my all-inclusive Americanism, which I admit sounded more Jackson

Pollock than, say, Aubrey Beardsley or Allen Jones. He wasn't done with me quite yet. He got down to business, rattling off his memorized script: "Do you promise not to engage in paid employment during your residence in the United Kingdom?"

"I will avoid paid work like the plague."

After a few more similar questions from him and (mostly repressed) cute answers from me, he stamped my new temporary twelve-month residence permit and handed it back to me across the desk, explaining that if I left the country I needed to have this card "on my person" if I expected to reenter during the period of my residence, and that if I wished to stay beyond the allotted time I would have to reapply at this office, etc.; that I was to take this card to the police station nearest my residence and register with them there as an alien, etc., etc.

I need not have worried that Srta. Sanchez would get away ahead of me. I lingered outside the building, smoking a Craven "A", for another length of time. As long as it had taken me to get away from the desk, it was taking her much longer. Every time I risked a glance in her direction, she was there with her hands in the air, or on her hips, or gripping her intelligent temples, her fingers deep in her sleek hair. I wondered if it felt as silken as it looked.

I pulled a slim volume from the pocket of my corduroy coat and pretended to read one of Herrick's poems. I glanced up and she was still there. I lit another cigarette, flipped to another page and read another, with more absorption, drawn into the erotic fantasy of "The Vine":

> *I dreamed this mortal part of mine*
> *Was metamorphosed to a vine,*
> *Which crawling one and every way*
> *Enthralled my dainty Lucia.*

For the line to scan, the name—so light, so Latin, so possibly Spanish—had to be twisted into an ugly three-syllable Anglicization—*loo-see-ay*—but that could be overlooked. Might that be her first name? The poem continued:

> *Methought her long small legs and thighs*
> *I with my tendrils did surprise;*
> *Her belly, buttocks, and her waist*
> *By my soft nervelets were embraced.*
> *About her head I writhing hung,*
> *And with rich clusters (hid among*
> *The leaves) her temples I behung,*
> *So that my Lucia seemed to me*
> *Young Bacchus ravished by his tree. . .*

Thus halfway through, I glanced up to find that she—Ms. Could-be-Lucia Sanchez—was gone. Gone?

Next time this Don Juan would try not to be so stupid, so callow, so faltering, so dumb. Knowing this was an empty vow, I walked dejected into Holborn. I was about to cross the street when I felt a hand on my arm.

"You must look *both* ways before you cross," said the voice behind me, its slightly lisping, almost British accent already familiar. "It could be very dangerous."

It was her. She continued across the street, and I fell over myself trying to follow in the wake of her trim hips like some stray puppy.

"So will you be staying long in London?" I expected her to ignore me now that we were out of the protection of the Immigration Office, but she was all confidence and dignified self-assurance. She simply tossed her head as we reached the other side of the street and smiled. I wanted to know: "Does everything I say amuse you?"

She ignored this question and asked one of her own instead. "Have you been to London before? No? That's what I thought." Then she stopped, faced me, put her hand on my arm again, and said, "Shall we take a coffee together? My name is Concha."

That seemed like a good place to start. Why didn't I think of that?

3 / Americans in Ashley Gardens

> Most familiar, for they have always come here, are the Americans.
> We do not know and they do not know whether they are foreign
> or not.
> —V. S. Pritchett, "London"

I lived with five or six other students in a mansion flat at 214 Ashley Gardens, Emery Hill Street, Westminster SW1, just behind Westminster Cathedral. Considering my research, I couldn't have picked a more appropriate address, although I hardly realized it at the time. Built in the 1890s, the apartment blocks with their clean lines of red and white brick represented the very summit of middle-to-upper-class late-Victorian urban modernity, everything that was then New at the close of the century. One discriminating connoisseur of the city admired the Cathedral but considered it unfortunate that it was "hemmed in behind the Army & Navy Stores, off Victoria Street, and long ranges of expensive flats, called Ashley Gardens, built in the *art nouveau* style which I have deplored."[7] I subsequently learned that Thomas Hardy had accommodations in one of those expensive flats for the season, when Parliament was in session, during which he found time to accept the dubious honor of laying the foundation

---

[7] Richard Church, *London, Flower of Cities All* (New York: John Day, 1966), 158.

stone of Westminster Cathedral next door in July 1895. Ten years later Anthony Powell was born in a furnished flat at number 44, "in one of the several redbrick blocks in that rather depressing area between Victoria Street and the Vauxhall Bridge Road."[8]

The entrance to our understatedly *art nouveau* building was not grand but respectable and inviting, the address announced in a quiet cement scroll above the door. There were two flats on every floor served by a tortoise-slow lift with its accordion metal doors and polished hardwood interior. It was reminiscent of the *ascenseur* in the building on rue Jules Verne (actually rue l'Alboni) where the American Paul and the French Jeanne collide in the empty apartment in *Last Tango in Paris*. The film, which I had seen on my twenty-first birthday in Los Angeles, defined for me my idea of romance: accidental, cross-cultural, by turns mournful and tender and brutal, and fatal. The lift ascended at a stately, unhurried pace which, as we would often discover, since it held only a handful of riders comfortably, could still beat any but the most athletic staircase climbers at a hare's trot to the top, where my and my mates' fourth-floor flat overlooked the rooftops north and west toward Victoria Station.

It was a convenient location for exploring the city, the country, and indeed the world, since one could easily depart from Victoria by bus or train for just about anywhere. Most of my research was done at the British Museum Reading Room in Bloomsbury, much more than a brisk walk away. For pleasure I preferred to go in the other direction to the Tate Gallery in Chelsea, which was closer, and where I immersed myself in the work of the Modernists, as well as more recent artists of the London School, like Francis Bacon, Leon Kossof, Frank Auerbach, Lucien Freud, and R. B. Kitaj, with the last of whom my new friend and fellow Fulbright scholar, Lauriston, was studying painting.

Laury and I had planned at first to find a flat together and looked at several, including one in Earls Court on Trebovir Road. It was a

---

[8] *To Keep the Ball Rolling: The Memoirs of Anthony Powell* (1983; Chicago: U of Chicago P, 2001).

treble attic room in a hostel for foreign students run by the Church of England. If you climbed up on a step you could just see out the sole dormer window with a view of the stately Brompton Oratory.[9] The concierge who showed us the space assured us that, if we were interested and for only a slight increase in price if we split the difference, we would not have to take in a third roommate. It was clear that he was tactfully suggesting that we would not have to share a room with a "foreigner," all the other residents appearing to have come from various parts of the former commonwealth, the Indian subcontinent, Africa, and the Caribbean. When it came to mixing with the "the brute, / The abysmal Fecundity" of the far reaches of Empire, the jingoist sword of William Ernest Henley was still singing if not swinging,[10] though concealed beneath the cassock of missionary benevolence, in Earls Court. (It would not be the only time my rosy picture of a prejudice-free enlightened multicultural metropolis was ruined by racist comments, and not just by skinhead louts. More than once I was shocked by the conductor on the #38 bus, as he punched out tickets on his cumbersome Gibson A14 machine, openly berating some person of color and complaining to me, as though I would naturally agree with him, about "all these bloody *foreigners*." Startled, I thought he was referring to me, as an American, but of course he meant those others, those not us, those non-whites, not me but those colored *Pakis* and assorted *wogs*.) All in all, the Trebovir Road accommodations were a depressing prospect, but the journey there had been pleasant enough. Nothing like hunting for flats to give one a sense of the inner workings, the prisms of prejudices, as well as the geography of a place.

 We spent our first few nights in a modern glass and cement block for student housing in Middlesex House near "sunny" Goodge

---

[9] Consulting maps now, I realize that this view is highly unlikely, if not impossible, the Brompton Oratory being over a mile away, but I retain the reference as noted in my journal here as occasionally elsewhere, since mistaken perceptions can be revealing.

[10] See Henley's imperialist anthem "Song of the Sword."

Street. Maybe it was the jet lag, but nothing could have been less colorful or sunny, or less like the setting of the psychedelic Donovan song. Still, the coincidental (though not referential) nature of the name of Middlesex House was not lost on me, in spite of the fact that its origin, I soon discovered, is a corruption of the Old English for "Middel Saexe" or Middle Saxon and has no more to do with an in-between or mixed gender than Essex, Sussex, or Wessex (i.e., East, South, and West Saxon).

After breakfast Laury and I tried looking in the newspapers for more flats to let, but no luck there. Then we went to Baker Street to open checking accounts at the Midland Bank. Having accomplished that task, we felt the glow of success and dropped by the Fulbright Commission offices nearby at 6 Porter Street, where a small lunchtime reception was being held in honor of this year's batch of Fulbrights. The commission was housed in a cozy warren of offices, run by what could not have been more than half a dozen staff.[11] Isabel was in charge of babysitting the new Fulbrights during our first days in country. The beaky and bespectacled accountant Mr. Sedgwick, wry and dry when he chose to speak, was in charge of all things financial. They were led on a long leash by Mr. Herrington, the besieged director, whose job was to smooth ruffled feathers and avoid all hints of impropriety.

With a plate in his hand and a dab of mayonnaise on his lip, Mr. Herrington approached Laury with the friendly possibility of commissioning a portrait of his wife, Mrs. Herrington.

Laury blinked, paused, pursed his lips, and emitted a short guffaw.

"But perhaps you don't do portraits," offered the diplomatic Herrington, somewhat taken aback, willing to let Laury decline the offer graciously.

I wanted to intervene to let our host know about Laury's quirky time delay. The man in charge was after all a decent fellow only try-

---

[11] The US-UK Fulbright Commission has since moved across the Thames to the Albert Embankment in Vauxhall, and expanded its staff to a dozen or more.

ing to keep everyone happy, above all Mrs. Herrington, who was clearly the woman in charge. I wanted to say that this was how Laury reacted to everything. It would take a long moment for him to process what was said to him, which could be disconcerting for anyone not used to it. Mr. Herrington naturally took the extended pause for reluctance, so he added, "You would be compensated, of course." This gave Laury a ledge, so to speak, on which to stand and speak, but first he motioned to his own lip as a way of alerting our host to the mayonnaise, a courtesy that he could well have foregone without injury to the boss. Mr. Herrington blushed as he dabbed it away.

"I'm only working in charcoal these days," said Laury, as though that might be unacceptable and save him from the task.

"I think that would be fine," concluded Mr. Herrington, relieved, but not without checking his lip again. "It's settled. I'm sure we can come to terms on reasonable compensation."

As we were leaving the reception, Isabel bestowed on each of the attendees a banana and two cans of ale in doggy bags to take home—those of us anyway who had found a home. When I mentioned that we were still looking for a place to stay, Debbie who had gone to Princeton said she thought there was room for one more in the mansion flat where she was staying just behind Westminster Cathedral. If we were interested, we should ring her and stop in later that evening. I could tell that she was directing her invitation to Laury, to whom she had been attracted from the first, and why not? Many women were. He had hair thick as a topiary wave, a thin upper lip that disguised or rather delayed his emotions, and intent eyes. He was serious and handsome and preoccupied almost to the point of inaccessibility, like the young Lucien Freud photographed contemplating a stuffed zebra head at his house in St. John's Wood. But right now Laury was intent on peeling his banana and weighing the prospect of the portrait of Mrs. Herrington, whom he had not yet seen, the trouble it would take versus the pounds of reasonable compensation.

"Compensation," he muttered to himself around the bite of banana in his mouth. "Of course I'll be compensated. Did he think I would do it for free?"

Next stop, the British Council. The young man at the front desk tried to discourage us, claiming that they only found flats for couples. Laury and I looked at each other, draped an arm each over the other's shoulder, then peered at the young man expectantly. "Well, we're a couple, aren't we?" Within moments the entire room of female clerks was in an uproar.

"Here's one," called out a young woman from her desk, taking a card from a file.

"Here's another," said another. "I'll bet it's the better one."

The competition was on.

"You might try Mrs. Toomey. A bit eccentric but I think she's very nice. In Maida Vale. And the place is inexpensive. Not too chic, I'm afraid."

"Hey, are you takin' me coostoma away from meh?"

"I think you might try Mrs Toomey, though, truly. She's a bit bloomy. I don't know how she'll take to havin' two gay young American blokes in her rooms. No offense. She's had such trouble with students in the past—Nigerians and Pakistanis bringin' in their families 'n uncles 'n such, and emptyin' their bedpans out the window in the garden. You wouldn't do that, now would you?"

The fellow at the front desk conceded defeat. "See how everyone jumps, do you? It's because you're American."

The Manchester girl who was helping us said, "I'm going to America, you know. Or Canada, I think. There's opportunities there."

On the way out, as a way of saying thanks, we left our cans of ale on the desks of the most accommodating of the female clerks, who whooped in surprise. I left my banana on the desk of the young man who had greeted us so doubtfully at the door, and winked.

* * *

That evening I showed up at Debbie-from-Princeton's mansion flat by myself, since Laury was sure he would be able to find something cheaper in the East End. It didn't take me long to decide to join the menage in Ashley Gardens, even though the rent seemed more than I could afford at £80 a month. The flat opened onto a long hall with a left turn at the end, with a couple of spacious bedrooms and a large sitting room opening off on the right, and two smaller rooms at the end. One of them would be mine, an L-shaped room, probably part of the servants' quarters back in the day, shared with another American, an actor, fresh out of Yale. It took several days after I moved in, however, before I met all of my new roommates, all of whom had busy schedules and complicated lives. Above all, I liked the central location being close to the British Library, the theaters, and all the distractions of the West End.

Like Goldilocks, it took Laury three tries to find accommodations that were just right for him. At first he moved into a very basic flat that fit his idea of a bohemian artist's studio in Hammersmith, but he soon realized that it was overpriced, under-heated, and unlivable. Eventually he found better deals in the East End, first in Wapping near the docks, and then another, even cheaper and more comfortable furnished flat in Hackney at 10 Martello Street, overlooking London Fields, next to a reggae venue called the All Nations Club. A few blocks away he was able to rent a cheap studio space as well, the two for about the same price as the original Hammersmith tenement.

Once we were settled in, I would take the #38 bus a couple of times a week from Victoria Station to Laury's studio. Laury had been doing a series of black-and-white architectural abstractions, especially studies of the bombed-out industrial areas on the Thames. These huge charcoal impressions of Shadwell Basin with its locks and garbage and monstrous mechanical forms, bridges and protrusions of metal, resembled a hybrid of Piranesi and Franz Kline trying their hands at the Euston Road School of cranes in industrial landscapes. There was a violence in the lines that was surprising coming from mild-mannered Laury, and he was not sure that it would translate well into the tradition-laden respectful representationalism of the portrait. With Mrs. Herrington in mind, he thought he needed additional practice with the human figure, so I agreed to sit for him in exchange for beer and sandwiches and conversation afterwards, although I somehow ended up paying most of the time.

Mrs. Herrington's busy schedule allowed her to sit for him only once a week when she was not involved in one of her clubs or charity works, so her portrait progressed slowly. Also, after an initial infatuation with the novelty of his artist's studio, she soon found it merely cold and uncomfortable and began to fidget and complain, ending with her asking to leave before the time for sitting was over, which Laury did not think he could prevent. Worse, she was constantly wanting to see his progress at the end of each curtailed sitting, a small enough request but one that Laury was uncharacteristically quick to say that he was unwilling to grant. No, she could not see the work yet. That was not, he said, how he worked.

All fall and winter I sat for him in the raw space of his increasingly frigid studio. The space reminded me of William Orpen's studio as he had painted it in 1912, the high ceilings and the wall of square warehouse windows throwing a kaleidoscope of shadows onto the dappled wall and onto the half-nude model whom Orpen depicts himself depicting. Laury insisted that I stay perfectly still, as he attempted to abstract my three-quarter profile in charcoal, the friction of that process shredding both the paper and his fingers before he would allow me to move. I could stretch my legs, since those were out of frame, and I could talk as long as I played the ventriloquist by not moving my lips. We traded stories about our childhoods and families in California, our experience living abroad, the women we were meeting here as well as the loves we had left behind. We debated the purpose and practice and future of art.

We had several things in common. We both had grown up in California, although Laury was raised in the lush coastal forests (and cannabis plantations) of Humboldt County, while I came from the suburbs of Los Angeles. His father was a famous nuclear physicist at Berkeley who had worked with Oppenheimer, while mine was an ex-Marine, an Okie from the Dust Bowl migration who now worked on cars and trucks for the Department of Water and Power. We both had left girlfriends behind in the States and genuinely missed them (indeed, I was also still married, if only barely) but behaved as if we were free. Art was the only mistress to whom we pledged our complete devotion, but we were human after all, and young at that.

My story of meeting Concha, our subsequent relationship and her unambiguous tastes, provided him with endless opportunities to be shocked and confused, sometimes envious, sometimes amused. But at least these tales of the erotic picaresque kept us warm when the December sun left little warmth during and after its brief arc on the horizon.

We shared stories of our foibles as well as our conquests. As when I had ventured into a bakery near Clapham and, following the example of the three heavily bundled old women ahead of me in the queue with their little shopping carts beside them, requested what they (I thought) had requested: a "French dick, please." What a charming locution these ladies had come up with, I thought, for those long slender crusty loaves! Each came away from the counter with her stiff and formidable baguette. But when I requested the same, the girl at the counter said, "Come again? Ah, haha, you want a French *stick*! He wants a French *stick*!" she announced to the shop at large to the great amusement of all. I was laughed out of the shop, my hard-won French dick clamped firmly under my arm.

At each of these anecdotes, Laury's time-delay reactions could take several seconds of him looking blank as he processed the story and its punchline before he burst into an appreciative guffaw or a judgmental "*Rich*ard!" The first syllable of my name could be accented in any number of ways to register disbelief (a high bark), disappointment (a low growl), or delight (a chuckled chirp). This defining quirk caused many people to see him as slow—"Laury? Oh, the space cadet!"—but it was just that he was brilliant in his own, deliberative sort of way. I suppose he was always painting in his head or analyzing the composition of words being thrown up in the air between us like a hologram. Sometimes I imagined him as a cartoon character watching the bubble between us fill with words, like a balloon filling with water, before the meaning burst upon him with a splash and he would wake up and react with his bark, growl, or chirp. It was disconcerting and somewhat draining being with him for any length of time for this reason, but we got along.

Because of this the best times were when we were both silent in the silence of the studio, only the scratch of charcoal on textured paper to distract us. It was a form of sitting meditation, I suppose, as anyone who has worked as an artist's model knows. The smile of the Mona Lisa is the interior smile of every contemplative throughout time. Walter Pater understood this. In his much-quoted passage describing *La Gioconda*, he suggests what was to become scripture in the fin de siècle cult of experience based on his philosophy of life.

> *She is older than the rocks among which she sits; like the vampire, she has been dead many times, and learned the secrets of the grave; and has been a diver in deep seas, and keeps their fallen day about her; and trafficked for strange webs with Eastern merchants; and, as Leda, was the mother of Helen of Troy, and, as Saint Anne, the mother of Mary; and all this has been to her but as the sound of lyres and flutes, and lives only in the delicacy with which it has moulded the changing lineaments, and tinged the eyelids and the hands. The fancy of a perpetual life, sweeping together ten thousand experiences, is an old one; and modern philosophy has conceived the idea of humanity as wrought upon by, and summing up in itself, all modes of thought and life. Certainly Lady Lisa might stand as the embodiment of the old fancy, the symbol of the modern idea.*[12]

At these times, I too was Lady Lisa, thoughts arising and dispersing in air, reaching back into the origins before origins and forward into whatever the future might hold, taking form and emptying out, along with each visible breath.

Never mind that what was taking shape on the paper on the easel was more Frank Auerbach than da Vinci. And rightly so. All I could see was the fine snow of black charcoal dust accumulating in drifts

---

[12] Walter Pater. *The Renaissance: Studies in Art and Poetry*. The 1893 Text. Edited by Donald L. Hill. (Berkeley and London: U of California P, 1980), 99.

beneath the easel. By this time my bones had set up in the cold until I could at last unfold them, cracking like wishbones. Then came the good stuff, what I had been waiting for, the reward, when we would retire to the warmth of the nearest pub for bland baps of butter and ham and lettuce and a couple of pints of bitter.

During the brief stint in his second studio, we favored the Prospect of Whitby, in Wapping Wall, a six-hundred-year-old pub famous for being frequented by smugglers and Samuel Pepys. As we downed our pints, we watched the Thames at low tide shrink below us to reveal a murky muck reminiscent of Dickens's mudlarks, Gaffer and Lizzie Hexam in *Our Mutual Friend*, while the evening view of the river took on an artistic Whistlerian haze.

"Did you know that Captain Kidd was executed here in 1701 at Wapping's Execution Dock," said Laury as though this were common knowledge, "by being left hanging for three low tides?"

"Now why would I know that?"

"It's written on the stall in the loo." Whenever Laury delivered one of these punchlines, his expression never changed. It was as if his usual time delay had come at the end of a sentence instead of at the beginning.

Whenever I left the third studio, the one in Hackney, I would grab a chocolate crispy Lion bar for dessert on the way to catch the double-decker bus back to Victoria Station.

27–29 January 1981.
Sitting for Laury in his studio, Martello Road, London Fields. (During the plague, London Fields was where people who lived outside town would bring food and other supplies to be picked up by plague victims in the city. A kind of no man's land.) Modeling for an artist is a kind of no man's land, too. Staring into space, I am not allowed to move. My job is to do nothing. It reveals what is in nothing. I told Carin, "Thing is, I've discovered that I'm perfectly happy sitting still, doing nothing. I feel I could do this again and again. I could see myself craving it. Addicted to nothing."

Taking the midnight #38 bus back to Victoria, I can see my reflection in the window superimposed on the passing cityscape. I reflect on the night's sitting. Laury never lets me see his drawing in progress. Tonight he did. Something authentic emerges, volcanic, serene and intense from the body, an energetic, almost atomized chaos of marks forming the upper torso, a touch of diabolism about the eyes. A new self-image, even when I don't see what he has drawn. It is the mirror of nothing in which the self-portrait is glimpsed, not the artist's depiction.

The fog as the bus floats past Hyde Park is authentic London fog.

Each time I sat for that portrait I was transformed. It was not that Laury had got hold of my soul; I am not superstitious (no more than the next atheist who reads his horoscope with some trepidation every morning) and did not believe in the soul (at least not one that could be saved or stolen). Nor had Laury given me a new vision of myself, since he rarely allowed me to see the work in progress. It was the sitting itself that did the trick, just sitting. Afterwards, I felt exhausted, depleted, empty, and yet exhilarated too, brand new. I would not have this feeling again until I began sitting zazen twenty years later.

4 / An Obsession Is a Hypothesis

> That the Greeks made a temple to the backside of Venus, that anyone who knows what a fine thing sex is knows.
> —Stevie Smith, *Novel on Yellow Paper*

Concha worked as an au pair in St. John's Wood. She was not exactly Mary Poppins, but her situation was similar, and her attitude often took on that air of practically perfect superiority. In the mornings she would get the children ready for school, and then she would study until lunchtime. In the evenings the parents often entertained and counted on her to keep the children amused or at least out of the way. Her afternoons were free and thus the best times for her to get away. So we met in the afternoons, usually around Oxford Street or Leicester Square because she liked to look in the shop windows.

Her father was an anarchist who had lost his professional position during Franco's fascist regime. "He is a bitter man," she said as casually as she might have said he was a coffee drinker. She showed me a picture of him and her mother. The woman was a blur who bore no resemblance to her striking daughter who had some of the same daunting presence as the man in the photograph. A typical bourgeois Spanish couple, stern and maybe slightly stiffer than was strictly necessary. "I hate my father," she stated without rancor. "I don't want to owe him anything." We had stopped at a construction site so she could look it over. "I will tell my father about this," she said as though she didn't hate him after all. "He is an architect, an engineer. It will interest him." The only other comment she ever made about her father was when we were eating fish and chips, a cryptic coda that seemed to come out of nowhere. "He would kill me if he saw me eating with my right hand." She never mentioned him again. Her mother she never mentioned at all.

In the beginning, I thought Concha was just materialistic, a wannabe Chelsea snob, although her look was far too androgynous for the usual Sloane Rangerette. "I like those shoes, but they are too expensive," she would say as we lingered in front of the shops in the West End. "I don't like those shirts. That jumper is too hairy. Those trousers are too American." She was a discriminating raven-haired Goldilocks. Rarely was anything "just right."

I should have been basking under the blue dome of the British Library perusing esoteric manuscripts on alchemy or Neoplatonic encomia on androgyny for background. I began to wonder why I was wasting my time with this opinionated window-shopper. Then she would stop in the middle of the pavement, oblivious to the foot traffic that now had to flow around us, and lock her arms around my waist as though we were alone on an Andalusian beach. I would feel the silk of her hair on my lips and breathe its faint sandalwood fragrance and my loins would turn to fire and all my dissatisfaction would melt away in the isolated beauty of that moment.

"I feel so stupid," she said, turning her face up to me. "Please, don't listen to me. Feel me instead." Her slanted eyes were pure seduction, and her boy's clothes and boy's manner and boy's figure (and girl's breasts) made me feel a little depraved and not a little confused as I sank into her kisses and felt her perfect teeth sink more than gently into my lips.

She would only wear the best quality clothes, but no matter what she expressed an opinion on, her opinion was the best, the only opinion allowed. I couldn't figure it out in advance. Whatever she decided was the only way it was supposed to be, whatever the topic. Whatever she liked was good; whatever was good she liked.

As for me, I was always at sea. I could see her point, but I could also entertain the possibility that the opposite viewpoint was equally true. Holding two contradictory views at the same time, wasn't that true wisdom? Wasn't opposition true friendship? Or was that all Romantic nonsense? Concha made me question that philosophical position, just as all supremely confident people made me question myself.

"Taste is tautological," I told her. I often hid my own lack of confidence behind a snippy assertion.

She asked me to explain, but I didn't have the heart. Or the courage. Or the words. I was always afraid of hurting her feelings even if she was never afraid of hurting mine.

"Whew! You Americans!" That was her answer whenever we reached an impasse in communication, which was not infrequently.

Later she admitted that the reason she was so opinionated and that much of her conversation was limited to saying she liked this or disliked that was due to her linguistic constraints.

"I feel so stupid," she said. "I would like to talk with you, deeply, about things. But all I know how to say is 'I like this, I don't like that.' I like it when you talk. It makes me feel like I am talking too. I don't like feeling stupid."

She was finally able to get away from St. John's Wood for the whole night, the family she worked for having left town for the weekend. We went to the Marquee, a popular music club in Soho, to hear a reggae band, then back to my flat and to bed. After hours of foreplay and slow undressing, she said, "Do you prefer women? Have you ever slept with a man?"

I told her about two homoerotic experiences, neither of them consummated, both when I was in graduate school.

"There was a beautiful German boy, long and lean with pale skin and long black hair—a little like yours, come to think of it. I thought I might be infatuated with him." Echoes of *Death in Venice*, I wanted to say, without the tragedy, and this Tadzio was not much younger than me; but all these comparisons and contrasts would have been too complicated to get across clearly. "It was summer, and I remember how beautiful he was at the beach, playing in the waves with my girlfriend, Mnemosyne. There was something awkward and unathletic about this Adonis, something androgynous, feminine and fragile. But nothing ever came of that."

"You should have gone to bed together, the three of you."

"It occurred to me," I said. "Then there was an undergraduate student of mine when I was a teaching assistant. He was black and I was drunk and we made out in a booth in a dark Italian restaurant just off campus. But I found that oddly unsatisfying, unaesthetic, or rather anesthetic, like touching myself on novocaine."

Concha had opened Pandora's box. I continued to free-associate. She had unlocked some part of me that wanted to find the key to every sexual experience, its place in the puzzle, how it contributed to the motif in a pattern. As though she were a guide, like Virgil, or some sleek, alluring spirit creature I couldn't help but follow, descending deeper into the infernal circles below the surface of my research.

"I'm not sure if this counts as a homosexual experience," I offered. "It was so long ago. I was young, maybe fourteen, maybe younger. I had a dream that I was with Ann-Margret in a hayloft..."

"A hayloft, what is a hayloft?"

"In a barn, like an attic, way up high, where hay to feed horses is stored."

"Yes, I see. And Ann-Margret?"

"An actress. Very sexy, very voluptuous, very feminine. Probably the biggest sex symbol at the time. She was in *Viva Las Vegas* with Elvis, and the rock opera *Tommy*, and *Carnal Knowledge* and..."

"Yes, yes, I know now."

"She was Lady Booby in *Joseph Andrews*, the film."

"Oh, we read that book at university! Enrique Fielding, yes?"

"Well, in my dream she and I are kissing and I'm feeling her breasts and she is feeling me. It's very sensuous and lovely. I am excited and I want to see her take off her clothes."

"Her clothes are not off?"

"Not yet."

"Continue."

"She's wearing a white shirt tied at the waist and cutoff jeans. Her breasts are heavy and I can see the nipples against the fabric. She is on her knees, straddling me, like this, the way you are now. She unbuttons her shirt, but doesn't take it off—it's still tied at the waist—but she allows one heavy breast to emerge, filling my hand like ripe fruit from a tree."

"What kind of fruit?"

"Like no kind of fruit anyone has ever tasted."

"I like this story. But I don't like the big . . . *boobies*," she added with a look of distaste.

"Neither do I," I said, running the palms of my hands up under Concha's unbuttoned shirt (the only thing she was wearing) and over her mere suggestions (like a Japanese ink painting) of breasts. Not planets or pyramids, but pink-tipped ancient burial mounds worn smooth by the centuries and dusted lightly with bright furze like peach fuzz, velvety.

"The big boobies are so . . . animal," said Concha, her judgment final. "Like cows."

"Bestial?"

"*Sí, sí, bestial.*"

"Well, *you* don't have to worry about that," I said, letting her shy, inverted nipples trace circles in my palms. "I prefer these. Your breasts are downright *espiritual.*"

"Like heaven?" she said, pleased. "I don't believe in heaven, but breasts, I believe in them, yes."

"Yes, heavenly," I confirmed, stretching upward to kiss them. "Anyway, after Ann-Margret lets both of her big '*boobies*' out of her shirt, she unzips her jeans and begins to pull them down. I am pretty excited at this point, as you can imagine."

"*Por supuesto.*"

"But wait. As she unzips her jeans and pulls them down—she is wearing no underwear of course—"

"*Por supuesto.*"

"—out flops a rather large, pendulous, half-erect penis."

Concha let out a shriek of laughter, a bit maliciously, I think, as though this was exactly the sort of trick that I, the dirty little dreaming teenage boy, deserved. But she was also fascinated, so her laughter took on a stifled kind of choking sound.

"What did you do?"

"I didn't do anything. I woke up."

"But you must go back and finish this dream!"

"It was a long time ago. I can't go back to it now. I tried at the time, but I couldn't get back to sleep."

"Oh but I want to know what happened!"

"So do I," I said.

Concha tried to interpret the dream as a desire for homosexual experience, to consummate what I had missed out on with the beautiful German boy and the black student. I said I didn't think it was that simple since this dream predated those events. After all, I had fantasized and experimented but those sparks never took fire in my loins, only in my mind as an intellectual exercise, in imitation of Byronic bisexuality. Yet the dream, unlike the German boy and the black student, still haunted me.

"An obsession is a hypothesis," I said. There it was again, my defensive assertion, something definitive to disguise my uncertainty, pedantry to hide my ignorance.

"What?"

I tried to explain what I meant while I caressed those parts of her that obsessed and confused me—the slim hips, the sleek hair, the pert breasts—but the more frustrated we became intellectually the more intimate and aroused we became physically.

(For a fleeting moment, mixing up reality somehow with the story I was telling and the point I was trying to make, I imagined Concha in the role of that ambiguous creature Bellino, whom Casanova discovered, despite the decoy of a "monstrous clitoris," to be not the male castrato she pretended to be but a beautiful impostor. For even though castrati were known to develop incipient breasts, what he felt when he managed to slip his hand between the ruffles of Bellino's shirt was the real thing, declaring: "The chisel of Praxiteles had never formed a finer bosom!"[13])

While Concha did not seem to like extended kisses, she suddenly goes down to show me what else she can do with her lips—all this while I am trying to demarcate some fine distinction between homosexuality and homoeroticism. She is listening but her hands are busy, lubricating her thumb in her mouth, which then slips without warning or fanfare into me. I'm startled into silence by this sudden penetration.

"*Que piensas?*" she asks, climbing up to sit on my abdomen again. I can feel her mounted there, warm and slippery. I am a welcoming saddle to this grinning Lady Godiva, her hands behind her holding onto the aroused saddle horn, which she keeps releasing to have it thump the small of her back.

What am I thinking? What I'm thinking is, of course, that we are both ready to move beyond foreplay, so I place my hands on her slim hips and make a move to hoist her onto my petard for the next stage in our lovemaking, but subtly, the way a priest might remove his staff from the altar to the sanctum sanctorum.

"Not so fast!" she says, blocking me and pulling away. "I don't like it that way, It makes me feel like a machine. You know the way the Greek boys do it to each other? I *love* that."

I stall, pretending ignorance through pedantry. "Intercrural? Like this?" And I try to describe and then demonstrate the ancient method of non-penetrative intercourse between her thighs (an oxymoron: better to call it *outercourse*) traditionally used as a jesuitical equivocation to protect virgins and pregnant women, as well as boys

---

[13]Said Casanova: "This alabaster breast, my dear Bellino, is the enchanting fruit of a seventeen-year-old girl." *The Story of My Life*. Trans. Stephen Sarterelli and Sophie Hawkes (New York: Penguin, 2000), 88. When Bellino finally reveals her true sex and her true identity as Teresa, Casanova has her don the decoy again, turning her into an artificial hermaphrodite that excites him even more than her unsupplemented self: "What I saw then was incredible: a girl whose charm was visible in all her person, but who, with that white appendage looked even more appealing to me, for it posed no obstacle to the reservoir of her sex. I told her she had been right not to let me touch it, for it would have plunged me into a drunken state and made me become what I was not" (108).

and boyish girls from harm and hairsplitting pedophiles and predators from feelings of culpability.

"Do you have some cream or oil?" she asks.

I get up and throw something around my waist. Luckily there is no one in the kitchen. I come back with a bottle of olive oil I have found in a cupboard.

"It's extra virgin," I say, not without sarcasm, pointing to the fine print: "and Greek."

After that I called her *mi catamita*, but I was a little afraid of her. She was so opinionated and European, perhaps even "classic" (in the Greek sense), and I was so tentative and callow and, well, *American*. With Maria, my Mexican first-grade crush, I felt like Gene Kelly the Smitten dancing in the rain; with Concha, my Spanish sophisticate, I felt like Gene Kelly the Rube in the Big City dancing with the siren Cyd Charisse, dressed all in serpentine ebony and chartreuse, in the sexiest dance number in the history of film. I half-expected Concha, like the slinky Cyd, to take off my glasses at some point and polish them on the inside of her naked thigh before disappearing with a diamond-necklace-dangling mafioso.

Concha always made me feel a little depraved, taking her small-breasted boyish figure in my arms, as though I were embracing my hermaphrodite in the flesh. Unlike the statue in the Louvre, though, even if she was boyish above she was all girl below, even if she made that part of her anatomy off-limits to penetration, even as she reveled in being taken from behind while having her bright pink cashew polished between thumb and forefinger to a stiffened explosion.

"You are not sensual," she once told me when I lost interest in prolonging a long night of lovemaking. I think she meant that I was not being sensual at that moment, but it sounded like another one of her absolute generalizations. As much as I enjoyed her way of doing things, I longed for a little variety in our games. Perhaps she was not sufficiently polymorphous, or I was not sufficiently perverse. I wanted to tell her that I was nostalgic for the missionary position, but I didn't want to sound like one of those puritanical *Americans*.

Concha prided herself on her Spanish "sensuality." Yet perversely, it seemed to me, she considered her own "concha" (she had to explain to me the double entendre) to be little more than a well-oiled "machine." Rejecting not only the assigned gender roles of a patriarchal society—she rejected her own femininity through the clothes she wore—she also rejected the reproductive function of her sexuality by taking the role of Ganymede. This is why she avoided using her given name, Maria de la Concepción, which she hated because it reminded her of the distasteful union of sperm and ovum, child-bearing, family, and all that devolved from the oppressive apparatus of the patriarchal hegemony not only of Spain but of all societies everywhere.[14]

Yet she enjoyed the sexual act, the physical intimacy (or was it the invasion?) of penetration, as long as it was divorced from any hint of the reproductive function. She was in every way as mysterious and enigmatic as Conchita in Pierre Louÿs' *Woman and Puppet*, as evasive and frustrating, yet I recall with real fondness the uncomplicated times we spent on the streets of the West End looking at shops or holding each other in the finely floating rain. Gerald Brenan, who is considered a perceptive observer of Spanish character, makes this dubious but provocative proposition: "though Spaniards have more virtues than other people and fewer vices, it so happens that their virtues are passive and their vices active. This is a view that is worth considering."[15] Whatever one might make of that ambiguous thesis, Concha still glows with the warmth and fragrance of an unforgettable sensory experience etched in my memory, like an espresso bean

---

[14]Delcourt compares the legends of the medieval female "penitents in disguise" and finds that they share the same symbolic value of male dress: "breaking with the feminine past, hostility towards the family and authority, renunciation of sexual life." For example, Antoinette Bourignon, who disguised herself as a hermit, taught that "God created man at once male and female, capable of self-reproduction like the plants; it was sin that brought about our fall from that ideal state, and inflicted copulation and woe." Marie Delcourt, *Hermaphrodite: Myths and Rites of the Bisexual Figure in Classical Antiquity*, Trans. Jennifer Nicholson (London: Studio Books, 1961), 96, 93.

[15]*South from Granada: A Sojourn in Southern Spain* (New York: Farrar, Straus, and Cudahy, 1957), 94.

floating in an unctuous blue flame of sambuca.

"You don't like me," she concluded that first night with finality, although it was far from our last night together. I protested that this was not true: I was quite taken with her. Fascinated, if not petrified, by her. "It's all right," she said. "It doesn't matter. I like you." She stretched out on top of me, covering my body with her body like a marble slab. "Can I sleep here like this? Do you mind? I like to sleep like this."

In fact she fell asleep immediately, like an exhausted child or a switched-off robot, her slight frame deceptively heavy on my chest. I envisioned the *Hermaphrodite endormi* in the Louvre lying on the exquisite trompe l'oeil mattress of Bernini. Through the window above our heads, the sun rising somewhere behind the gray skies managed to light the curve of her slimly sinuous hip and thigh before I managed to fall asleep in the incense of her raven hair.

5 / Mnemosyne and Mary Poppins

Mais vous êtes une femme, nous ne sommes plus au temps des métamorphoses;—Adonis et Hermaphrodite sont morts,—et ce n'est plus par un homme qu'un pareil degré de beauté pourrait être atteint;—car, depuis que les héros et les dieux ne sont plus, vous seules conservez dans vos corps de marbre, comme dans un temple grec.
—Théophile Gautier, *Mademoiselle de Maupin*

Given the foundational experiences of my sexual prehistory, my head having been filled by my brother's fantasies, popular culture, and my own subconscious fears and desires, it is no wonder that I was taken with Swinburne's poem "Hermaphroditus" in my first graduate class in Victorian Poetry. I don't know what personal chimeras my fellow graduate students were chasing with their dissertation topics, but it is clear that mine had a long prelude. Not that I realized it at the time, but there were deeply etched experiences buried deep in my subconscious that I only now realize were like a vast subterranean root system that fed my obsession so that it blossomed everywhere with images of dual sexuality.

My mentor, Robert Peters, held an enigmatic position in the Department of English and Comparative Literature at UC Irvine, which included a well-regarded MFA program. Physically imposing, with a head like the marble of a wall-eyed decadent Roman emperor,

Bob was a colossus who straddled the often antagonistic worlds of criticism and creative writing to the perplexity of the faithful of both camps. What to make of this ambidextrous talent who had begun his career with a prize-winning book on Swinburne, followed by a first book of verse by a mainstream publisher before unleashing a flurry of pugnacious reviews of contemporary poets as well as his own volumes of proudly gay poetry from numerous small presses? Other faculty and their students were more prudent, considered their careers, chose their weapons and allies carefully, their enemies (and lovers) circumspectly. But Bob followed his own idiosyncratic counsel. Mine was one of the few dissertations he directed; he was more popular with the poets.

After circulating unsuccessfully at some of the more prestigious critical journals, the paper I wrote for Bob on the hermaphrodite in the work of Swinburne and Rossetti sat in a drawer until I finished my PhD qualifying exams. The detailed and often contradictory critiques of their readers did little to clarify my command of the topic. The "toy of double shape" still obsessed me, for personal as much as professional reasons, so it was natural to propose this as my dissertation topic. When he was in my place as a graduate student at the University of Wisconsin, Bob had won a Fulbright to Cambridge to work on what would become his edition of the letters of another ambidextrous colossus of letters, John Addington Symonds. Bob encouraged me to follow in his own footsteps. A research grant to London would not only hasten my path to the degree, it would also allow me to escape the escalating complications of my personal life. I had always dreamed of traveling to Europe, but with commitments to a wife and daughter before I was twenty-one, it was a dream long deferred. A Fulbright could be my chance to fulfill that dream.

*   *   *

As an undergraduate at the University of Oregon, while writing an honors thesis on time ("that double-headed monster of damnation and salvation") in Beckett's trilogy, I took my daughter Cyleste every day to preschool on the back of my bicycle. I almost fell off one morning when she began chanting behind me: "Sam-u-el Beckett, Sam-u-el Beckett." One must be careful what one discusses around children: they will put almost anything left lying about in their mouths, and whatever topics are in the air they will pluck and absorb and process, regurgitate and express if not fully digest.

She gave me a similar shock when I was writing and revising my second or third paper on the hermaphrodite. What a bore I must have been, talking about my work all the time, because one morning I found a drawing she had made of a dual-gendered creature. Her image was split vertically like a sideshow freak, or the Ardhanarishvara form of Shiva/Parvati, or one of Aristophanes' three original genders before the man/woman had been split down the middle.[16] In Cyleste's drawing, the figure shared a single head, split down the middle, while the bodies diverged, dressed in their gendered roles: bow tie and trousers for him, pearls and a dress for her, a baby crying "Waa!" on her arm. His mustache and glasses are mirrored by her lipstick, rouge, and pink bows adorning each of her eyelashes. It was instructive that she identified gender not with primary or secondary physical sexual characteristics but with superficial social markers, fashion, hairstyles, and accessories, especially around the eyes, the organ that sees gender and categorizes it. There was, for a stick figure, an uncanny if caricatural resemblance to me on one side and to her mother on the other. An illustration of my verbal musings and monologs? Or a child's mythographical self-portrait, the DNA of complementary chromosomes unsynthesized, yet to morph completely into a separate, blended self?

In graduate school my marriage with her mother had stalled, thanks in part to a polyamorous drama with another couple—a beautiful, dynamic and dramatic punk poet and performance artist and her theatre director boyfriend. This was perhaps the logical

---

[16]The technical term is gynandromorph, often seen in nature in butterflies and lobsters, and not as uncommon as one might think.

conclusion of our marriage, one that began full of hope in the free love era of the sixties and then slept through the seventies, only to awaken, disillusioned, at the dawn of the eighties.[17] We began 1970, fresh out of high school, by running away from home to Venice Beach, living on very little, scavenging discarded groceries from supermarket dumpsters, and giving everything we had to our idealistic notion of love, poetry, and life. Our tiny apartment at 15 Horizon Avenue overlooked an alley and a parking lot—and beyond that the glittering Santa Monica Bay. Posted on the front door was an announcement encouraging all who entered to abandon hope of worldly ambition—these lines from Ezra Pound's "An Immorality": "Sing we for love and idleness / Naught else is worth the having." We lived by that—for awhile.

Ten years later we were singing a different tune, abandoning simplicity and instead lusting for experience of a different kind, in which the texture of complexity seemed irresistibly seductive. Thus the short-lived symmetry of the *ménage à quatre*.

I moved out of our Irvine campus apartment in married student housing and into a blue bungalow at 133 Turquoise Avenue a block from the beach on Balboa Island with three other graduate students: a poet, a novelist, a theorist, and me. The poet was Little Jimmy, as we called him, who also worked as a scientist and performed as a morris dancer in an Elizabethan troupe every summer at the Oregon Shakespeare Festival until he broke his neck on his bicycle one day on his way to the biology lab. For months he went around with a stainless-steel halo and collar with screws fastened to his skull. The novelist was Carolyn, divorced and sprinting to forty, who chain-smoked and tapped fiercely at her IBM Selectric every morning until breaking out the jug wine and endless conversation every afternoon when the writing workshops concluded. The theorist was Mnemo-

---

[17]Nico (of Velvet Underground fame) might well have been providing context when she said, "The 1980s are an extension of the 1960s, as if the '70s didn't exist, as if it went straight from the '60s to '80s. Somehow." Interview on the *South Bank Show*, 1986.

syne (let's call her that), broodingly beautiful, with a brilliant analytical mind and a caseload of psychological problems. Of course, it was her I fell for, glutton for extremes that I was, when the romance with the intense punk poet paled.

How can I describe Mnemosyne? She had grown up in one of the mountain states, an irreligious Jew who rode gymkhana and loved country music, which I at the time hated as my father's music. It was she who taught me to love Waylon Jennings, Willie Nelson, and Jerry Jeff Walker, the pathos and bathos of outlaws and honky-tonk heroes. After her Ivy League degree (and sexual assault by her psychiatrist), she went on to one of the best medical schools in the South, before dropping out and taking on the brave new world of critical theory, of which Irvine was a major if unlikely frontier. But all this does nothing to describe her unique blend of sensuality and intellectualism, intense rationality and mild psychosis. I keep coming back to one snapshot of her sitting up in bed in the house on Balboa Island, wearing a soft yellow turtleneck, her rich auburn hair falling softly around her cheeks, sucking her thumb and reading Derrida. That was Mnemosyne to a tee.

It was a lively household. At the dinner table, over wine and cigarettes, the four of us talked poetry and promiscuity well into the night, the ocean mist wafting in through the open windows. We wrote screenplays together and assembled exquisite corpses. We held dinners and impromptu parties for faculty, graduate students, and visiting writers. Carolyn was an old friend of the writers Stan and Anne Rice from their days in the Bay Area, so when the couple came to give a reading of his poetry and her fiction at the university, we threw a party for them afterward. The brash and still vivacious author and bonne vivante Eve Babitz (who once played chess with Marcel Duchamp in the nude—at least in the photograph that became her first claim to fame) came down from L.A. to visit "the Vampire Queen." Queen Anne held court in our modest beach bungalow till the wee hours when she said she had to retire to the fancy beach hotel where the university had put her and Stan up, and where (someone quipped and she confirmed) her coffin with its spadeful of earth was presumably kept.

When Donald Heiney, who published his novels under the thin disguise of MacDonald Harris, came to dinner, he was especially interested in the sexual dynamics of our household. He would ceaselessly—and sometimes crassly (he wasn't known for social graces nor what would later be known as political correctness)—interrupt the conversation to ask about who slept where and with whom, as he snapped the SLR camera, the recording eye, that he always wore on his wrist like a prosthetic limb.

On hearing about my research on the hermaphrodite, he quizzed me tirelessly, while keeping his own work-in-progress close to the vest. I was not entirely surprised, then, when I returned from London to find that he had published *Herma* in 1981, a novel depicting in his characteristically detailed and voyeuristic (the reviewers said "keenly observed") style a genitally ambidextrous "couple" (if one can call Jekyll and Hyde a couple) named Herma and Fred Hite (get it?).[18] I don't claim that Heiney's observations of our household or his interrogations of me and my research led directly in any way to his sexual dimorph in *Herma*.[19] He clearly must have been already at work on his 500-page opus in 1979, since *Herma* is much more wide-ranging and obsessively researched than what he might have wrung from his brief visits to our household on Balboa Island.[20] In

---

[18] *Herma* was reissued in 2015 with a preface by Michael Chabon, a student of Heiney's at Irvine. Chabon says that he met Heiney in 1985, yet I clearly remember both Chabon and his first wife the poet Lollie Groth from my time at Irvine (1977–82). I moved to Baton Rouge, Louisiana in 1982, and completed the dissertation in 1984. So how do I remember so clearly knowing Chabon and Lollie? This is not the first and will not be the last footnote to point out an irreconcilable difference between geographical or chronological memories and the evidence to be found in maps and other documents.

[19] The only intersection between my research and his might be the Beardsley print on Herma's wall in her Paris apartment on page 336, "just risqué enough to be interesting without offending anyone."

[20] The brilliant poet and author of the memoir *Tales of an Ancient Go-go Girl* (2015) Joan Jobe Smith tells me that I was credited with "'diagnosing' Don Heiney as 'banal-retentive.'"

the end, Heiney seems in *Herma* to be more interested in the behind-the-scenes workings of opera and the mechanics of early aeronautics than the literary or art historical dimensions of his doubled characters anyway, whatever his interest in our household dynamic might have been.[21] Still, the timing was interesting, if only to show that the dual-sexed figure was at that period everywhere and continues to pop up periodically as LBGTQ issues refuse to be relegated to freak status.[22]

Michel Foucault had notoriously taught at Irvine's summer School of Criticism and Theory a few years earlier, when (it was said) he had taken a bevy of young men and a blotter of LSD to Death Valley in a red Cadillac convertible, there to cavort in what became legendary fashion (let's just say the desert sun was supposed to have burnt more skin than Foucault's shaved head). A few years later, in 1978, Foucault published *Herculine Barbin: Being the Recently Discovered Memoirs of a Nineteenth-Century French Hermaphrodite* in French, its translation appearing to great fanfare in 1980. Not that Heiney would have needed the translation. He was perfectly at ease in French and Italian, as I knew, having taken his French translation seminar.[23]

---

[21] There are, notably, errors and omissions in his references to dual-sexed figures. Heiney asserts that Guanyin is the male version of Tara, when actually Guanyin is the Chinese version of the Tibetan Tara. Both bodhisattvas of compassion, they are female counterparts to the male (and Indian) bodhisattva Avalokiteshvara. Heiney also mentions the dual-sexed creature of Plato's *Symposium*, whose male and female halves, once split apart, then seek to reunite, explaining the origin of heterosexual desire—but he neglects to mention the other two creatures that account for homosexual and lesbian desire.

[22] Another 500-page novel on the same theme appeared twenty years later, Jeffrey Eugenides' *Middlesex* (New York: Farrar, Straus, and Giroux, 2002). This pseudo-autobiography is as well researched on the genetics and medical history of pseudohermaphroditism as Heiney's was on opera and early aeronautics, and thus more on point.

[23] Each graduate student was assigned a chapter of Suzanne Prou's novel *Les Demoiselles sous les ébéniers* (1967). Our difficulty in translating the title, it seems, had already been solved through evasion in the 1971 translation *Mlle Savelli?* The ques-

Mnemosyne and I were in the middle of a tumultuous love affair, an *amour fou*, if not an *égoïsme à deux*, and we lived more or less together until I left for London. Like addicts, we would quit one another for a time only to find it difficult to live without the dangerous stimulant each provided. We knew we were not good for each other, but that was part of the attraction. We would relapse for that fix of passionate sex and intense intellectual identification in a mutually self-destructive spiral. We got along in many ways, the physical attraction was magnetic, the intellectual affinities compelling. We just couldn't live together without insult or injury. There were too many past and increasingly present emotional wounds, some but not all of which we inflicted on one another. After a series of particularly unsavory, even surreal fights, we agreed to live apart, even if we could not resist sleeping together.

In the end it was my daughter who was the indirect cause of the collapse of our relationship. I could have dismissed Mnemosyne's threats to jump out of my van on the San Diego Freeway, or the time during an especially dramatic fight she pretended to call a cab to take her to a hotel and sat on the porch with her forest green North Face backpack for hours waiting for the taxi she knew would never arrive. I could even have forgiven her frequent infidelities with cowboys and famous critics. But I could not forgive her calling me a "bad father," even if it was true.

*   *   *

"Goodbye, Mary Poppins. Don't stay away too long," said Bert, near the end of the second showing of the film. Cyleste and I had watched it twice, but she was still agog with the magical London we had just seen (again) in the hard-candy hues of Disney's Technicolor.

"Want to see it again?" I asked.

---

tion mark is appropriate, serving as a disguise of sorts that emphasizes the story's mystery. As far as I know, however, none of us knew that the book had already been translated, or else we surely would have made comparisons if not cribbed from it.

The eyes of this seven-year-old said, "Can we?" We went out into the lobby to have our tub of popcorn refilled for a third viewing.

In a few days I would board an *aeroplane* for England. Cyleste had never been on a plane, although she had a vivid imagination, once telling her grandmother that she and I had flown to New York over the weekend, describing the buildings and bustle with credible accuracy, entirely made up. Now she believed that I might actually be moving to a place where a man could float up to the ceiling on the wings of his laughter and where foppish penguins danced in the park.

My own preconceptions about London were no less fantastical. The son of parents who had come to California like Steinbeck's Joads, I had never been aboard an *aeroplane* either, much less abroad. All of my expectations came from literature, especially a sliver from the late nineteenth and early twentieth centuries, although a few Gothic accents intruded, Monk Lewis and Beckford's *Vathek*, for example. But it was Blake and Byron, and their successors in the form of latter-day romantics and dandies from the Pre-Raphaelites to the fin de siècle and its afterglow who set the scene for me. The mythos of London that I had in mind was based on everything I had read in Dickens and Thackeray, Collins and Beerbohm, Firbank and Waugh, no less than on the cardboard Edwardian setting of the movie version of the Travers novel about a magical nanny. The taffy-textured world of the Disney production that so entranced a seven-year-old was not far removed from the mental constructions in the mind of her father, four times her age. Never mind that the cinematic spectacle we were taking in for the third time in a row was filmed on a set in Burbank, not fifty miles from this multiplex theater in Costa Mesa, California.

Mnemosyne was right: I was a bad father. Like many fathers separated from their young children, knowing that no atonement can ever be enough, I tried to make up for my absence with extravagant gestures, like sitting through three showings of *Mary Poppins*. Not that spending several hours in Disney's mythical London was a chore for me; I'm sure I enjoyed it at least as much as she did, maybe more. In fact, I suspect that by the third viewing, it was she who was humoring me.

I might as well have been Mary Poppins myself, descending on Piccadilly Circus from the sky with my brolly as parachute, except that she was *practically perfect in every way*, and I was not yet fully formed, almost an embryo whose sexual and intellectual identity had yet to take the shape of an identifiable self—practically *imperfect* in every way, from my failed marriage and disastrous love affairs to my shabby corduroy coat and less than stylish shoes. In a year from now, who knows how everything might change: I might catch a wind "blowing dead on from the west" and arise renewed from the ashes of my time in London, having created what? The intrepid Poppins had created order. What if my only souvenir was the chaos of memory? Would I return to California any wiser? Even if I did not discover who I was, I might come away with a better sense of who I was not.

As the TWA flight rose up over LAX and the Pacific Ocean before heading east northeast, I knew that, packed in my bags, among my research notes, was the gynandromorph that Cyleste had drawn for me. In that form I hoped to take my daughter with me. What, I wanted to know, had inspired her to take up pencils and colored pens and put to paper her personal impression of the primordial myth? Was it simply that she had overheard me droning on to her mother about my research? (Thus our sexual mythologies are unwittingly passed on to a younger generation who are always paying attention, even when we are not. What they do with those mythologies is always a mystery, whether they are edified or horrified by them, whether they adopt or reject them.) Or was it something more profound? Perhaps it was simply an attempt to connect with me, her soon-to-be absent father, and my interests. It is possible that I told Cyleste a PG-rated version of the myth of Salmacis and Hermaphroditus from Ovid's *Metamorphoses* as a bedtime story, as I was to do decades later with my younger daughter Izzy with Kafka's *Metamorphosis*.

It was September 13, 1980. I was 35,000 feet over the North Atlantic. I had just turned twenty-eight.

6 / London with its Foolscap Crown

> A huge dun cupola, like a foolscap crown
> On a fool's head—and there is London Town.
> —Byron, *Don Juan*, Canto 10

My Ashley Gardens flatmates, all students, included several Americans like me on graduate fellowships to study drama or economics, a Polish fashion design student from Canada, and studious Nikki, our only indigenous resident, from Newcastle. I shared the L-shaped room with the only other male, Eric, an awkward American actor with a wide smile, a bad complexion, and a strong but unobtrusive faith in the Bible, which he would study in a fervent whisper when he wasn't immersed in semi-silent rehearsals for some play. These sibilant monologs for divine or human audiences could occur at any time of day or night. We made an odd couple, I suppose, the enthusiast and the atheist, since we had so little in common. We were polar opposites really, but since we did not impose our views on each other, the arrangement worked out well. Though we had been thrown into close physical proximity, we were so distant in personality that the invisible wall that separated us provided us with quite a bit of privacy, as though our room comprised two different spiritual planes. We hardly talked, and hardly saw each other, in part, because our schedules were so erratic, but really because we were invisible to one another. We never bumped into each other, perhaps because we passed through one another, like ghosts. Even Concha seemed not to notice him sleeping around the corner of the same room, although I am sure he was well aware of her since she was not shy of expressing herself, especially in her more ecstatic moments.

Mariola struck me as neither Polish nor Canadian; she was the most American of us all, at least on the surface. Her brash voice and her unapologetic materialism—she was the original Material Girl avant la lettre and avant Madonna—provided one's first impression of her. But once you had talked with her for a while her European assertiveness appeared, along with her Canadian accent oddly enough, and you began to understand her background as a Central European Catholic immigrant. Unlike Eric, who kept his born-again sentiments to himself, but was always silently judging everyone, Mariola tossed out predictions on everyone's future prospects based on their behavior, dress, and diet like some sort of benevolent Baba Yaga fortune teller—"Richard, you'll die alone if you keep this up. Man cannot live on girls and Guinness alone." Yet she never held these judgments against us. Instead, she embraced our peccadillos, enfolding us in her forgiveness even as she pointed out our flaws, as though she were Mother Mary herself drawing us to her substantial bosom.

As a budding fashion designer with an outgoing personality, Mariola brought a whole cast of interesting characters through the flat, not just her fellow fashion students and artists, but also refugees from the Eastern bloc, political and social dissidents, homosexuals, hairdressers, and models. I went out with a few of her friends, including Charlotte, a cold Swedish beauty, and Lena, the diminutive daughter of a Greek shipping magnate. Mariola never had any romantic entanglements of her own that I recall, but perhaps that is because she was always advising us on ours. Mariola herself was too valuable as a friend and confidante for me ever to consider becoming intimate with her in any other way. Anyway, there was something forbidding and forceful about her that put an inviolable space between us, like two repelling magnets, a force field that kept our friendship safe. And there was a fleshly solidity to her, cheeks like chipmunks', from which she emitted endearing giggles, that kept me in a state of confusion as surely as the mustache on Marian Halcombe's lip in *The Woman in White* put poor Walter Hartright at bay.

It was Mariola's friend Carin, a sweet gamine teenager from Detroit for whom cynicism was a form of romanticism, who claimed me at once with the petulant toss of her shingle bobbed hair à la Louise Brooks. She wore a forest green wool jacket with a leather band collar with matching leather piping on the pockets and fawn jodhpurs with delicate black boots. In addition to the way she blew smoke from the moue of her pursed lips, I was attracted to what I thought of as her "idle intelligence," which was not idle at all; it was just not put to the scholarly plough, as Mnemosyne's had been. It was, in a sense, intelligence for its own sake, pure, detached, fun, and, as I wanted to think, immune to me. Soon after meeting in early winter, we became inseparable.

Nevertheless, the fall was difficult. Separated from Mnemosyne and my daughter, I tried to devote myself to work, but with little success. To save bus fare, I walked to the British Museum, but by the time I got there, I had taken so many detours drinking in the sights of that tradition-rich but always trendy city that the Reading Room would be close to closing. I would order books, most of which could not be fetched until the following day from the stacks south of the Thames, promising myself that I would attempt to get there earlier tomorrow. Sometimes I actually did, but en route I would fall prey to the city's iconic palate—splashes of color against the backdrop of convention—and lose my way, led astray perhaps by a pink polkadot punk mohawk in the midst of Savile Row.

The vast metropolis of this ancient city on the Thames was endlessly seductive, more like an aggregation of small neighborhoods than a big city, each with its distinctive personality and attractions to be infatuated with. I was happy just to wander aimlessly, taking in its constantly changing aura, like a lovestruck boy following one crush after another.[24] My direct route took me from Victoria to Bloomsbury, through St. James Park and along the Mall to Trafalgar Square, where the sirens of the National and Portrait Galleries called my name. From there I might veer to the left into Chinatown and the temptations of Soho or more often to the right into Covent Garden towards the eccentric Sir John Soane's Museum. If I managed to avoid this Scylla and Charybdis to find myself in the neighborhood of Tottenham Court Road, I knew I would make it to my destination. Of course by that time I was in need of a coffee, if not lunch, before making my way into the Museum itself.[25]

One day I arrived at the tall entrance gate after dark, only to be stopped by the guard. I knew the museum closed before the library, which stayed open until nine in the evening, so I pulled out my Reader's Card. The guard said, "At'll do ye no good now, mun. The Readin' Room closed an hour agoo." So it had. My only excuse was that I had wandered with a fresh infidelity of Mnemosyne's in mind. Her betrayals made me long, more painfully than ever, for the Slavic solidity of her jaw and body, and underneath that velvet flesh the cold steel of her often confused Nietzchean will.

Upon entering the great storehouse of stolen artifacts, I had to keep myself from peeling off to visit the Rosetta Stone or the Elgin Marbles or the hieratic Egyptian statues of black granodiorite one more time, in order to make my way into the inner sanctum: the

---

[24] Richard Church's impression of London's sprawl, the result of "capricious organic growth," is more sinister: "A spider's web, drooping under rough weather, and broken by continuous ingurgitation of victims, is an orderly structure by comparison with London's mesh of streets." *London, Flower of Cities All* (New York: John Day, 1966), 157.

[25] Google Maps tells me that the distance from Victoria to Bloomsbury, just over two miles, should take a brisk forty-five minutes to walk by heading along Victoria Street to Westminster Cathedral and the Houses of Parliament, left along Parliament Street to Trafalgar Square, continuing north to St. Martin's Lane through the theater district, then along Shaftesbury Avenue to zigzag finally onto Museum Street. I must certainly have gone that route more than once, yet I rarely made it from the gate of our lift to the gate of the Museum in less than two hours. On too many days I never made it there at all.

Reading Room of the British Library with its rows of polished reading desks radiating from the central information hub like spokes in a great wheel, the circular array pointing to the book-lined walls, all under the expanse of its famous sky-blue dome, light (on a good day) flooding through its neo-Gothic arched clerestory windows.

In the evening, upon leaving, I had to run the gauntlet of inviting pubs and wine bars just outside its gates. The Museum Tavern, for example, where many a researcher had ended their workday, including Marx and Engels, as the brass plaque claimed, and who knows how many thousands of others who had, like me, no claim (as yet, if ever) to any sort of fame or notoriety. With that thought, feeling my insignificance in the universe of scholarship after a day standing on the toes of giants (I didn't flatter myself that I had reached as high as their shoulders), I faced the walk home through the same temptations and detours on my return trip, like Odysseus, except that now the nightlife of London was lighting up, igniting ten thousand more temptations. More than once I found myself at Rumours or Tutton's having a "dinner" of Guinness, in spite of Mariola's oracle. Sometimes I even made it home that night to my own bed, ready the next morning to get up and do it all over again.

I confided in Mariola my loneliness and depression. Weeks passed with no tangible progress in my research, days passed with no unforeseen adventure to excuse my uselessness. I felt adrift and drained, jaded and lost. She encouraged me to try to meet more people and not worry so much about what I had left behind. She could see that I would wait for hours for the post to come or for the telephone to ring, only to be disappointed and feel abandoned if there was no communication from America, or worse, when a letter or phone call did come and Mnemosyne informed me of how she had taken refuge from her own loneliness and depression in yet a new lover. Conversations with my daughter and her mother similarly left me feeling more tender and nostalgic than when I merely longed to hear their voices.

These long-distance conversations were rendered absurd by the loud click of the primitive timer that we had British Telecom install so that we could divvy up the bill accurately. The first bill had been staggering with so many American roommates calling home and no way of knowing who made the calls. As the sole native, Nikki was sure that she should not have to pay an equal portion of our bill, and Eric and I seldom made long-distance calls, preferring to wait for our calls from abroad. Once the timer was installed, each of us signed in and out on a log, entering the beginning and end times of our call. The timer helped to keep us honest as it heckled us all during the conversation, like a housemother clicking her tongue to inform us of every five pence being spent. For a local call, this was not particularly distracting—5p, 10p, 15p, 20p, at most—but a call to the West Coast meant that the housemother's tongue clattered like a card in the spokes of a bicycle. It was nothing for wealthy Debbie-from-Princeton to call her mother in Los Angeles or her father in New York, but for those of us on a tight budget, the timer felt like the empty chambers of a revolver being spun in a game of Russian roulette.

Concha broke the monotony of that autumn, her intensity a welcome shock after several days of my own company, but even she left something to be desired.

My sittings for Laury only reminded both him and me of what we had left behind.

Mariola was sympathetic and tried to convince me to live in the present for a while. "Isn't that why you came here?" she said. She was right, of course.

To equip me for life in London, Mariola gave me fashion advice. "Richard, you know if you're going to go out with my friends, you need to think about what you're wearing. That old corduroy pea-coat is hideous, and it's not enough to keep you warm in a London winter anyway. You need a proper wool coat. And your shoes. You really have to think about your shoes. Shoes tell the whole story of a man."

"What do my shoes tell you, Mariola?"

"You don't want to know," she said dismissively. It seemed that my dandyism, like my homosexuality, was all in my mind. "You can get away with everything else, even your hideous cloth coat, but you must buy some decent shoes. Promise me you will."

I promised and I tried. Splurging on clothes seemed extravagant and possibly unhealthy, since I had so little to spend on food. My budget was especially strapped in the beginning because my stipend from the Fulbright Commission was not what it should have been for the cost of living in London. I had been assigned to Professor Ian Fletcher, the legendary late-Victorian scholar at the University of Reading, but I had good reason to be in London, where most of my research materials were to be found. Besides, who would willingly reside in Reading when you could be in London? Professor Fletcher was an invaluable resource, and I should have made better use of him, but he was not in the best of health and later apologized for not being of more use to me.[26]

On the occasions when I did take the train to Reading to consult with him, Professor Fletcher would usher me into his anachronistically spacious, book-lined university office, and invite me to settle into one of the two overstuffed armchairs. Then he would bring down a bottle of whiskey and a single glass from one of the shelves overflowing with manuscripts, and offer me a drink, saying how sorry he was that he couldn't drink with me, due to his failing health. I consented to drink for both of us.

I'm afraid I might have been too insistent on expounding the positive aspects of the "erotic hermaphrodite," which had recently become the centerpiece of my dissertation's argument, citing Georges Bataille's view that eroticism is the activity of a conscious being, the physical paradox of the figure of double sex in the art and literature I was studying (Beardsley, for example) being more about awakening the critical consciousness of the viewer than aspiring to some spiritual state of perfect balance, much less exciting the mere manipulation of flesh.

---

[26] Ian Fletcher (1920–1988) specialized in authors of the fin de siècle, such as Aubrey Beardsley and Walter Pater. His only degree was a PhD, with a 1965 dissertation on the history of the little magazine. He left England, no doubt for the change of climate and his health, in 1982, and took a position at Arizona State University in Tempe, where he died six years later.

"Just be sure you are not playing some sort of anagrammatical game with 'erotic' and 'rhetoric,'" he said. "Those kinds of critical puns are fashionable, but they are the kind of glitter that is not always gold."

I warmed to this wordplay. I acknowledged that the two words were two sides of a coin, that eroticism was a form of persuasion and that rhetoric was a form of seduction, but that was what made them so suitable to the subject: they were like the hermaphrodite that had been split, and I wanted to see the erotic and the rhetoric reunited so that words carried a kinetic charge and the physical conjunction became the embodiment of words. I also wanted to draw sharp distinctions between the *analytical* hermaphrodite of the Decadence and the *synthetic* androgyne of the Romantics. In other words, I was trying my best to sound like I knew what I was talking about by creating oppositions that did not necessarily exist (it's what academics do, after all). And the whiskey tricked me into thinking that I might be able to put something over on this brilliant and generous man.

I followed up on this harangue by reverting to something a little more ancient, the "learned ribaldry"[27] of the Renaissance Italian Antonio Beccadelli, whose poetic compendium of erotica, *Hermaphroditus* (1425), was dedicated to Cosimo di Medici, condemned by the Council of Constance, and subsequently honored by book-burnings in Ferrara, Milan and Bologna. Beccadelli saw his book itself as hermaphroditic, in form as well as content, as he pointed out in a poem dedicated to Cosimo di Medici: "In two parts, Cosimo, I've divided my book / Just as the Hermaphrodite is divided too / . . . The first holds the penis, the second the vulva."[28] John Addington Symonds, Bob Peters's research subject as a Fulbright, had extolled

---

[27] Donald Cheney, "Spenser's Hermaphrodite and the 1590 *Faerie Queene*," PMLA 87 (March 1972), 194.

[28] Antonio Beccadelli, *L'Hermaphrodite de Panormita* (Paris: Isidore Liseux, 1892). The original Latin was translated into French, which I have here translated into English. A more recent English translation, and more loyal to the Latin, by Holt Parker, is more blunt: "Our book has at the same time a cunt and a cock." Antonio Beccadelli, *The Hermaphrodite* (Cambridge & London: Harvard UP, 2010), 9.

the virtues of Beccadelli's work as deserving "a prominent place in the history of Renaissance manners," calling it a signal instance of the value attached in this age to pure scholarship, irrespective of moral considerations."[29] That judgment resonated with me in more ways than one. I was always responsive to the argument to purity, *argumentum ad puritatem*, anything done for its own sake: education, scholarship, *l'art pour l'art*, sex, intelligence.

Fletcher pointed out that I might consider the fact that Symonds' insistence on Beccadelli's scholarly purity might have been somewhat compromised by the Renaissance author's repudiation of his *Hermaphroditus* as a youthful—and immoral—mistake, writing in 1435, ten years after his dedication to Cosimo this recantation: "I dedicated to you a book / with the foul title of *The Hermaphrodite*. / I am now ashamed that I taught various filthy acts and / impious ways of Venus, which nature shuns. / . . . / Forgive me. Alas, I myself now recognize my offense."[30]

Rather brashly, if not impertinently, I said, "If we are going to always measure the wisdom of youth's *temerity* by the scales of maturity's *timidity*, we won't get anywhere. Or as Blake said, 'Prudence is an ugly old maid courted by incapacity.'"

Professor Fletcher smiled at the glitter of my newest less-than-gold alliterative critical comparison and did not seem to take my inconsiderate outburst personally. It was only later that I considered he could have taken my comment as a veiled reference to his own ill health. Back in London, I kicked myself for kicking's sake—and because I deserved it.

My youthful insistence, like Beccadelli's original enthusiasm for his boldness, was probably too strident, but it was in reaction to most of the critics on the subject who followed the mature Beccadelli by seeing in his work—as in most uses of the hermaphrodite—nothing but code for "various filthy acts." These critics seemed to prefer

---

[29]*Renaissance in Italy*, 2 vols. (New York: Modern Library, 1935), vol. 1, 445.

[30]Antonio Beccadelli, *The Hermaphrodite*. Translated and edited by Holt Parker (Cambridge & London: Harvard UP, 2010), 9.

the airbrushed ambiguities of the spiritual androgyne to the explicitness of the erotic (and rhetorical) hermaphrodite. I felt I had to make a stand. I was put off by those moralistic critics, like Mario Praz, whose *Romantic Agony* (1933) set the tone for seeing in the figure only sexual perversions like incest, cannibalism, vampirism, and necrophilia.[31] Following in Praz's footsteps, Mircea Eliade, considered the use of the hermaphrodite in late nineteenth-century art and literature as a "degradation of the symbol."[32] Closer to home, A. J. L. Busst (in an essay published in a collection edited by Fletcher himself) saw only indications of decadence, degeneracy, and "moral ambivalence," adding to Praz's catalog of sexual paraphilias: "As a symbol of evil and vice, the hermaphrodite represented not only promiscuity, but indeed all sorts of perversions: besides cerebral lechery, onanism, demonality and incest, which have already been mentioned, it symbolized homosexuality, sadism and masochism."[33]

All of these old fogeys seemed to protest too much! Their obsessive fascination with what they called perversion and degradation struck me as itself perverse and degrading to their profession as critics. How they justified their preoccupied stare by a show of moral outrage! Busst, in particular, appeared outdated and puritanical, but I might have taken his preaching too personally. Cerebral lechery indeed!

Offering to refill my tumbler of Famous Grouse yet again, Professor Fletcher seemed to guess what I was all about, but he was indulgent with me and more charitable than I deserved. All he said was:

"Don't you think you're being a little hard on old Busst?"

As he tipped the bottle to fill my glass, there was a sparkle in his

---

[31] *The Romantic Agony*. Trans. Angus Fletcher (New York: Oxford UP, 1970).

[32] *The Two and the One*. Trans. J.M. Cohen (New York: Harper & Row, 1965), 100. Eliade's examples are easy targets, such as Joséphin Péladan and Aleister Crawley [sic].

[33] "The Androgyne in the Nineteenth Century," in *Romantic Mythologies*. Ed. Ian Fletcher (London: Routledge and Kegan Paul, 1967), 55.

eye that might have been mixed with a drop of envy for my passion, my headlong bullheaded argumentativeness, my ignorance, and my youth, as though he knew well what it was like to be hungry and thirsty and full of both physical and intellectual lust and would like to go back and do it all over again. Then, to end the discussion on a much-needed lighter note, he said:

"You know what the notorious Nina Hamnett used to say: 'I wish sometimes when I am tight / That I were an hermaphrodite.' But I would not recommend her as a model. She was a die-hard bohemian who did not end well."

"How was that?" I was not familiar with her or her work.

"Fell—or jumped—out of her apartment window—not in her beloved Fitzrovia, where she was called the Queen of Bohemia, but in Paddington, where she ended up after being made homeless after a fire. Impaled on the fence below, I'm afraid. Interesting writer, though. Have another dram against the cold for the trip back?"

* * *

I finally appealed to the Fulbright Commission to increase my stipend to the level that my fellow Fulbrighters were getting in London. I had missed out on several months of the higher stipend by that time, so when the Commission came through with the difference in a lump sum, it was as though I had managed to save brilliantly. It was this windfall that would allow me to take a trip, however frugally, to Morocco for the winter holidays. Friends from graduate school, JoAnn Balingit and Francis Poole, wonderful poets both, were now living in sunny Tangier, teaching at the American School there, and had invited me to visit. But first I bought a beautiful pair of jazz saddle oxfords on sale at a boutique in Bloomsbury, very well made and stylish, a light beige suede, completely wrong for three seasons of the year in London. Mariola approved, however, and I kept them for over a decade. It would have been more sensible, though, to buy a wool coat.

Carin, the fashion design student from Detroit, must have generously overlooked my many fashion faux-pas. Throughout the winter we explored London together, seeing the city anew through each other's eyes. We went to jumble sales and street markets and bought odd little items we could afford, like toast racks or the matching ashtrays we found at two different street markets, a pair of porcelain dice with white pips, found among the miscellaneous trash and treasure at Portobello Road, Petticoat Lane, or Camden Market. We reunited them as though they were long lost brother and sister twins separated at birth. Mine was black and resided at Ashley Gardens, while hers, pink, was kept at her place in Princess Mews.

My enthusiasm for this conceit of the twins, I think, startled Carin but also amused her. I pointed out (somewhat pedantically) that Pausanius, in his *Description of Greece* (9.31.7–8) asserted with lawyerly logic that Narcissus was certainly old enough, and not stupid enough (nor is there any mention of mental illness in the record) to have been fooled into thinking that his reflection in the pool was some pretty girl (or boy) that he longed to merge with, sexually or otherwise. Pausanius very sanely, although without any evidence, speculated instead that Narcissus had a twin sister whose loss he grieved. This is a far more generous and plausible theory for Narcissus's drowning than his famous vanity.

"However, if we believed Pausanius," I said, beginning to wrap up my disquisition, "we would have to reconsider our entire definition of 'narcissism' and lose a pretty useful mental health diagnosis." Ignoring Carin's look, which was at first curious and grew incredulous as I went on in this vein, I concluded in a parody of the language of literary criticism: "Thus an early scientific explanation for the reunification of the separation of the sexes as reflected in the variation on the Narcissus and Echo theme that the myth of Hermaphroditus and Salmacis seems to be. Q.E.D."

Carin just laughed at me. I loved her for that. That these innocent ashtrays could remind me of my research into sexual mythologies showed that I was, she said, "either brilliant or barmy or obsessed or perverse. Or—*check* and *check* and *check* and *check*—all of the above."

Even if she couldn't always take me seriously, Carin did take her fashion studies seriously. Bent over her sketchbook, pencils and pastels in one hand and a cigarette in the other, blowing smoke at the ceiling, she would sometimes lock herself in with her projects and not emerge for days. She would fly off on field trips to Milan to study with Pucci, or to Florence to see what was current in the ateliers on the Arno. She laughed easily, but self-consciously, which added to her attraction, as she aspired to be detached, sophisticated and debauched, but she could never quite pull it off. She enjoyed life too much to be *ennuyée*. To be bored in London would not just have been to be bored of life, it would have been boorish and ungrateful. *S'ennuyer est ennuyeux*. She was too smart for that. She was genuine. She was really a bright Midwestern girl from the better suburbs of Detroit, although she had lived in England before, when her father, "a captain of industry," she said with a mixture of pride and irony, was transferred. "Thus my bad case of transatlantica," as though it were a terminal but not debilitating illness, this affinity for England, this love of London. As we gazed into the mirror of each other, I suppose she saw some similar aspiration, longing, and vulnerability in me, an Okie mechanic's kid from the lesser suburbs of Los Angeles who aspired to be a European decadent, or at least a scholar of such.[34] We met on the outskirts of our aspirations, where we could be authentic, and played there like incestuous brother and sister.[35]

We wondered: was London the catalyst that sparked our chemis-

---

[34] Maybe Joseph Brodsky was right: "only a really provincial person can become a true dandy." Emmanuel Carrère, *Limonov*. Trans. John Lambert. (New York: Farrar, Straus and Giroux, 2011), 118.

[35] It occurs to me that there was another childhood pre-sexual experience— repressed until now, it seems—that belongs to the period between Maria and the 50-Foot Woman, between desire and fear. A neighbor in Upland a few years older than me, whose name I can't recall, would take his little sister into the backhouse and molest her; I'm not sure exactly how, since I declined his invitations to join him. "C'mon, Uncle Mousey! It's fun." I adjusted my recently acquired glasses, seeing him in a new light, and fled his leering insouciance, which even then struck me as a portrait of casual evil. That said, I can imagine a fraternal-sororal incest that is consensual and neither evil nor tragic, but as pure as Adam and Eve before the fall.

try? Would we fizzle in another environment? To find out, we spent a weekend at a bed-and-breakfast in Bath, playing tourists, visiting the Museum of Costume, touring the eponymous mineral baths with their Roman foundations and their eighteenth-century overlays, and frequenting the Pump Room for tea and cakes and chamber music. So civilized. We ventured out by taxi one damp day to see a country house called Dyrham, part of the National Trust, and laughed as we danced with peacocks in the garden along the gravel paths, me clowning around, strutting with my black umbrella, fanning it out like some gloomy peacock's display.

Carin lived with a Canadian friend, Louise, in a mews flat near Swiss Cottage, which amounted to a bit of a trek for me all the way from W1. Sometimes I would make the long walk home in the middle of the night by myself in my shabby corduroy coat to save on taxi fare. The line of mews flats where they lived had been stables once upon a time, and now the ground floor housed the cars and drivers of mini-cabs, who would keep odd hours, but they never bothered us since we kept even odder hours ourselves.

We never tired of each other's company. We never felt cramped thrown together in small spaces. We would climb up the ladder and through the trapdoor in the floor of the attic, which was her bedroom and where we slept or avoided sleep. It was not much bigger than a coffin. We couldn't stand up, but we didn't really need to. Reclining under the low sloped ceiling with a bottle of wine, we flicked the ashes from the tips of my glowing Dunhills or her Silk Cuts[36] into her pink porcelain die with the white pips and talked all night about the bands we had heard (UB40 or the English Beat) or the movies we had seen together (*Raging Bull* comes to mind, which we saw with Louise and Laury on Carin's nineteenth birthday) or the authors we were reading (Ronald Firbank or Penelope Fitzgerald). I

---

[36]Silk Cut's brilliant advertising was understated, sexually suggestive, and iconic. There was no text to these ads, but no one could ignore the effect of the billboard displays and cinema ads of undulating landscapes of purple silk slashed with a smooth slit. This is known as Charles Saatchi's "Silk Cunt" campaign, launched in 1983. How is it part of my memory of 1980–81?

suppose my literary tastes made up in Carin's mind for my lack of a fashion sense. I can't guess what else she could have seen in me, an older man with a past and a daughter, an estranged wife and an estranged girlfriend, and strange obsessions that became hypotheses.

She could be genuinely annoyed with me, especially when I neglected to call her, but more often she would toss her head in faux perturbation, flipping her Louise Brooks bob, her eyes positively feline, her head turned to present her signature profile pout as she blew smoke at the low ceiling. And then, laughing at her own posturing, she would break character, revealing her true sweetness, mischievous and elfin. She was nothing if not self-aware. I don't think she was aware, though, of how wonderful she was. Otherwise she would not have been jealous when I joked around with her roommate. Louise was fun, but not as fun as Carin. Louise was funny, but not as funny as Carin. Louise was lively and opinionated, but Carin was sensitive and intelligent. Even if I had been attracted to Louise, which I was not, I would not have done anything about it. I loved Carin, I realized, the person sitting there in Carin's clothes, smoking Carin's cigarettes, smiling Carin's smile, looking out of Carin's elfin eyes, the one who smelled like Carin and laughed exactly like Carin.

As the December cold set in, though, the familiar commute between Ashley Gardens and Swiss Cottage began to take its toll. I longed for sunshine, the surprise of new places, unfamiliar faces, and open spaces. Morocco was calling me.

Lady with a Fan, c. 1635–40. Diego Velázquez. Wallace Collection, London.

"... what spoke to me was the black glance that shone from her slightly blushing visage, the dark sanpaku eyes, which could only spell misfortune." (p. 75)

7 / Visiting Velázquez in London and Madrid

> There are two sexes. The unpalatable truth must be faced. Your attempts at a merger can end only in heartbreak.
> —Joe Orton, *What the Butler Saw*

Among the myriad museums of London, my favorite is the Wallace Collection in Marylebone. There are other museums with more extensive collections, like the National Gallery, the British Museum and the Tate, and a few that are more idiosyncratic, like Sir John Soane's Museum. But the Wallace Collection is the most intimate. I met another Spanish woman there, and it was love at first sight. I was drawn into the room where she was as if by a spell when I spotted her through the door of one of the galleries. I was beckoned at first by the flared gauntlet of her white gloves as though pointing to her breast and the creamy froth border of lace décolletage. But it was her eyes that drew me in and have haunted me ever since. Her widow's peak directed one's gaze to her full red lips, but what spoke to me was the black glance that shone from her slightly blushing visage, the dark sanpaku eyes, which could only spell misfortune. Her expression never changed but never settled into a definite expression, seeming to hover between sadness and indifference, depending on my mood. I am almost ashamed to admit that for a while she became a goddess of love; she was an ideal form for me who never gave much credence to Platonism.

It seems that scholars have been unable to establish the identity of Velázquez's *Lady with a Fan*. I'm not surprised. It has been suggested that she was French and had come to the court of Philp IV after fleeing France disguised as a man.[37] Imagining her in male clothing instead of the low-cut bodice trimmed in lace, I found the suggestion of transvestism intriguing. (No such seductive backstory seems to have been attached to Velázquez's portrait of the same woman dressed in less elegant costume in his inferior *Lady in a Mantilla* in Devonshire). Of course, I associated her with Concha and both of them with Gautier's charming Mademoiselle de Maupin. Still, I prefer to think of her as Spanish; she could have been Concha's more feminine sister—or ancestor. Whenever I had the chance, I returned to visit this haunting, long-dead lady with a fan well after her living replica from Salamanca had tired of me (and I of her). Perhaps there was something to Platonism after all, or at least Neoplatonism, which posits art as the bridge between our senses and what we otherwise *sense*. This ambiguous intersection was, after all, one crux of my research.

*   *   *

I ran into Concha in the Green Park tube station just before Christmas. I was on my way home from Carin's in the precocious winter twilight after a long debauch that had begun the day before with two hours of squash with my flatmate Debbie-from-Princeton, followed by an extended visit to Sir John Soane's Museum with Carin, where we marveled over a small-scale plaster copy of the Villa Borghese *Sleeping Hermaphrodite*, in addition to endless architectural fragments with figures of ambiguous gender and animal-human blends that could have come fresh from the island of

---

[37] It is unlikely, though, that the *Lady with a Fan* is the same Marie de Rohan, Duchess of Chevreuse (1600–1679), who in portraits by other artists is depicted as a rather run-of-the-mill aristocratic milady.

Dr. Moreau. Then, after cappuccinos and shandies, off to the Arts Theatre near Leicester Square where we saw Joe Orton's *Loot*. Afterwards, we discussed his playful life and pathetic death and the satisfactions of farce. Finishing with a late meal and drinks in Soho, we slept like ancient statue fragments in her attic-coffin-bedroom at Princess Mews until two the next afternoon when I dragged myself to the tube station just as the briefest of winter so-called sunlight began to flag.

I was exhausted by the time I ran into Concha, all my muscles aching, mostly from yesterday's unaccustomed exertions in the squash court, but she insisted that we have a drink in Leicester Square, at an Australian wine bar called Bin 11. She told me about her new friend, "a Jewish boy who takes me to fancy places like the Playboy Club. But I don't care about that. He says, 'you have to wear a skirt.' I will not. 'You know I like to wear boys' clothes,' I say to him. 'I do not wear skirts and dresses. Full stop. Sorry.' No Playboy Club for me, I guess. Boohoo."

Then she apologized for our last meeting, which had begun with such promise and genuine affection, but ended like so many others, in frustration. "I am sorry, I was cruel, selfish. I want to go to bed with you tonight. The right way."

"That's sweet of you," I said. Sated and still saturated with Carin, I nevertheless longed for the detachment of Concha's impersonal sensuousness, so adept and emotionally undemanding. The fact was I was falling in love with Carin, and Concha provided the perfect antidote. "Come to my place," I said.

"I can't," she said. "I want to but I am ill."

It took me a moment to understand what she meant. I told her I didn't mind. I would welcome her tombstone weight on my chest as I slept the sleep of the dead.

"But I do mind," she said, wrapping her arms around me the way she had in the very beginning, her fragrant hair nuzzled silkily under my chin. Then she let go of me, and pushed me away slightly. "I will call you next week," she said, as she slipped into a taxi.

I would soon be leaving for Morocco, but I hadn't time to tell her that, so a rain check with Concha would have to wait for the new year. As the cab pulled away from the curb, I was glad I had betrayed Carin only by intention. I had a feeling I might never see Concha again, although I took comfort in the fact that I could always visit her doppelganger whenever I found myself with time to spare in the neighborhood of Mayfair or Marylebone.

* * *

It was almost the day of my departure for Morocco when I got a telephone call from Virginia, whom I had met back in October. She and her friend Hillarie had been passing through London and Oxford before heading to France and Italy. Now Virginia was back in town for a few days before their flight home to the States. Hillarie was delayed in Germany but would be along soon. In the meantime, Virginia wanted to meet me for dinner. Carin was with me when I got the call; she wanted to know who this mystery woman was and why I'd never mentioned her. To ease her suspicions, I told her that she was welcome to join us for dinner, and filled her in on how I had met the two American art students at the Tate Gallery restaurant on their way to Oxford well before I met Carin.

Virginia and Hillarie could not have been more different. Hillarie was an Amazonian Alice in Wonderland, an artist for whom life was a constant adventure, much of it underground—through rather than in front of the looking-glass because she lacked the vanity of self-consciousness. Robust and athletic, eternally youthful, she exuded sunshine and American health, her bright hair tumbling about her face like amber waves of grain. Virginia, a budding da Vinci scholar, was Hillarie's foil and complement. Prematurely gray, she wore her hair and her erudition like a nun's wimple. Her sallow skin had come to resemble the rare parchments she perused in libraries all over Europe. Her vast knowledge of art history rested in the high forehead like a shelf over her brow. And yet she was not unattractive—her features were sharp yet delicate, if the lips were a bit thin—more like a blank but primed canvas or one of those

Renaissance pages of ambiguous gender and minimal affect. Her dignity made Hillarie's energy look like frivolity. A makeover, or a little makeup and a smile, would have done wonders. Virginia had the stark beauty of a tree in winter, whereas Hillaire offered up the bounty of profligate blossoms midsummer.

The two were a study in contrast. I couldn't help but be reminded of Firbank's impressionistic description (typically somewhat slippery to grasp but effective nonetheless) of the title character in a book of his I was reading at the time, *The Artificial Princess*, whose title character bore some resemblance to Hillarie: "Often the fugitive marvels of the Sunset would linger with her in an afterglow entirely personal, and some of her lunar effects were extremely fine." Virginia was not simply tolerant of her more attractive friend, she genuinely admired her. But Hillarie's insatiable need for attention sometimes caused Virginia to cast a glance that conveyed the same ambivalence as the Artificial Princess's servant: "'She is a Cobra,' thought her maid, who understood her to perfection."[38]

I followed them to Oxford, using the excuse of their invitation to conduct some of my own research there. Virginia introduced me to treasures from the vaults that were not on display. In the Christ Church Picture Gallery she knew just which cartoons by da Vinci to request from the librarian, who was happy to bring these rarities out for us to examine. Earlier in the day I had discovered on my own in the same gallery Gaudier-Brzeska's wonderful *Dancer* (1913), cast in lithe bronze, along with a Procaccini oil of *Susanna and the Elders* (always a disturbing subject, but this treatment especially so: the head of one of the voyeuristic elders must surely have been modeled on someone's erection, his bald pate a protuberant obscenity, purplish, tumescent, undeniably phallic. I turned away in sympathy for Susanna and from the Elders in revulsion). But to be able to handle the portfolio of da Vinci drawings—that was a revelation.

That evening Virginia and I went to a concert at Holywell Music

---

[38] Ronald Firbank. *The Complete Firbank*. Intro. Anthony Powell. (London: Duckworth, 1961), 19.

Room to hear a Pierre Boulez solo for clarinet called *Domaines* performed by Roger Heaton. (Hillarie had meanwhile met a couple of undergraduates and was off testing her Zuleika Dobson mojo in some pub or club.) Heaton began at one of the six music stands, producing a long double-toned growing note that sounded half clarinet and half speaker-system feedback. But there was no speaker system, it was all clarinet. After finishing a few strange phrases, he would stop, pause, make a face perhaps while pondering the fermata, and then proceed to the next music stand, where he would produce another seemingly random harmony, a kind of improvised evocation of something found in man, city, abstraction, or nature. Random, and yet these dozen or so dissonant fragments created a unified mood, manic, nervous, and deserving of the no less than three curtain calls (although there was no curtain, the performance having been presented in the round).

This was followed by Gabriel Fauré's "Elégie," Opus 24 (1883) for cello and piano. All during the performance, triggered by the date, I imagined a dance between two very different books published in the same year: Carlo Collodi's *Adventures of Pinocchio* and, strangely enough, John Addington Symonds's *A Problem in Greek Ethics: Being an inquiry into the phenomenon of sexual inversion, addressed especially to medical psychologists and jurists.* The female cellist was quick and stoic, a beautiful marmoreal calm to her taut features. The male pianist's face was an expressive Roman mask. Together, their sound was a doomed marriage consummated in air, which was an impression more appropriate than I knew since the famous elegy (I later learned) was written for the composer's dead wife.

Back in my dank Oxford lodging, Virginia and I sat on the narrow bed to be as close as possible to the inadequate heater plugged into the wall overhead. It was the size of a rolled up scroll and we took turns placing our hands on it to warm our fingers. We pulled the rough wool blanket and quilted counterpane onto our laps and added a pillow to prop up the catalog of drawings she had bought so that we could examine it in detail.

She gave me a quick lecture tour through the current Leonardo scholarship, with particular attention to his allegories and their relevance to my interest in hermaphrodites. His series of the three double-sexed beings, she explained, together make up the three original beings described in Aristophanes' allegory of love in Plato's *Symposium*. She assured me that in Leonardo's *Allegory of Statecraft*, Prudence is depicted as half-man and half-woman, and Justice as a female holding up a mirror in which a male image appears, although I admitted that I couldn't make out any of this from the palimpsest of overworked cartoons. Undaunted, she went on to assert that Leonardo's *Allegory of Pleasure and Pain*, reminiscent of Swinburne's sadomasochistic interests, depicts a hermaphroditic (at least in the sense of being doubled) male figure, an effeminate younger torso along with a more weathered older torso bifurcated at the waist of a virile lower body ("as you know," she said, "the legs are the last to go in men"—in fact, I didn't). Finally, she pointed out how the Leda myth lends itself to hermaphroditic interpretations, since the hermaphrodite is often symbolized by a swan in classical and Renaissance iconography. This is especially relevant considering that the progeny of Zeus-in-the-form-of-a-Swan's coupling with Leda led to the birth of one set of male-female twins, Helen and Pollux, along with her husband Tyndareus' male-female twins, Clytemnestra and Castor, conceived, so it is said, on the same night.[39]

Pursuing the rape theme, I told her how smitten I was recently with two huge cartoons by Agostino Caracci in the National Gallery, studies for the ceiling of the Palazzo Farnese in Rome. These two scenes complemented one another, male and female switching roles as rapist and raped. The violence of *A Woman Borne Off by a Sea God* matched that of *Cephalus Carried Off by Aurora in Her Chariot*, the male's rape of the woman in the former mirrored by the female's rape of the man in the latter. Both drawings are highly charged and erotic, done in sensitive pencil that seems to make each muscular

---

[39]See Byam Shaw, *Drawings of Old Masters at Christ Church*, Catalog I (Oxford: Clarendon Press, 1976). Cat. #17 recto and verso.

contraction visibly twitch. The swirling force of the Sea God's departure is about to sweep the mortal woman away, resistless, especially if he can latch his hand between her thighs as it appears he is about to do while his cheek nuzzles her plump breast. "When I saw it, the movement of the drawing was dizzying," I confessed. "I can't imagine anyone looking up and seeing it on a ceiling without keeling over. But maybe that's because I had a cold when I saw it." The companion piece had a similar effect, as Aurora wraps her muscled arm around her prey to abduct him for an eight-year absence. Still, her arms and face (suspiciously similar to Cephalus's own) make it hard to believe that this is a wholly female rapist. On the arm of dawn's chariot is carved a diminutive face, neck distended above breasts which could be either male or female, hermaphrodites being popular decorative motifs of that period. Neither of us noted, not aloud at least, the remarkable similarity between Caracci's figures and our friend Hillarie, but we exchanged an unvoiced glance.

Such was our time in Oxford, I assured Carin, a cultural smorgasbord of erotic references and representations but no actual orgies. The only intercourse I shared with Virginia was intellectual. Carin remained suspicious until she set eyes on Virginia in the flesh. When she sensed no sexual tension in the air, the two of them hit it off immediately.

We met up with Virginia at Jimmy's Greek Restaurant in Frith Street, Soho. Carin and I often came here for the stuffed vine leaves, moussaka, and retsina, which were plentiful and cheap. The service was usually charmingly indifferent when it was not actually rude. Tonight it was rude. One sometimes wondered how they stayed in business.[40]

"I spoke with Hillarie on the phone today," said Virginia, once we had managed to place our order with the surly and hirsute waiter. "She called from Baden-Baden and should be here in a few days before our flight back to the States. She asks if you miss her."

Carin could not hide a frown at this new threat, but I laughed.

---

[40] An East Soho institution for over sixty years, Jimmy's closed sometime in 2011.

"Of course she says nothing about her missing *me!*" I pointed out.

While Hillarie and I had once slept in the same bed together, nothing overtly sexual had occurred between us. Perhaps our cuddling had not been as chaste as my intellectual intercourse with Virginia under the scratchy wool blankets and homely counterpane in Oxford, yet neither had it been in its way as intimate, but I had no designs on that free Amazonian spirit and she had no designs on me. It was the special charm of our acquaintance that sex was taken for granted as not being in the picture, not our picture anyway.

Over dinner Virginia painted for us a vivid verbal tableau of Hillarie's and her adventures in France and Italy. All of her stories seemed to involve a Hillarie misadventure with men: like Caracci's rape cartoons, either they were carrying her away or she was carrying them away. Hillarie was larger than life, as though she had obeyed the "Eat Me" command but forgot to take the "Drink Me" antidote. I could see her, Aurora-like, with her athletic build carrying off a man under each arm, one French and one Italian; or just as easily, her being carried away by two men, one French and one Italian—(it would take two to wrangle her if she bothered to resist: she was what my father would have called, in a down-home flourish of understatement, "a handful")—looking bewildered, wondering what they were to do with so much woman.

One actual adventure in Naples involved the two of them being hustled off the street and into a car by several men. Rape was avoided only by Hillarie deciding to deprive the men of their sport by enjoying the moment, taking on one man after another in the back seat. When one of them reached for Virginia (I imagined her cowering in the corner like Christina Rossetti posing for her brother's *Ecce Ancilla Domini*), Hillarie grabbed him by the arm and said, "Leave her alone. Fuck *me.*" Yanking him away from Virginia, she forced him between her own powerful thighs and held him there for the duration. Did I detect a hint of regret in Virginia's voice? Or was it admiration for her creatively courageous friend, whom she viewed (and not only in that instance) as a figure of heroic proportions if not always altruistic intentions. Afterward, Hillarie made light of the event, declaring victory by saying she had "beat their spadas into harmless ploughshares." (If only she had been able to perform at will, as in my brother's fantasy, spada captiva, and then to clip their stems off, one by one, with a spasm of her vagina dentata, what sweet vengeance.)

After dinner, we were supposed to meet Laury at the Black Friar pub in The City, famous for its *art nouveau* reliefs, but it was closed and he never showed up. (It would be weeks before I found out why he couldn't make it.) We found another, less picturesque pub nearby, where Virginia told the story that came to be known as The Ruins of Rome.

One evening, after an uneventful day of sightseeing, she and Hillarie were walking at sunset among the ruins of the Roman Forum (in my mind the setting is near the Temple of Vesta) when a man, presumably Italian, headed straight in their direction. Hillarie was always oblivious to such dangers, but this time it was Virginia who was looking up and admiring the broken columns and architraves, much as Thales had been marveling at the constellations before he fell, philosophically, into an open cesspit. The Italian who had fixed Virgina on his radar managed to bump violently into her with perfect timing, an extraordinary effort of coordination between navigation and masturbation. Virginia, who was usually the one to warn Hillarie of mashers, upbraided her friend for not taking care of her this time. When she saw Hillarie's expression, she looked down and realized that the man had gushed a little Vesuvius over her clothes. Such would forever be their memory of the ruins of Rome.

"Ewww!" said Carin, who knew something about Italy. "The ruins of Rome will never be the same."

"Nor will I," said Virginia, flicking at her blouse with a napkin as though a vestige of the ruins remained. But it was only a little foam from her beer.

* * *

When Hillarie arrived from Baden-Baden, we went to a pub for a drink, this time without Carin, who had an assignment for school to complete. Hillarie was affectionate but tired from her months of travel and knowing it was almost at an end. That night Virginia took my narrow mattress and Hillarie and I slept in Debbie-from-Princeton's bed because she was visiting her movie-mogul mother in Los Angeles for the holidays. I was not interested in betraying Carin with Hillarie, who had enough French and Italian scalps hanging from her belt already. We slept together, cuddled half-naked but chastely, like a couple of Arctic fox twins in the womb, yin and yang, for the asexual affection, this Amazonian Alice and I.

The next day we went to the British Museum, where we found an Attic clay wine jug from around 600 BC with Hermes posing in profile between two sphinxes. We noted his strange garment resembling a black garter belt and stockings.

"Sexy!" said Hillarie. "Why don't you try that?"

"Oh, is that what it takes to turn you on?"

Afterward, we trekked to the Whitechapel Gallery to see the Max Beckmann triptychs on display, which knocked me out (as the German Expressionists often do), but she claimed to be unmoved, devoted as she was to Cézanne's "integrity of painted surfaces," as she called it. Whatever that meant.

My last few days in London before leaving for Morocco were thus a whirlwind of activity, bantering with Hillarie, buying guidebooks and travelers checks, changing a few pounds for francs and pesetas, a final trip by myself to the Wallace Collection to visit the *Hermaphrodite* ("after the ancient") and Concha's twin, my *Lady with a Fan*, ending with a visit to the Warburg Institute Library with Virginia to hunt out some manuscript she lusted after in her headstrong scholarly way, before showing up at Evelyn's for pasta with mussels and mushrooms, filberts and French wine.

The climax of the night was not saying farewell to Hillarie and Virginia, who were flying out of Heathrow the following day, but the long goodbye with Carin at her place. My body, I realized, had fallen in love with her and it was saying so, insistently, even if I could not yet utter the words aloud. She gave me a Christmas present, a vintage Dunhill Rollagas silver cigarette lighter, which I was to take with me on the trip in her stead. Every cigarette would be a reminder of her. The next morning, once I managed to extricate myself from her embraces, I raced home for a quick shower and shave, packed light in a flash, and shouted my goodbyes to my flatmates as I slammed the door on my way to nearby Victoria Station. On the boat train, reading *Prick Up Your Ears*, John Lahr's biography of Joe Orton, I made it to Calais by early afternoon.

* * *

I had had enough of London. It was oppressive, and not just the weather. As V. S. Pritchett has said, "London has this power not only of conserving the history of others but of making one feel personally historic." By which he meant, it seems, living in the past rather than currently living what would someday enter into the history books. Certainly one lives among or amidst the past, for better or worse.

As I explained to Robert Folkenflik, one of my graduate school mentors who was in London for the fall semester as an honorary fellow at the University of London, I felt oppressed by the past, constrained by the Regency and Victorian architecture that seemed to lord it over us merely human temporalities, sniffing at our mortality. Flesh withers away; things endure. This in contrast to my native (and Folkenflik's adopted) Southern California, where everything built was so recent and so fragile, so rootless and so temporary, as to make the healthy human body seem significant and puissant, if not immortal, free of history, and therefore nakedly innocent. It was not just the surfers who rode the wave of the California mythos of the heroic body pitted against the instantaneity of a pristine nature. Indeed, it allowed the recently constructed University of California at Irvine to thumb its nose at tradition and embrace the trend of a romantic deconstruction in which the individual, for all his or her insignificance in terms of creation, reigned supreme in the realm of interpretation. In any case, Pritchett tells us, "London has always turned the mind inward. Londoners vegetate."[41]

As I visited Folkenflik and his family in their sumptuous Mayfair sublet, I had noted that the professor was not vegetating. Excited about his research, he lived each day to delve ever further into how the eighteenth-century artist-as-hero interpreted Renaissance allegory, such as Sterne's "ludic self-fashioning" through Tristram and Yorick.[42] Whether I had embarked on such a task of self-fashioning at the time, I am not sure that I knew, and we did not discuss anything in those terms, always deferring such discussions to the literary realm. Neither was his wife, also a professor at Irvine, vegetating. She too was luxuriating in London culture. Nor was his son, David, a bright eleven-year-old who was called upon to perform for their visitor, not by reciting Shakespeare or playing the harp, but by rattling off every tube station on all the lines of the vast London Underground, including their relative length, depth, and date of construction. A stellar and memorable performance worthy of any future London cabbie expected to imbibe The Knowledge. Or in David's case, worthy of the brilliant National Public Radio journalist he would grow up to become.

Certainly I was vegetating, and not in a good way. The dull leaden chill of an English winter had me hungering for sunshine and southern warmth. My friends from graduate school, JoAnn and Francis, had invited me to visit them in Tangier as far back as October and I was finally taking them up on it.

I reached Paris before midnight, just in time to miss the train

---

[41] *The Pritchett Century* (New York: Modern Library, 1999), 200.

[42] The phrase is Ian Campbell Ross's, from his biography *Laurence Sterne: A Life* (New York: Oxford UP, 2001), but I recall Folkenflik using the term "self-fashioning" in regards to Sterne and other authors well before this in his seminar on the eighteenth-century novel. Ludic was a term much in fashion in critical theory circles in the 1970s, like liminal. After Huizinga's *Homo Ludens* (1938), everything could be seen sub specie ludi. Just add ludic or liminal, and these terms, like bacon, could improve the taste of almost any theoretical recipe—*ludic irony, ludic eroticism, ludic law*. See also *The Culture of Autobiography: Constructions of Self-Representation*, edited by Robert Folkenflik (Stanford: Stanford UP, 1993) in the press's Irvine Studies in the Humanities series.

connection to Spain. A little Parisian gentleman in a beret saw my battered green backpack and welcomed me, trying to make conversation. "Ah, la première fois que vous êtes ici, à Paris! Mais les mauvais garçons, gardez, gardez-vous! Il y a trop, trop, trop de mauvais garçons. Ils vous tueront, vous voleront." After making little stabbing and shooting gestures with his fingers, he pointed his finger at me and wagged it in my face, as though to say, like some prophet of doom: "Heed my words, my boy, or disaster will ensue!" Lesson over, he dropped his Ancient Mariner role, politely doffed his beret, shook my hand and took his leave, shaking his head over the state of his beloved city as he made his way down the boulevard de Magenta, waving without looking back. "Bonsoir, Monsieur! Bonsoir!" I thought of Henry Miller and how he loved Paris and Parisians.

Unwilling to waste what little cash I had on a hotel for mere hours, I rambled with my backpack through the streets of Paris in a circumambulating loop from the Gare du Nord to the Place Bastille, then crossed the Seine to the Sorbonne. Sometime after 2:00 a.m. I stepped into a little bistro in the rue Descartes called Le Bateau Ivre. After the boat and trains from London, a simple meal of salad, bread, and a bottle of wine sated and rejuvenated me. Now full of determination to continue walking the streets of Paris until dawn, I happened onto the famed rue Mouffetard, a long narrow street that winds up a hill, with its bookshops, bistros, and boulangeries, all closed now, but the street was full of garbage trucks and garbage-pickers. Through the Luxembourg Gardens and thus around Saint-Germain-de-Prés, listening in on any number of spirited discussions and lovers' quarrels in the rooms above street level before crossing the river again to roam the Tuileries and the Louvre, its courtyard, the Cour Napoléon, imposing and empty.[43] One last lap along the Seine, past Île de la Cité, with a nod to Shakespeare and Company.

At dawn I sat down at an outdoor café facing the Gare d'Austerlitz. I picked up a newspaper someone had left behind, drank café

---

[43] This was of course before the addition of I. M. Pei's glass Pyramid (1987).

au lait, and devoured the petit déjeuner I'd asked for, a basket of brioches, croissants, *beurre et confitures*. Famished, I loaded up on these until it was time to board the train for the Spanish border at Irún. I was shocked to find I'd consumed 100 francs worth of breakfast, not knowing that I would be charged by the piece for the basket brimming with baked goods on the table.

*   *   *

The train from Boulogne to Paris had been modern and luxurious, like an airliner. But this one to the Spanish border was antiquated and quaint, squealing, sluggish and slow. It was full of Portuguese workers, homeward-bound for the holidays. They carried baskets of food and big white straw-covered jugs of red wine. At first I thought I was having trouble understanding their Spanish. Someone had told me that I should never speak Spanish to a Portuguese; they would prefer to be mistaken for French. Long history of the Iberian peninsula. So when I heard that mellifluous language, so close linguistically to the clipped consonants of Spanish, but distinguished by its buttery vowels closer to French, I ventured to speak to them in my rudimentary (literary and somewhat antique) French. They smiled and replied in a French that was understandable to me, relatively unidiomatic and pronounced slowly and clearly, as one non-native speaker to another.

They informed me that this was not the express train to Madrid that I was prepared to buy a ticket for. This was a chartered train for Portuguese workers only. As a consequence, no *contrôleur* ever appeared to ask for my ticket, this leg of my journey coming compliments of the Portuguese proletariat. Not only had I saved money on a hotel by walking all night, but what I had lost on my breakfast boulangerie binge was now more than regained on the free train ride. There was no dining car, but that too turned out well, thanks to the generosity of my fellow travelers. After several hours of our slow crawl south, they took pity on me. Pulling out a much-used pocket knife, its blue blade sharpened to a scythe-like sliver, one of the older women in the compartment carved for me portions of cold roast chicken, linguica sausages, fragrant white cheeses, and chunks of bread; and poured the thick syrupy rustic wine into a metal cup. I thanked her heartily, ate heartily, and fell into a profound slumber.

I woke up at the border at dusk. Here at Hendaye, the last French town, I had to change trains. I was tempted to abandon my itinerary and go all the way to Lisbon with my new friends and benefactors. A guard picked me out of the crowd and asked in French where I was going. "Madrid," I said. Whether he was confused or malevolent, the direction he pointed me in was the wrong one. Once I figured out where I was supposed to go, it turned out that I would have to wait for a short train ride to Irún. While waiting, I bought a bottle of wine, an apple and some cheese, which I ate on the two-kilometer hop before I could change trains again to Madrid.

The ride to Madrid lasted all night and then some, from before dark until midmorning. The moon was full, as it had been in Paris, but the moonlit northern Spanish countryside was eerie, barren and severe, a dream from *Don Quixote*, nothing like the moonlit cityscape of Paris which fulfilled a much different romantic fantasy for me, followed by the sunny, rolling hills around Tours and the Loire Valley that I had been enjoying all day. I drank my wine and slept fitfully, the local (and perhaps, as I thought, *loco*) train jerking to a spastic stop at what must have been every station, then jerking forward to continue the journey. Every time the train lurched forward I had the impression it was laughing at me, convulsed with glee at my series of miscalculations on my journey into the heart of Spain.

A fellow passenger occasionally tried to make conversation with me and the other passengers, but he had even less Spanish than me, so I provided some rudimentary translation. He was a lanky American basketball player who was living near Lyon. "It's horrible," he said, running his hands through his hair and pulling on his ears. "I have this 100-franc-a-day patisserie habit. I'm not sure how much more I can take." He played his whiny Neil Young tapes all night, even when the other two passengers in our compartment, a Spaniard and a Portuguese, were trying to sleep. Every now and then I'd ask him to turn the music off in the interest of international relations. But his Neil Young compulsion was equal to his addiction to *mille feuilles*. He clung to me because I could understand some Spanish until he met his girlfriend at the Charmartin station in Madrid. Then he was off, but not before leaving me with a couple of day-old Parisian pastries in gratitude for putting up with him.

I walked from the Charmartin station to the Atocha station, changed some pounds for pesetas and bought wine, bread, cheese, oranges, and olives. There were no lockers at Atocha, so I had to lug my backpack everywhere again. Luckily I packed light. I rode the Metro to get to the Prado, buying a *sacacorchos* to open my wine and parking myself on a bench in front of the great museum's eighteenth-century edifice, which an architecture student was studiously and meticulously sketching. I sat near him and glanced at his sketch, commenting on his skill in rendering the accuracy of his detail. We talked for a while, long enough for me to trust him. I expressed my regret that I wasn't allowed in the building with my backpack, and he offered to watch it for me while I went in. "It would be unfortunate if you came all this way to visit the art and had to settle for the architecture student," he joked.

Awed by this palace of renowned art treasures, I wandered among the sepia saints of Murillo and Zurburán, and the grotesques of Goya and El Greco, until I gravitated to the Velázquez room. On one wall hung official portraits of kings and their families. Facing them were their modest countrymen of no fame or special infamy. All of them, though, showed Velázquez's tendency to stylize his subjects just enough to turn his living models into types, like my French-or-Spanish goddess back in the Wallace Collection. I lingered a bit longer in the presence of Breughel, and then gaped awhile at Rubens' grisly *Saturn Devouring His Son*, so much more graphic than the more famous depiction by Goya, more realistic and therefore more terrifying. How terrified that old graybeard Time, grumpy Chronos, must have been to be driven to devour his children before they devoured him.

The climax of my visit, though, to my surprise, was finding the

Hieronymus Bosch collection. First the *Temptation of St. Anthony*, then his magnificent *Table of Seven Deadly Sins*. But I spent the most time contemplating *Extracting the Stone of Madness*. Finding it here was like running into an old friend. This painting had been a favorite of mine since it inspired one of my first published poems, "Interregnum or The Stone Operation," four years earlier, while I was still in college.⁴⁴ The painting's Flemish inscription, *"Meester snijt die keye ras / Myne name is Lubbert Das"* ("Master cut the stone out / My name is Stupid Fool"), had served as the epigraph to my poem. Part I was datelined (prophetically) Madrid and begins: "Watching them enact the grisly script / In the gold and black design / She stands in the Prado perplexed . . ." Less perplexed than pleased to be in the presence of the painting at last, I drank in the grisly scene depicted on the canvas with a new understanding. The dunce of a surgeon is supposedly removing the stone of madness from the patient's head, but now I could see it was really a water lily flower (not the tulip I mentioned in my poem), a symbol of fleshly desire. And the verb *lubber*, meaning to castrate, I now discovered in the museum's label, made the removal of the "stone of madness" in the form of a lily, a primitive sort of emasculation through lobotomy. One wonders what the poor lumpish peasant (whom I unaccountably identified with) did to deserve such a fate at the hands of the dunce surgeon with the blunt scalpel, the drunkard priest with his beer tankard, and his halfwit wife with the book balanced on her wimpled head.

Outside, my backpack and the architecture student were still on the bench. We shared the rest of my *pan, queso, aceitunas,* and wine, as young soldiers in tight-fitting uniforms strolled and strutted by. I made no mention of my experience inside, the two of us preferring to observe the world in front of us. He explained that these young men in uniform, strikingly fascistic figures, with the patent-leather space-hats perched on their heads and the submachine guns tucked under their arms, were members of the famous Guardia Civil of

---

⁴⁴*Angel's Flight* (1:2, Summer 1976; 23-7), the undergraduate literary magazine of California State University Northridge.

Madrid.[45] It was hard not to think of Lorca murdered, who in his famous ballad envisioned the Civil Guard "advancing, sowing flames, / where young and naked / imagination is burnt out," while "The Virgin heals children / with spittle from a star."

On that bench in Spain I felt my bones at last beginning to thaw. Madrid felt a lot like my native Los Angeles, hot, dry, and smoggy. The Christmas decorations in the Plaza Major seemed out of place. On every other vendor's table was offered what must have been a popular item: plastic dog shit, in piles or hamburger buns, as you like. Was this a temporary fad or some long-held local yuletide custom? I bought a bottle of Four Roses bourbon, a canister of Pringles, and a box of banana Nesquik, since these were the items JoAnn and Francis had requested I bring to them in Tangier.

---

[45] The Civil Guard patrolled public buildings in Madrid. The distinctive black leather tricornio cap, traditional at the time, has since been replaced. On February 23, 1981, just a few weeks after I was at the Prado, two hundred armed Civil Guard officers attempted to overthrow the government in a coup known in Spain as 23-F (named after the date of the attempt, abbreviated somewhat in the manner of the bombing of the Atocha Station in 2004 as 3/11 or our own attack on 9/11).

94　　　　　　　　　　　　　　　　　　　*In Search of the Hermaphrodite*

The Stone Operation (Extracting the Stone of Madness), c. 1494–1516. Hieronymus Bosch. The Prado, Madrid.

"... the removal of the 'stone of madness' in the form of a lily, a primitive sort of emasculation through lobotomy." (p. 92)

8 / That Was the Kif Talking

> He seemed to have been a fine, stable gentleman, sir. No hanky-panky, if you know what I mean. Oh, regular habits, sir. Well, far as anyone knows.
> —The Constable in *Mary Poppins*

Christmas Eve found me on the Mediterranean, crossing from Algeciras to Tangier. Sunning on the deck, I regarded the calm sea, the single cloud over Gibraltar like a halo, and the dark blue water reflecting the clear blue skies. Such a contrast after the monochromatic grays of London and Paris and the blanket of brown smog over Madrid. And when we pulled into the dock at Tangier, a cubist cascade of white buildings.

Old men in whitish djellabas seemed scattered everywhere, watching, lounging, walking, existing, not to hustle the tourists, just to oversee the proceedings, like objective observers from another galaxy. Once I passed through customs, the zoo began. Here, everyone is your friend, everyone wants to take care of you, everyone offers you their sincere assistance, everyone will sell you whatever you want in any language or currency: money, hashish, opium, kif, carpets, promises, perfumes, girls, boys, friends, themselves.

I had to remind myself that this was Africa. I could never live in this chaos; that was part of the attraction. Constant dislocation, the

Dada camel and the Dada gas station, the streets laid out in an effort to disorient the invading visitor. Was it California à la Tangier, or Tangier à la California?

When traveling I follow the advice someone once gave me to buy some small item as soon as you arrive in a new country or in this case a new continent. It helps to stave off the chaos for a moment or two, gives you time to reorient the disorientation, a postponement, time to get your bearings before the inevitable shock sets in. I order a cup of mint tea served in a glass at the first relatively calm café I see, find a plastic chair just outside the door, and assume a stoic pose, my legs stretched out in front of me. The drowned mint leaves are muddled with not too much sugar. I hold the glass beneath my nose and breathe in the fragrance, observing the crowd through the steam that fogs my sunglasses. I watch the buses bound for Rabat, Casablanca and Marrakech fill with people. When the buses have filled to overflowing, passengers pile on top, lifting or pushing one another up, flinging shapeless bundles and bags, and cling to the luggage and luggage racks, calling down to their fellow travelers seated inside in aggressively friendly barks of Arabic.

Two nights ago, departing from the Atocha station in Madrid I shared a compartment on the overnight train to Algeciras with a New Yorker, Larry Samuelson; an Englishman in overalls and sandals, Martin Foster; and a married couple with their dog Foxy—Mustapha from Casablanca and his wife Marguerite from Amsterdam. Arriving in Algeciras, we went directly to the harbor and bought our tickets for the next boat. Mustapha frowned when he saw that the boat was Moroccan.

"We may not make it today," he speculated.

"But we have our tickets," I said.

"It doesn't matter," replied Mustapha knowingly. "But let's wait and see. Possibly I am wrong. I hope I am wrong."

As it turned out, he was right. The first barrier of Spanish officials checked our tickets and stamped our passports as having left Spain. We still had to pass through Spanish customs, where the officials took their time, questioning each passenger, examining their papers and sometimes their luggage, looking dubious.

As the boarding horn blasted for the last time, the Moroccan boat seemed to let out a resigned sigh as it pulled away from the dock, leaving about a hundred of us to watch its bright white surfaces and canary-yellow accents depart without us. It was an odd feeling. We had officially exited Spain, but could not get to Morocco, which we could see across the water—unless we swam.

"Now," Mustapha explained, "we will have to stay another night in Spain and take a Spanish boat in the morning. It is economics."

"That's clever," said the Englishman.

"Corrupt, if you ask me," said the New Yorker.

In protest, we vowed to spend as little money in Spain as possible. Mustapha found a cheap hotel that would take all of us with rooms for about four dollars each. In the morning the five of us had *cafe con crema* together at an open café, and spent the rest of the morning and early afternoon picnicking on the Spanish bluffs watching the planes taking off and landing across the water on isolated, fortified Gibraltar. We passed around a bottle of the local wine, as the ships made their way between Algeciras and Tangier and Cueta, the Spanish enclave on the Moroccan coast. Mustapha and Marguerite told us how they made their living running hashish between their respective cities several times a year. Martin, the Englishman in overalls, revealed why he was going to Morocco: "I fancy a pet tarantula."

I was eager to see my friends, JoAnn and Francis, who were also known by their pen names, Total Eclipse and Dr. Panik. They published a pocket-sized xerox magazine called *Skullpolish* and an even smaller one called *Blades*. When they wrote to invite me to come to Tangier, back in October, they included the latest issue, *Blades* 10 © 1980. Its cover was of "Henry relaxing in heaven 1891-1980" and featured a drawing of the recently departed Henry Miller reading *Blades* with a cover drawing of Henry Miller reading *Blades* with a cover picture of Henry Miller reading *Blades*. It was a matter of good things coming in small—and sometimes even smaller and still smaller—packages. When I wrote to ask what they missed most from civilization, they responded that if I could just eat a burrito from Taco Bell and fart in a Pringles can, that might bring them a Proustian moment. That was Panik-Eclipse humor in a nutshell—or rather a Pringles can.

I found the American School by asking a cab driver to take me to La Scuela Americain, mixing Spanish and French, in rue Christophe Colomb. I was tired. But he understood me perfectly. JoAnn and Francis were not there. It was Christmas Eve, after all. One of their colleagues was in the office. She told me they had an apartment in the old section of town, the medina, but it would be impossible for me to find it on my own. In any case, they weren't there at the moment. They were housesitting a villa outside of town in Ibn-Battuta. She would take me to her apartment in the school compound, she said, and go get them. I waited on the balcony of the apartment, drinking from a bottle of duty-free Johnny Walker I'd bought on the ferry, saving the Four Roses bourbon for Francis, and listening to the sounds of the evening prayers broadcast from the minarets in the white city below.

When they arrived, I handed over the banana Nesquik to JoAnn and the Four Roses to Francis, and apologized for bringing them a can full of only Pringles. They hugged these icons of Western mass consumption to their breasts like old friends. We stopped off at their apartment in the medina, 4 rue Bergach, where I took a quick shower in an open room with a drain on the ground floor. We finished off the Johnny Walker, saving the Four Roses for a special occasion. Then we set off for the country house in their borrowed Citroen 2CV.

I woke the next morning to the smell of chlorine bleach. A servant girl, Najat, had taken out all the carpets to air and was mopping the stone floors, as she did every morning.

"I've tried to tell them that they don't have to do this every day," said Francis, lounging on tapestry covered bolsters on the tiled banquette, "but they insist."

It was warm outside, but I wandered through the cool house, admiring the wet and shiny mosaic floors and the arched doorways. I was still disoriented. We were somewhere outside the city limits of Tangier. It was quiet, with only the sounds of chickens, horses, and sheep—and of Najat emptying a bucket of dirty water onto the drive. Outside, I met the caretaker, Kadir, Najat's father, who lived with his family in a small house away from the villa. There was a dog in the yard, a gangly Irish Setter whose sole trick was to jump into the lemon tree and pluck the fruit, gobbling the lemons whole.

"I'm told," said Francis, "that the dog has leukemia or something. The lemons somehow make him feel better. Self-medicating."

We drove to Asilah, about thirty-five kilometers down the coast, a beach town with an ambiance of indolence like beach towns everywhere. There were camels en route, which was not like beach towns everywhere, but their presence soon became commonplace. We climbed up to the small clean uncluttered medina overlooking the Atlantic. Asilah was once a Portuguese port and still had portions of its alcazar. We ate in a seafood restaurant at outdoor tables in an unpaved garden in the shadow of crumbling fortifications. Peacocks and pelicans roamed about under the palm trees, unmolested and occasionally aggressive. A teenager offered to sell us hashish, and asked if we had heard about Bob Marley. "A tragedy," he said, smiling and pulling faces. "He has died. A tumor of the brain, I think."

Francis remarked that Moroccans' expressions never seem familiar, as though they possess emotions that are not like ours and are therefore, like certain Arabic idioms, untranslatable.

* * *

The previous night we had gone to the apartment of the famous writer Paul Bowles. He lived in a cement high-rise in the European section, with Bulgarian guards, right across from the American consulate. In spite of having lived in Morocco for so long, he had none of the affectations of an American "gone native." Except one. As we entered the door the pleasant, persistent herbal aroma of kif hit us.

A diminutive man in brown corduroy slacks and Hush Puppies, wearing a cable-knit turtleneck sweater and an old tweed sport coat with patches at the elbows, Bowles would have looked more at home in a New England seaport or on a college campus than here in this modern Moroccan apartment. In place of the academic pipe, however, he held a *pipa*, an ebony cigarette holder with one of the kif cigarettes that he chain-smoked. He emptied the tobacco from two filtered CasaSports (about twenty cents a pack), then with a few deft twists refilled the empty tubes with powdery kif from a small round red leather box.

Handing a kif-filled CasaSport to us to share, he stood at the fireplace and smoked the other joint himself, one hand on the mantle as he delivered pronouncements on literature and music and on the catalog of composers and poets he had known in Paris and elsewhere before coming, at Gertrude Stein's suggestion, to Morocco. The list of celebrities included but were not confined to the Beats who sought him out here. This recitation he seemed to think was expected of him, and he was affable enough to deliver, even in his kif-induced state, or because of it.

I asked him whether he had ever met Edward Dahlberg, then one of the writers I thought much of, and whose work I knew well (unlike that of Bowles, who, I'm ashamed to say, I had read for the first time the night before at the villa, and then only a handful of the Mohammed Mrabet tales. This was long before I had been knocked over by *The Sheltering Sky*).

"A pleasant person," said Bowles, like a lepidopterist placing two pins in a specimen, "but I found his use of arcane and obsolete words in *The Sorrows of Priapus* to be unnecessary and annoying, an indication perhaps of a writer not entirely confident in his material."

This judgment did not square with my impression of Dahlberg, who seemed to be anything but pleasant. And yet it did, in a way, square perfectly. The patrician Bowles had put his finger on the very thing that attracted me to Dahlberg, an erudite contrarian critical of anyone without his self-taught classical education. I identified with his upstart appropriation of high cultural discourse, and I took the poke personally. In my ignorance, I preferred such stylistic excesses and posturings as Dahlberg displayed over the economical style of Bowles (except when he tries to describe altered states), although I have since come around.

I happened to have a quotation from *The Sorrows of Priapus* fresh in my mind, having used it as an epigraph to a chapter of my dissertation I had recently finished: "Man is double, and who may know his heart: he is a moral hermaphrodite."

"It is difficult to disagree with that," said Bowles, puffing the kif cigarette through his *pipa*, tilting his chin, and blowing the smoke over our heads.

When I went on to mention my research, Bowles paused for a moment, as though he were flipping through index cards behind his high forehead. I half expected him to connect my research with his own "lavender marriage" to Jane, to bisexuality or ambidexterity or even amorality, paradox and the polymorphous, or to put me on the scent of some racy Moroccan folktale along the lines of the more licentious tales of the *Arabian Nights*.

"You know," he said at last, once he had located the mental files he wanted, "this kif is from the Rif." He smiled to himself at the rhyme. "It's called Beldia, or Landrace. It's been around for centuries. Very hardy. Easy to grow in almost any soil through droughts and the Rif's baking heat. You can smoke the leaves or the flowers. I prefer the flowers." He held his cigarette up as though it were the stem of a wine glass, the smoke curling up into his nostrils. "You might notice it has a sweet floral smell, with spicy layers underneath, somewhat minty. Its effect is not long lasting, but it is quick and happy, if you are prone to that sort of response."

Where was he going with this train of thought? Maybe he was tired of talking about literature and wanted to change the subject. Maybe he was lost in the clouds of kif.

"This particular strain is from Chefchaouen," he continued, at once appearing to be gazing into the distance and yet at the same time quite present. "The old-timers there cultivate a pure lineage of vintage seeds. Very desirable. The plants from which this particular kif comes are the result of three generations of open pollination. This enhances the genetic diversity of the plant. It also weeds out the weaker plants and the hermaphrodites."

I marveled at the virtuosity of his discourse, how he had managed to begin miles away and yet to beckon what appeared to be the errant flight of his thought back to the subject at hand, like a falcon come home with a sudden swoop to roost on the glove of the falconer.

I had, of course, read of hermaphroditic plants and animals, in mythology and scientific texts. The self-reproduction of some hermaphroditic plants and cirripedes fascinated Darwin, for example, and helped put him on the scent of natural selection. I had read about hermaphrodites, admired sculptures of hermaphrodites, dreamed of hermaphrodites, even slept with something resembling a hermaphrodite. This was the first I heard about smoking hermaphrodites.

Bowles went on to tell us about former residents of Tangier. Like the man who would kidnap girls from the mountains and take them to his house, doing whatever it was he did with them until he gave them a fine kaftan and let them go. "A young girl cannot get married until she has saved enough money to make or buy a good kaftan to get married in," Bowles explained in his deadpan, nonjudgmental way. "So I suppose he rationalized he was doing them a favor."

He once went to a party given by this man, complete with entertainment by a bevy of dancing girls in transparent gowns, "each of whom was more beautiful than the next, each with finer features, more striking eyes. Beautiful, beautiful." Bowles savored these details more as an aesthete than an eroticist. "Then a very short man, almost a midget (Jones, I think his name was: Welsh) appeared, striding out in high boots, wielding a whip, cracking it while the girls cowered like great cats. When the show was over, the host walked the beautiful girls to the gate of his estate and said to each of them in turn: 'Good-night, my dear, fuck you.' A few years later, when Morocco became independent, the man left what had been the International Zone, afraid of repercussions from the new Moroccan government."

Another man Bowles knew, a Brahmin, walked from Tangier to London in mid-winter, wearing only sandals and a saffron robe. He made it, but died three days after collapsing in Piccadilly Circus.

"I hope that won't happen to you," he said, suddenly returning to the present moment.

Another kif cigarette for him, and one for us, rolled expertly even more quickly than the first, as if by the hands of a magician—*presto-digitation*. During this process, he mentioned the legend about the feral women from one of the mountain tribes, who would roam in packs hunting lone men who ventured onto the mountains. Finding one, they would ravish him and move on to the next. I lit our newly rolled cigarettes with Carin's gift, which seemed to bring her ravishing presence into the room with me.

"The British consul's wife met a man in church, St. Andrews, who invited her over for tea," said Bowles, following his own peculiar association of ideas. "Not in itself an uncommon invitation. In the living room was an ice-box where he kept his refreshments handy. He opened the box and asked if she would care for some blood. She kept her composure: she was British, after all. 'No, I don't think I should care for any just now,' she answered. 'But if you don't mind,' she inquired, 'where on earth do you get it?' 'Oh,' he said, 'from the boys in the neighborhood.' Each of the jars of viscous red liquid had a label: MUSTAPHA, AHMED, MOHAMMED, MOKDIR, and so on. Evidently he paid the boys well for their samples, in one coin or another."

Once or twice Bowles became a little too poetic in his descriptions, or a little too speculatively philosophical in his observations. He would catch himself, pause, and say, "That was the kif talking," stabbing the air with his *pipa*, as though someone (presumably himself) had blown an annoying bubble he was glad to burst. Then, for my benefit, he added, "a scenic detour: maybe there was a touch of the hermaphrodite in that kif." Taking up his discourse at the point where his own voice had left off and the kif had taken up, he continued in a terse style more like that of his best lean prose.

We would see him again in a few days, for his seventieth birthday party, but it was a relatively unmemorable event, with a crowd consisting primarily of admiring expatriates.

* * *

On our return from Asilah, Francis wanted some bourbon, but when he went to fetch the Four Roses, the cabinet was bare. The next morning yellow roses appeared in the living room, one on the kitchen drain, and another at the gate to the garden. JoAnn asked Kadir to see what he could find out. When we got back from the medina in the afternoon, Kadir told her, "*Najat dit que le chat fait la bouteille casser.*" Francis insisted on seeing the broken bottle. Kadir brought Najat, and she told them she threw the shards of glass into the ravine behind the house. When they could find nothing there, she tried to tell them that it had broken into tiny little pieces "*comme sable.*" JoAnn asked Kadir if he really believed that. Kadir looked at Najat and said: "*Ce n'est pas possible.*" Najat shrugged her shoulders and would not raise her eyes.

The mystery of the Four Roses remained unsolved. But we could no longer lay it on the djinn or the cat. Najat obviously knew something and wouldn't tell. A thirsty boyfriend? Covering for her little brother? Did she covet the bottle for its pretty label with the roses, replacing it with the yellow roses from the garden? Surely that was a fair trade? Of the gifts of this faux-magus from London, only the banana Nesquik remained. Francis was having none of that, though, his palate having prepped for the charred white-oak kick of Kentucky bourbon.

* * *

Time was running out on my brief journey to Morocco.

JoAnn and Francis took me shopping in the medina. It was a feast for the senses. I felt like Des Esseintes in *À Rebours*, but assaulted by scents rather than orchestrating them. I bought some phials of oil, essence of henna, *ambre, fleur d'olive*, Malvaloca (geranium), and two packets of kohl with a carved kohl applicator. Here the men also wear scents and kohl. Not that I was interested in them for myself, but Carin and Mariola might be. The choices of scents were endless: oils and distillations of flowers: narcissus, chipre, tuberose, rose, and musk from the glands of gazelles, they said. I also bought a rug and a large tapestry, which would triple my luggage back to London. The tapestry was from Ourzazate, in a banded design, wool with silk running through it. The vendor took some threads and burnt them with a match, saying that it was fifty or sixty years old and *tout de laine*, probably *fabriqué par deux personnes* over a one or two-month period. The much smaller rug was from the Moyen Atlas, a rich blood-red, *de fabrication récente*. In the Grand Socco we drank *nana con shiba*, mint tea with shiba, the mint from which absinthe is made.

We ate kefta at a little café in the medina, a dish that I became fond of during my stay. Kefta is made of ground meat seasoned with saffron, cumin, hot paprika, parsley and celery leaves, shaped into silver-dollar sized patties, fried in oil, and often served with lemon and two fried eggs over onions in tomato sauce. I was tempted to try to improvise this dish in London but doubted it would translate there, even if I took all of the spices back with me.

Later we had martinis at Madame Porte's so-called *salon de thé*, really an Art Deco era bar where all transient European literati are said to have hung out in decades past and thus an obligatory pilgrimage for present-day wannabes like me. Alec Waugh would have his daily martini there, solo, at precisely the same time every day. People could set their watches, if they cared about time, by his evening promenade to Madame Porte's, in his white linen suit and Panama hat, through the confetti-like sensory barrage of the streets of Tangier. His meandering march to the storied *salon de thé* was one of the picturesque sights of the city, *de rigueur*, like the Changing of the Guard, not to be missed, and as predictable as Greenwich Time.

On the way to Paul Bowles' seventieth birthday party, we ate majoun, kif prepared with figs, dates, sugar and butter.[46] It had an

---

[46] In one of his novels, Bowles describes majoun as "a combination of figs, cinnamon, ginger and licorice," although I don't remember any hints of ginger or licorice in the confection I ate. *Let It Come Down* (Santa Rosa: Black Sparrow Press, 1994), 210.

odd odor but tasted delicious washed down with warm milk. Silent sirens were sent speeding to all the districts of the body. Soon my extremities were being stretched like warm taffy. The feeling lasted for some time, as I realized that the next day, New Year's Eve, I would be leaving for Spain again on my way back to London. I suspect that the majoun might be why my memory of the famous writer's party is so sketchy.

*   *   *

Early New Year's Eve we were awakened by Najat, who told us to come quickly, *vite, vite!* Kadir was in front of the house with a towel pressed to his forehead, bleeding profusely. A huge gash and swelling was revealed when he took the towel away. We immediately piled him into the car to take him to a doctor. Francis had the presence of mind to tell me to get my bag, as well, since this was likely to take a while and he knew that my boat left in just a few hours. I had packed early, however, and had already stowed my bag in the car's trunk. Kadir had been kicked between the eyes by one of the horses, La Chica.

Finding a doctor involved going first to the American School, then to the Consulate, then to the doctor's house-office, then to the Italian hospital for x-rays. At that point, JoAnn said she would stay with Kadir so Francis could take me to buy my ticket and catch the boat. We had just enough time left over to get some mint tea and gateaux at the same quiet café where I had bought my first glass on arrival.

Whiffs of hashish and kif kept breezing by us, the old men in djellabas puffing away at their posts, observing the passing scene. I had come to relish the sensuous textures of Tangier, the climate, the visual excitement, the melange of languages, the odors of animals and hashish, the partly deformed population, the feeling of dislocation, the sun, the colors, the air, the wool, the oils, the scents. I admired the disdain of these proud Moroccans, a desert and mountain people, a race of hustlers, whores, and holy men. I had arrived thinking I could never live here on the left eyebrow of Africa; as I prepared to board the Moroccan ferry back to Europe, I could see why Paul Bowles had not been able to bring himself to leave.[47]

---

[47] Bowles died in Tangier at the age of 89 after 52 years in Tangier. Francis Poole went on to become head of the Film and Video Collection at the University of Delaware. He co-edited a collection of essays on Bowles and conducted one of the last interviews with the author in 1999 before his death. JoAnn Balingit would have a distinguished career as a poet, serving as Poet Laureate of Delaware (2008–15).

Sleeping Hermaphroditus, 2nd century. The Louvre, Paris.

"Bernini's statue is doubly erotic: not only because of its ambiguous appeal, but because our perception involves a double-take. It is not so much the plastic qualities of the sculpture which attest to its eroticism, but the composition, the spiral curve of the reclining body, directing the way we are to view it: our experience of its subtle gestures brings us face to face with our own process of perception. In short, the sculpture is not an opaquely unselfconscious presentation of ritual; it is highly self-conscious rhetorical seduction." (p. 111n)

9 / Mencius of Hyde Park Corner

> A sexless thing it was, and in its growth
> It seemed to have developed no defect
> Of either sex, yet all the grace of both—
> In gentleness and strength its limbs were decked,
> The bosom swelled lightly with its full youth—
> The countenance was such as might select
> Some artist that his skill should never die,
> Imaging forth such perfect purity.
> —Shelley, "The Witch of Atlas"

Back in Paris, I take a room just off the rue Saint-Denis. First thing in the morning I make my way to the Louvre to see the Borghese *Hermaphrodite endormi*. After years of reading about the Hellenistic masterpiece with the marble mattress by Bernini, seeing it through the eyes of poets and critics, at last I have come to see her for myself. I say "her" because that's how she strikes me as I enter the room where she is displayed to great advantage, the light falling from the window behind onto her slight frame, the slim hip highlighted in its half spiral curve (not unlike Concha's in the light of my bedroom window in London). The head propped on a forearm is turned toward us, the eyes closed behind the locked door of a dream. The body forms a perfect serpentine S on the mattress, or the left *f* hole, if you like, on a cello. From this angle, the upper torso reveals only the suggestion of a breast, while the lower torso turns half away to give us a privileged view of her backside while depriving us of any instant satisfaction to our curiosity about what else is below. And there, near the lower lumbar region, a chip in the perfect simulacrum of flesh, like a scar, almost identical to the one on her cheek. Then, on her right shoulder, an indentation, like the crater of an old blemish or stab wound, to humanize her even more. As though she might at any moment breathe a sigh, snore, or turn in her sleep. The proportions, the pose, the polished surfaces, the drapery, all conspire to give the general impression of the half-taut bodily consciousness of a not quite nubile girl at rest. I wonder if Gautier or Swinburne or Shelley saw her in this room, under this window, in this light, or some other. It is only as we circle the deceptive bed on its rough plinth that we discover the secret she reveals with an arm entangled in the bedsheet, revealing one modestly responsive breast, while one leg extends to pull the drapery down, exposing the sleepy partial erection of the uncircumcised penis aroused in a reverie—of what exactly it is impossible to guess. Perhaps her body is the physical expression of a dream in which the simultaneous tug of contradictory or complementary desires meet, the pulse of the breast with the tug of the penis, both now undeniable in one body—or one fantasy—at once.

Even though there are guards at the door and DO NOT TOUCH signs near the statue, the marble is brown in places and shines with the oils of hands that have traced the inviting hip, almost as dark now as the more accessible pillows. A Spanish woman, fascinated, cannot resist patting the figure's buttock, and comments, "*Que flaco!*" Someone laughs. The taboo remains. No one dares openly touch her penis, and yet there it is, diminutive and daring us to extend a finger in a parody of God's touching Adam's to give it the galvanized touch of life, an invitation not everyone has resisted because there it is, blackest of all, evidence of years of curious furtive fingerings. The museum guard looks away and smiles, amused. He understands as well as anyone the *Sleeping Hermaphrodite*'s magic spell and does nothing to break it.

*2 January 1981. Le Louvre. Paris. L'Hermaphrodite endormi.
After reading for years about the Borghese masterpiece with the
marble mattress by Bernini, seeing it through the eyes of Swinburne
and Gautier and Marie Delcourt, at last I get to see for myself what
she's got. The modestly responsive breasts, the extended foot that
pulls the drapery down to expose her secret, the sleepy partial erection of the uncircumcised penis that points toward the window,
where the sunlight promises to illuminate but never to burn her
everhard marble, if sterile, cock....*

Back in my room, I scribbled my impressions in my black and red Chinese journal, notes that would eventually be transmuted into a passage of my dissertation.[48] I pulled my copy of Delcourt's *Hermaphrodite* from my backpack to compare my fresh impression of the most famous sculpture of the figure with that of the art historian. She writes: "In literature, Hermaphrodite is more an idea than a person.... The sculptors were less discreet. They brought into the world of forms what should have remained in the world of the imagination." But why should it have remained locked up in the imagination? Why shouldn't it be put on display for all to learn from, to stroke if that's what we need to confront the dream in ourselves? Delcourt's moralizing concludes: "In the reclining figures, an all-enveloping sensuality displays itself without discretion.... The very insistence of the artist betrays the frivolity of his art; for him, the subject is no more than a game of skill, an opportunity to gratify unhealthy fancies and to pander to tendencies in his public completely foreign to primitive feeling, for which the union of the sexes was the survival

---

[48] "Bernini's statue is doubly erotic: not only because of its ambiguous appeal, but because our perception involves a double-take. It is not so much the plastic qualities of the sculpture which attest to its eroticism, but the composition, the spiral curve of the reclining body, directing the way we are to view it: our experience of its subtle gestures brings us face to face with our own process of perception. In short, the sculpture is not an opaquely unselfconscious presentation of ritual; it is highly selfconscious rhetorical seduction." Richard Collins, *"A Toy of Double Shape": The Hermaphrodite as Art and Literature.* University of California Irvine. PhD dissertation. 1984.

of the race."[49]

Pander to the unhealthy fancies of the public indeed! Primitive feelings indeed! How the crowds loved it! They couldn't keep their hands off it. They circled her like wolves around a dozing rabbit and pointed and stared, baring their teeth as they grinned to each other, and drooling at something deep inside themselves. It was that damned impertinent penis that pricked them. They didn't know what to do with it. None of us did. Pity the poor people who don't bother to take the time to go around to the other side of the statue to discover that impertinent prick. What they miss is a mirror into themselves. Too bad. C'est dommage. Que lástima! Que flaco!

* * *

I don't recall where the streetwalkers congregated in Henry Miller's time, but these days it was right outside the door of my hotel off rue Saint-Denis. Maybe it has always been the place, the lowest chakra of Paris in the first arrondissement, le premier. I asked one petite and soon-to-be-haggard blonde if she was working tonight. She held out her Gauloise for me to light; I lit it with the Dunhill Rollagas, Carin's gift. Her response to my stupid question was crisp: "Cent-cinquente." 150 francs, fifteen quid, or about thirty-eight dollars for five minutes in a room with a naked girl with whom you can "talk about anything you want to," *talk* being that euphemism for human intercourse that rarely requires anything more articulate than a gasp and a grunt. In Soho it was all mediated simulacra—peep shows, porno films, and magazines—at least on the surface. Here the sex was on display, frankly exhibited for sale, like oysters on ice in a fish market, raw as an open vulva. I think the garish scene attracted some men like moths to naked bulbs, yet scared others who avoided the women like vampires. To judge by the hollow eyes and blue skin, emphasized by clotted mascara and indigo shadows,

---

[49] Marie Delcourt, *Hermaphrodite: Myths and Rites of the Bisexual Figure in Classical Antiquity*. Trans. Jennifer Nicholson (London: Studio Books, 1961), xi, 66.

some of these *putains* might well have been vampires indeed, these creatures of the night. The air was thick with the white lace of their smokey exhalations, the rank whiff of the Gitanes and Gauloises with which they posed, leaning in doorways, exposing a dark armpit or a bright thigh.

Buoyed up by my week on the Mediterranean and my morning visit to the *Sleeping Hermaphrodite*, I was in a good mood, but it was impossible not to connect the statue with this exhibitionism. Talk about pandering to unhealthy fancies and primitive feelings! In comparison to this living spectacle, the hermaphrodite is purity itself. I strolled by and greeted the working women who came in all shapes, colors, ages, sizes—and sexes: "Bonsoir, Mademoiselle! Belle nuit, n'est-ce pas?" I got more or less friendly responses. One even took up the greeting by answering with lines from the famous barcarolle of Offenbach, singing:

> *Belle nuit, oh, nuit d'amour*
> *Souris à nos ivresses*
> *Nuit plus douce que le jour*
> *Ô, belle nuit d'amour.*

Her voice wasn't half bad, if a bit rough around the edges like a serrated knife against a scratched phonograph record, but it suited the venue. I bowed elaborately—she bowed back—I continued on my way.

The more worn-out they seemed, the more worked-up and muscular, the friendlier they were. The prettier ones made it hard on themselves. Instead of working the clientele, they waited. For what, exactly? For their supply to be less in demand? For their ripe fruits to go bad on the shelf? The riper the fruit, some splitting at the seams, the more on display it was, which seemed the wrong fashion—or sales—approach somehow. I wished Carin was with me so that we could discuss the scene, its costumes, the customs, their conscious and unconscious fashion statements.

A couple of months ago I would have taken the petite blonde

up on her cent-cinquante. It would have been worth it to drown my despair in the oil of the cheap perfume between her legs. But in a few hours I would be with Carin again, sweet Silk Cut puffing Carin. I decided to skip the sightseeing planned for the next day and take the first train to Boulogne for the ferry. To hell with the Musée du Jeu de Paume, the Musée Gustave Moreau, the Musée Rodin, and other guidebook attractions. Carin was calling me, body and soul. Paris would still be there in a few months or years, painted canvases and painted women, crumbling buildings and bumbling *mauvais garçons, tous ou presque tous, qui vous tueront, qui vous voleront.*

Back in my hotel room, nestled under a floral bedspread, surrounded by floral wallpaper and floral drapes that did nothing to deodorize the accumulated human smells of the room, nor to suppress the nocturnal sounds in the flesh market below, nor to darken the ironic glow of the City of Light, I could hear the buzz of the cruising cars, horns honking, wolf whistles, far into the night. And, somewhere above it all, Carin's laughter.

* * *

Sundays, one could always go to Speakers Corner at Hyde Park. That's where Carin and I went when I got back to London. One speaker who could often be found there was a Socratic philosopher in the confrontational tradition of the Cynics. I thought that if I were ever to apprentice myself to someone, disciple to a master, it would be him. Dumbfounding the listeners who hungered for simple solutions to the world's problems, he would often quote the Chinese sages, peppering the crowd with paradoxes. I began to think of him as the Mencius of Hyde Park Corner.

"You just want to be entertained," he was saying to the crowd when we approached his soapbox.

"Then why did you come here?" a woman asked. "If not to entertain us? If not to be held up to ridicule?"

It was a fair question.

"I did not come for your amusement."

"Then why are you here?" she repeated.

"I am not here for your amusement. If you think I have come here to entertain you, you are sadly mistaken. Not so many hundred years ago, on this very site, people were being hanged. Crowds came to be entertained by the sight of broken necks and blackened tongues and erections caused by asphyxiation. Do you think that those who were being hanged were holding themselves up to ridicule? Not willingly. Do you think they dangled there for your entertainment? Not even for your edification, I'm afraid. I am not so different from those executed, and you are not so different from the executioners, or the bystanders who rubbed against each other for their perverse thrills!"

"Then why," a man piped up in the crowd, thinking he could put the question more clearly, "are you here? Why don't you answer the lady's question?"

"You're—not—listening," said Mencius, enunciating his words as though he were speaking to a foreigner or a child. "That the crowds were entertained by the spectacle of suffering cannot be doubted. But what had that to do with the intention of the victim?"

Again the woman insisted on an answer: "Well why do you come here then?"

"I do not come here to satisfy your curiosity."

This went on for some time, the same calls eliciting the same responses, slight variations on the theme.

"If you want to be amused," he said at last, "go across the way to Mr. McIlheney." He gestured in the direction of the popcorn-headed performance poet who looked like Harpo Marx but who was unfortunately not mute. "*He* will amuse you. Or why not try the Christians, or the Scientists, or the Christian Scientists, the Marxists, the Feminists, the Vegetarians or the Skinheads, or the Vegetarian Skinheads. They all have all the answers for you. But I did not come here to satisfy your curiosity."

"Then why did you come?" said someone in high-voiced mock-imitation of the woman who had spoken before. Everyone laughed.

Then the Philosopher fell silent, refusing to respond to any more provocations. Half the crowd trailed off, some taking his advice and joining the laughter around Mr. Harpo McIlheney-Marx's poetry show, or the pulpits of the pseudo-prophets down the row. The curious woman herself could not realize that our philosopher was being completely truthful to her. He had come to do just the opposite of satisfying her curiosity. He wanted to *unsatisfy* her curiosity. Perhaps he succeeded.

When the crowd had dwindled to just Carin and me and a few others, Mencius continued to stare into the crowd. Those remaining began to feel uncomfortable and to shuffle their feet. In the end there were only a handful of us left, staring at his silence, wondering how he would wrap up his reluctant discourse.

"Now that I have the audience I want, I'll tell you a story. A young man, delighting to wander in unknown mountains and unseen rivers, was traveling from one place to another as young men and even old men often do. Women too. On the way he espied a stone, a rather lovely stone as stones go, it was smooth and round and black and very light as he found when he picked it up to place it on the herm that formed the boundary of one land and another, as they did in those days. On the stone was written TURN ME OVER. Now he would have turned the stone over, as any of us would do once we had bothered to pick it up whether it had anything written on it or not, but that is immaterial. And when he picked it up he turned it over, as any of us might do, it is even a wise thing to do in certain territories, for you never know what will be lurking beneath a stone, whether or not you may want to know what it is that lurks or simply lies beneath the stone, and this is what the young man read inscribed on the bottom of the smooth round black clean stone: WHY DO YOU JOURNEY SO FAR IN SEARCH OF KNOWLEDGE WHEN YOU HAVE NOT YET MASTERED WHAT THERE IS FOR YOU AT HOME? That is my question to *you*. What are *you* doing *here*?"

At this the Philosopher fell silent again and, still standing on his little step ladder, opened his black Penguin paperback translation of Mencius and began to read to himself. Everyone assumed at first that he was searching for a passage to read to us. The diehard few who remained began to grow impatient, sensing that they had, in Aristotle's sense, been presented with a beginning and a middle, but had yet to be served an end. But evidently he had not come here to read to us, either.

"That musta been some rock, mate," said one of the stragglers.

"That was no rock," said another. "It was the Rossetti stone or some reasonable fax machine thereof."

"Nah," said an American. "It was a computer chip."

These few holdouts grew pleased with themselves for their clever interpretations and, gratified with their facile conclusions, let the curtain fall and dispersed.

Carin and I were the last to leave, like those in the audience in a movie theatre who won't give up until the last credits have rolled and the lights go on, just in case there is that parting shot, a gift, a bonus, a blooper or a big reveal.

The philosopher closed his book at last and said, as though to himself, "If you look for a fish by climbing a tree, though you'll not find it, no harm done. But if what you seek is enlightenment, don't come to me."

*   *   *

Days later, Carin and I went to Kenwood House to see its paintings, and an extraordinary thing happened. We were discussing the relative merits of autobiography over fiction, and in art the relative merits of self-portraiture over portraiture. We agreed that the Rembrandt *Self-Portrait* was fine but that Vermeer's *Guitar Player* which faced it was finer still. The comparison was almost a lesson on the difference in what could be learned between looking at oneself through oneself and looking at others through oneself. Our discussion loitered around these topics as we strolled Hampstead Heath, gathering not ye rosebuds of May but the dead leaves and feathers of January. As we talked, I kept hearing in the back of my mind the echo of the Mencius of Hyde Park Corner: *I did not come here to satisfy your curiosity.* Suddenly, this uncanny thing happened.

Carin interrupted a brief silence by voicing what was in my head: "I did not come here to satisfy your curiosity."

She had been doing that a lot lately, reading my mind, echoing my thoughts. Or maybe it was I who was echoing hers.

"Then why *did* you come here," I said, taking her in my arms, "you beautiful thing? If not to satisfy?"

"To satisfy," she said, tossing her hair and turning her lips away to deprive me momentarily of a kiss, "but not necessarily your curiosity." A kiss that she then bestowed more richly than I deserved.

* * *

In the Reading Room of the British Museum, I often spent more time observing the other patrons than poring over texts. One day I was skimming Burton's *Anatomy of Melancholy* when I looked up to find in front of me a pretty girl, blonde, in what could have been a school uniform. The short-sleeved pressed white blouse, the white socks and sturdy shoes, cast her perfectly for a certain genre of porn film; all that was missing were the pigtails and glasses. All of this was not unusual, I suppose. What was unusual was that she was sucking her thumb. Not just biting her nails or stroking her lips but full-throttle sucking her opposable thumb, thrust deep in her mouth's cavern, the ball of her thumb no doubt firmly stuck to her smooth palate, as her curled index finger stroked the length of her nose, exactly the way Mnemosyne did when she read Derrida in bed.

Not far from her was another scholar that I realized I had seen earlier when I had stopped for coffee on my way to the Museum. I hadn't at first recognized him at his desk, where he looked very different than through the greasy window of the trattoria as I drank my cappuccino. He had lumbered slowly by, like an elephant in the rain, slowly enough for me to make note of the two ridges of his upper lip that seemed to flow from his nostrils like columns of snot. I had assumed he was some workman on his way to repair someone's toilet. Even his bag looked more like a toolbox than a briefcase. Here he sat, not far from the thumb-sucking portrait of intellectual porn, looking like a disheveled deity. Hatless, intent on the pages of a history of the Puritan Revolt, he sat regally, as on a throne, his wooly head of hair a billow of steel cloud, matted, greasy, immobile. It would have taken the wrath of Neptune armed with triton pitchfork gales to comb it.

These descriptions amused Carin when I told her what I'd done all day. But when I suddenly complained about the straitjacket of my winter clothes, she didn't understand. I had been thinking of Breton's famous complaint: "I wish I could change my sex the way I change my shirt." It was more (and less) than that, though. I was chafing at the layer upon layer of clothing required to keep warm in the damp London winter. I was reminded of Tanizaki's débauché, who in his weakened state from too much physical and imagined erotic stimulation longed for kimonos instead of western clothes.[50] Carin was not from California and could not comprehend how much I missed the half-nakedness that passed for fashion in a Southern California beach town. She was a student of international fashion, after all. Clothes were a mode of self-expression to her, an art form, almost a religion. To renounce the sacrament of clothing bordered on blasphemy. She pretended to pout as she paraphrased Wilde: "If you can't be a work of art, you should at least try to wear one."

"Then I'll wear you. You know what the Koran says? 'Women are your garments and you are theirs.' I'll wear you, if you wear me. I'll slip into you if you slip into me."

"So I can become your straitjacket?" She was not appeased. "No thanks."

I told her the dream that had prompted my complaint. "I was at

---

[50]"First of all, his feet were cramped by these tan box-calf shoes that compressed them in a narrow mold. Western clothes were intended for healthy, robust men: to anyone in a weakened condition they were quite insupportable. Around the waist, over the shoulders, under the arms, around the neck—every part of the body was pressed and squeezed by clasps and buttons and rubber and leather, layer over layer, as if you were strapped to a cross." Junichiro Tanizaki, "Aguri," in *Seven Japanese Tales*. Trans. Howard Hibbett (New York: Knopt, 1963), 195. "Aguri" first appeared in the fashion magazine *Cosmopolitan*.

the beach along the boardwalk, and all these hustlers were trying to sell me T-shirts and postcards of Venice Beach. It was like Tangier, only worse. I shook them off, yelling, 'You can't sell me crap. I live here!'" But this was probably not about clothes or fashion or Surrealism at all but only the angst of displacement and nostalgia.

One Wednesday evening Carin and I looked forward to having her flat to ourselves after Louise and her boyfriend Peter left for a long weekend in the country. Before they left, though, Louise and she cooked a Chinese stir fry in a wok. I made the mistake of lighting up a joint as an aperitif. While stirring the sizzling vegetables and shaking the pot of rice, the two giggling roommates fell over themselves, shrieking "we're stirring the wok and shaking the pot on pot!" and "we're going stir-crazy!" and laughing hysterically at their witticisms—"We're martinis! You're shakin' and I'm stirred!" "You're not stirred; you're disturbed!"—dropping things on the floor of the tiny kitchen and laughing harder as they bent down to pick them up and finding their heads in each other's crotches.

After sending Louise and Peter on their way and finishing off the second bottle of wine, Carin and I went to bed for the first of a long series of "naps" that lasted the next several days. Constantly stoned and slightly drunk, I was stuck on a sensual loop of enjoying the generalized erogenous delights of our whole bodies, although the lower half of my body seemed to go at one point uncharacteristically numb, like one of those ancient herms—a torso, often ithyphallic, on a pedestal—used for boundary and fertility markers. When Carin showed signs of frustration, I laughed and the more I laughed, the more mock-desperate she became. "You're too patient for my own good!" she told me, urging me to "finish" her. I asked, "Would you rather I be too quick?"

We got out of bed at last on Saturday afternoon and went to Hampstead in search of artist supplies for her assignment that was due Monday. We kept running into Americans. The clerk at the Jewish deli which sold Premium Saltines, Oreos, and Budweiser, said, "That'll be two dollars—I mean, two pounds fifty." We had been craving reuben sandwiches for weeks, and here we got everything we desired: real corned beef, real Swiss cheese, real German rye, real homemade sauerkraut, even real dill pickles and real Russian dressing. We only lacked a couple of cream sodas and some frilly toothpicks to impale the pickle spears atop the sandwiches. Breakfast had been oranges and omelets with herbal boursin cheese, fresh apple turnovers and coffee laced with Bailey's Irish Cream. But this debauch from the deli crowned the day with greasy deliciousness. We lay on her mattress, sated, and crowned our oral fixations by savoring our cigarettes and each other for dessert. I kept making futile gestures to go home so that she could finish her project, but Carin didn't want me to, so we played house instead. I did the cooking for another day or so while Carin finished her drawings. All day Sunday we were in and out of bed, a little sore, a little drunk, and a little woozy. But we were happy and she, at least, could affirm that she had been productive.

We talked more than usual over that weekend, and I suppose in that way I could claim some progress on my work as well. We shared details about our childhoods, our families, our infamous pasts, sex in doorways and discos, creepy sex and sleepy sex, wet sex in showers and uncomfortable dry sex on beaches, sex with strangers and students and teachers, almost sex and first sex—in my case in a swimming pool.

"It was with an 'older' woman. She was only twenty-two, but I was fifteen. A family friend. She taught me one summer how to swim. She wore a bikini, bangles on her arms, and bright orange lipstick in the apartment pool while her husband was at work. Which seems strange to me now."

"What, that her husband was at work?"

"No, that she wore lipstick and bangles in the pool."

"You said you were fifteen—and you still didn't know how to swim?"

"I didn't know how to do a lot of things. I was twelve before I learned how to ride a bike. She was a very attentive teacher. She held out her arms to help me float while I learned to kick and paddle." I described how she let her forearms glide along my stomach and thighs and brush my crotch, and how the bangles caught in the waistband of my trunks, which came partly off as I kicked like mad. Her bright eyes and brighter lips laughed. "I laughed too and pulled the trunks back up. 'Someday I'll teach you the breaststroke,' she said, 'when you're a little older.' I remember how the water pooled in the top of her bikini bra. How her skin sparkled in the sun. How drops of water clung to her lashes heavy with mascara. Still, I didn't make too much of all the contact. I thought it was accidental. How else would one be taught to swim? I can't remember if it was that summer or the next that she was staying in my parents' house and found her way to my bedroom. It was pretty intense. I would call it a spiritual experience, if that didn't sound so callow and stupid. I walked around in a daze at school the next day and for several days afterward. The world had changed, like aliens had landed, or there had been a war, or hordes of people had been taken up by the Rapture after the tribulations, and nobody seemed to notice but me. I guess it was my own personal Rapture."

"You realize," said Carin, "that you just described the Hermaphroditus myth. The one I've heard you tell people a dozen times. Your age, the pool, the woman, naiad or nymphomaniac or whatever she was. The metamorphosis. The rape if not the Rapture."

It was true. It was pure Ovid with a contemporary setting. The parallels had, incredibly, never occurred to me before, not consciously at least: my age at the time, the swimming pool (the sex didn't occur there but the foreplay did), her forwardness, my cluelessness (I hesitate to say "innocence"), and the emotional and physical—I might even say, yes, spiritual—transformation.

It was a revelation. No wonder I was obsessed with the image. Was my research simply a repetition compulsion exploring the "trauma" of my loss of virginity? It sounded comical, and yet credible. In graduate school I had been fascinated (triggered?) by the myth of Hermaphroditus when I read Swinburne's poem, not realizing that it evoked the real-life Salmacis, the nymph (or nymphomaniac, as Carin so accurately put it) with the bright orange lipstick who carried her magical pool between her breasts.

I allowed this revelation to pass without too much attention, though, focused as I was on Carin's much briefer sexual history and on the making of our own history in the present moment. There would be time to return to this epiphany and reflect on it.

"You know," she said, not exactly changing the subject but certainly changing the mood, "I think you are the only one who doesn't know that I am in love with you."

There. The word was spoken. The spell was broken. A shadow suddenly passed over our playground.

We talked about what might become problems in our relationship. Carin was afraid of her freedom slipping away even though I had "done nothing to hasten it", which was a pithy thing for her to say. Or how she might not like my being so perceptive; "it might become intrusive," she said. "Half the charm of a stupid man is that he can't see through you; you can keep your *privacy*." She pronounced the word in the British fashion, as though it were related to a privy, which I suppose it is, instead of in the American way, which made it sound like it had something to do with privation or prying, which I suppose it does.

We determined that we should travel abroad together, perhaps to Italy or Spain in the spring. Or if we couldn't wait, to the Channel Islands in February. "I always wanted to go to Sark," she said. "It's tiny. No cars."

"Or Herm," I said. "It's next door. No cars there either."

"Herm?" she said, eyebrows arched.

"Don't worry," I said, "the name probably refers to the monks who lived there for centuries, hermits. Not sure if any were hermaphrodites, but with monks you never know."

"No, you never know."

"Maybe we could go to Turkey," I suggested, "to find the pool of Salmacis, the Carian spring."

"The Carin spring?"

"Carian! Nothing personal. Where Hermaphroditus lost his manhood."

"Don't you mean where he gained his womanhood?"

She was right, of course. Like when a mother says of a marriage, she has not lost a son but gained a daughter. It dawned on me that the myth intrigued me not because a young man was feminized but because the young woman had overpowered him and she as a result added his power to hers. That was the secret of the Louvre's *Hermaphrodite endormi*, which Shelley described so well, as he explored—in *The Witch of Atlas* and *Epipsychidion*—the unconscious depths of his own ambiguous desires.[51]

It was the imaginative supplementation, the passivity of the sleeping female body putting on the emergent dream of male power. (As Yeats asked about Leda and the Swan: "Did she put on his knowledge with his power / Before the indifferent beak could let her drop?") Surely this was why I was attracted to powerful women, women like Concha who were undeniably feminine but who could take charge and be assertive, or Mnemosyne with her sharp scientific and philosophical mind, or like Carin, who declared her cynical independence but succumbed to the tenderness of an inherent romanticism.

"Seriously," said Carin. "I want to go away with you somewhere. There doesn't have to be a reason. Not everything has to be about your research. I wanted to go with you to Morocco. I missed you. I wanted to see what you saw."

"I wanted you to. Maybe someday."

"*Maybe*," she said, doubtfully, pretending to pretend to pout but actually pouting for real. "*Maybe* may be the cruelest adverb in the language. I hate adverbs that wiffle-waffle."

I finally quit wiffle-waffling and made my way out the door around midnight. I checked my pockets for loose change. The tube shut down at midnight, and I didn't have enough for a taxi, maybe not even enough for a bus, assuming I could find the right route. So I buttoned up my shabby rust corduroy coat, pulling the collar up to my ears, and walked briskly all the way home, some four or

---

[51] Shelley most likely based his notions of the hermaphrodite in these poems on the statue in Florence, a copy of the one in Paris.

five miles, in the cold, dead London winter, conjuring memories of blue skies and bluer pools, sparkling eyes and a mermaid's sparkling skin.

126   *In Search of the Hermaphrodite*

Salome with the Head of John the Baptist, 1607. Caravaggio.
National Gallery, London.

"... Salome, with the head of John the Baptist on a platter, looks away, a troubled but not repentant look on her face ..." (p. 138)

10 / The Dark Night of the Spring

> Neither could ever say,
> No more than the god's bronze form,
> If that hermaphrodite
> Were the perfecting circle, or flurry
> Of self-pulverizing fury.
> —D. M. Thomas, "From a Greek Statuette"

I don't know when I first noticed the number of lost or discarded gloves on the streets of London, but it seemed an appropriate metaphor for my loneliness. There were leather gloves and kid gloves, red gloves and black gloves, mittens and fingerless gloves, always in the singular. Nobody ever seemed to lose both gloves at once, or if they did they were quickly retrieved together. No one wanted a lone glove. The more I noticed, the more they appeared. Soggy wool mittens in the mud, and even children's gloves with (ineffective) clips to attach them to their sleeves. It gave rise to an ongoing series of puns when I pointed them out to Carin. *Another lost glove*, I said. *It must not have been true glove*, she replied. *First glove, lost glove, glove 'em and leave 'em, glove of my life. Better to have gloved and lost than never to have gloved at all.* Thus we found ways to laugh at the melancholy.

As intimations of spring arrived, I looked back on the fall and winter with a sense of missed opportunities and time wasted. Fall had been a progression of shortening days of diminishing light and warmth. I had made an attempt at Thanksgiving, that American holiday so intimately associated with family get-togethers, to recreate its ambiance in our largely American displaced household by cooking a turkey with cornbread dressing. But everything about the process was foreign, from buying the bird live in a nearby outdoor market to having it beheaded there in the street and defeathering it ourselves. Nothing was familiar about that familiar holiday. Absent too was all the drama that accompanied such dinners in my family, from my drunken, mythographical brother and his mad wife to my mother lamenting in spite of it all that we didn't get together more often as a family. Late autumn, then, had come down like a coffin lid, slowly lowered over the London rooftops, with Concha slumbering on my chest. With the onset of winter had come darkness and hibernation, although I shared my isolation and my bed with Carin, who, along with Spain and Morocco, brought life-restoring light and warmth.

Those first five months—wandering the streets of London, working under the blue dome in the Library, waking up in Carin's cramped attic, and sitting for Laury in Hackney—stand out starkly like the bare branches of trees against a cloudbank. The solitude of fall and winter was very different from the solitude of spring, when buds began to appear on branches, office workers began to strip down to their bras in St James Park on their lunch hour, and I began to delight in being alone. One fine day, as I reclined in a striped lawn chair facing the lake, I was soon rousted by an attendant who wanted the chair's rental fee. I pleaded ignorance instead of indigence. Thus I was constantly reminded of my lack of funds. I was not exactly down and out, but not much had changed, it seemed, since George Orwell had "noticed one of the worst things about London—the fact that it costs money even to sit down."[52] I haunted again the used bookshops in Charing Cross Road and elsewhere, the subtle pleasures of which no one has described better than Arthur Ransome in his *Bohemia in London*. Just as his purchase of a two-volume edition of Burton's *Anatomy of Melancholy* caused his dinner for that night to vanish "as

---

[52] *Down and Out in Paris and London* (1933) (New York: Harcourt, 1961), 154.

the meats from the table of Halfdan the Black,"[53] and he had to walk home to Chelsea, so I often found myself choosing the company of a book over the comfort of a meal and an omnibus ride home.

Yet my memory detects no rhythm to the spring, no patterns that I can identify in retrospect. Only a succession of days and nights randomly illuminated as if by spluttering candlelight.

It turns out that Laury had been going through a similar bleak patch. His had begun the night that he didn't show up for that drink with Carin and Virginia in the Black Friar pub just before Christmas. We hadn't seen each other since then, the first of my portraits being finished. It seems that he had finished Mrs. Herrington's portrait before Christmas as well, or at least enough to allow her to take a peek at it that day in late December. Her reaction astounded him more than his usual default state of stoic astonishment. When she came around the easel to see his depiction of her for the first time, she gasped audibly and groaned.

"You, you, you have cut me into little pieces like a Picasso," she stuttered, "butchered me, like a Chaim Soutine piece of meat!" She must have had no idea that these hurled imprecations landed on Laury not as insults. At first he processed them as compliments and would have continued to do so if not for her sudden shriek. "Why, why, you've vivi-vivi-vivisected me!"

His time-delay reaction did him no favors in this case because his inability to understand her attack for what it was struck her as indifference to her displeasure for the crime he had committed in representing her as he had.

Such impudence, as the wife of an important man, she could not tolerate. The violence Laury had perpetrated on her image called for violence in return. She struck the easel with her handbag, causing it to fall to the floor with a crash. This shocked Laury out of his reverie, and now it was he who was moved to action. Not knowing what else to do, he bum-rushed her out the door of the studio and locked it.

She stood outside the door screaming, "You have disfigured me!

---

[53]*Bohemia in London* (London: Stephen Swift, 1912), 140.

You will pay for this, I promise you!" She continued in this vein until the Jamaican sculptor in the studio next door came into the hall with a smile on his face and a chisel in his hand and told her, "Please to kibbuh yuh mouth the fuck up, Mum, yeah?"

Laury told me all this as we stood in front of the offending portrait, scrutinizing it to see if we could understand what prompted her violent reaction. The figure in the portrait did seem uncannily to be shrieking "you have disfigured me!" like some agonized figure from a Francis Bacon painting. Perhaps the portrait was prophetic. I thought it was brilliant. I may have liked it better than my own, although an objective observer might not have been able to tell much of a difference between them.

We stood back and considered it from a distance.

"I rather like it," he said at last.

"So do I," I said. But I might have been prejudiced by the fact that it did not resemble the middle-aged matron who had expected a Singer Sargent and got a Leon Kossoff so much as it resembled me, or rather Laury's portrait of me. The two portraits resembled each other far more than they resembled their sitters. The originals seemed to have dropped off all the residue of individuality and gender, leaving only the skeletal remains of pained existence, like decomposed skeletal remains in their coffins, somewhat mummified to fragile dust, and not unlike the tortured bridges he had been drawing all autumn. Laury's expressionist technique lent itself to broad interpretation.

After Mrs. Herrington's fit, Laury spent several days wondering how she might make him pay. It was not that he was worried she would destroy the portrait, as Churchill famously did with Graham Sutherland's portrait of him—he couldn't care less about the fate of the work as long as he was compensated—but rather, like me, he was hoping to have his Fulbright grant extended for another year, and she might well try to influence Mr. Herrington to quash that hope. Laury had been so upset that day in December that he couldn't drag himself to the Black Friar for a drink.

In the end Herrington apologized for his wife's behavior and paid Laury the agreed-upon fee for the drawing. Laury asked how he wanted it delivered, to which Herrington said that was probably not advisable. "It may well be best," he said, "if you kept it after all. Nothing against your work, but it is unlikely ever to join the nation's luminaries in the vast gallery in St. Martin's Lane." Then he added, "No need to let anyone know about this little to-do, yes? Oh, and your extension has been granted, I'm told."

*   *   *

That spring Laury and I saw the historic eight-and-a-half-hour performance of *Nicholas Nickleby* at the Aldwych Theatre. Roger Rees was the only truly memorable performer, if only because of his starring role in the marathon Dickens adaptation. I do recall that we forgot to bring anything to eat during the dinner break intermission and thus welcomed the cast's parading through the audience, singing and tossing warm baps at the beginning of the second half because we surely needed some sustenance by then. We had drunk heartily during the break, though, which caused us to have to piss soon after the play had recommenced.

The impression of that spring feels like a series of false starts. Perhaps I was only working harder. Looking over my notebooks from the time, I seem to have finally found the pulse of my research. My notes are full of visits to libraries and museums, a visit to Cambridge and extended notes on the exhibition at the Royal Academy called "A New Spirit in Painting" in early March, where I deride a painting called *The Lone Ranger in the Jungle of Erotic Desires* for its lack of subtlety (of both color and narrative) and praise works by Sandro Chia, Julian Schnabel, and others. In a room full of Cy Twombly, I hear a woman exclaim as she enters, "Why these are just the scribblings of a child!"

I am disturbed by Balthus, whose work inhabits an oppressive silence, like the aftermath of a steamroller that has leveled everything in its path, surfaces, contours, bones, and morals. His painting *Le Chat au Miroir* (1977–80) makes me feel like Alice because, although nothing comes out of the painting, it seems that if one were to crawl inside it, there would be a world on the other side, even if it were only the two-dimensional fantasy of a playing-card world. There is a wooden quality to Balthus. If you were to drop his subjects, they would make a sound like a toy carved in balsa wood: *klok!* It is a universe of eyes without ears, of deep sadness without tears.

The eyes of Lucien Freud, on the other hand, have the effect of an injection of formaldehyde, turning flesh rubbery and green. His ulcerous color consumes his figures, as though by a disease that eats away at them from inside. There is something sickly about his work, like the ruminations of an adolescent masturbating to medical photos of chancrous breasts. I don't think I could hang Freud in my living room, but I might plaster my bathroom with him. But the masterpiece here is *Naked Man with a Rat* (1977). All of Freud's qualities combine for an assault on the viewer's gentility and sense of humor. The spread legs reveal the secret of his paintings, their ambivalent depiction of pansexuality, a nausea brought on by the realization that we are immersed in sex, in flesh, in the real. As Freud said of smoking opium with Cocteau, it was not something he needed to repeat since "I don't want to be out of this world, I want to be absolutely in it, all of the time." The rat, displaced object of masturbation, is a comic element, however dark. The naked man in his element, and furry rat in his. Is it a pet or a projection of the man's beady-eyed and whiskered fear? Bachelard said we live fixations, but I'm afraid they are not all fixations of happiness.

Other paintings elicited personal references. I could see how Laury had tried in his own painting to achieve something of the texture of Frank Auerbach's torturously worked canvases or Leon Kossof's streams and eddies of pigment, even though his Fulbright mentor was R.B. Kitaj, a very different painter whose work in the exhibition I found somewhat flat and stuffy and much more representational than Laury's work.[54] I have much more appreciation for

---

[54]Perhaps Kitaj was assigned to Laury not on aesthetic affinities but merely because he was another American expatriate in London. Kitaj had studied at the Ruskin School of Drawing at Oxford, where his teacher's lineage went back to Ingres, but

Kitaj now. But then Laury ended up spending about as much time with Kitaj as I did with my Fulbright mentor, Ian Fletcher, which is to say hardly at all. Indeed, I don't remember Laury ever saying much about any meetings he might have had with Kitaj or any admiration he might have had for his work, although he often spoke highly of Auerbach and Kossof and of their relationship to the texture of a canvas and paint. David Hockney's *Nichols Canyon 1979–80*, meanwhile, took me back to the scene of my wedding reception at the house of my high school history teacher Walter Bodlander there in Nichols Canyon on Jalmia Drive in the Hollywood Hills. Coincidentally, I had just received a letter from Robert Peters saying that he considered himself the Francis Bacon of American poetry. If Peters is the Francis Bacon of American poetry, then Philip Guston might be the Charles Bukowski (king of the "gab poets," as Peters put it) of American painting, especially in *Talking* (1979), with its collage of fingers, beads and cigarettes, and in *Desert* (1974), with its whiplash of fingernails, bandaids and boots, all with a boisterous humor that is infectious and honest, like the bursts of lightbulb motifs going off like bombs of expressionist color.

I concluded my visit with a long look at Sigmar Polke's *Kandinsdingsda* (1976), a work more erotic than pornographic in that it takes time to work one's way into the bed and the cunnilingus going on there, even though it's front and center. The mad bomber leads the viewer around with the expectation of a climactic moment, so you're set up for a tense search. And you're satisfied. Upside down, sideways, and backwards, you can get it or get lost in it from every angle. Here,

---

where he also "encountered the distinguished art history professor, Edgar Wind, known for his interest in iconology—the study of the history of images—who sent him in turn to the Warburg Institute Library, where he researched quirky ways of the visual past. From the beginning, he was interested in the meanings of pictures and not just their form" (Martin Gayford, *Moderns and Mavericks: Bacon, Freud, Hockney, and the London Painters*. London: Thames & Hudson, 2018, p. 200). From this description of Kitaj's interests, which were allusive, iconographical, philosophical, and literary, it would almost seem that he could as well have been assigned to my research, drawn as I was eventually to Wind and the Warburg in my research of "quirky ways of the visual past."

free of gravity, you are *free to be geometric*. What more can you ask of art? Relax, have a cigarette, have a martini, or sip on something more heady. Have yourself a rotten little demented laugh, because it's you who are the mad bomber, the viewer as incendiary, arsonist, anarchist, troll. I thanked the artist for a dangerous moment.

Aside from the time I spent in galleries, there is also evidence in the journals of an increasing ability to congratulate myself on having finished the draft of a chapter or having come upon a new idea, not all of them relevant to my research, or only tangentially. My cup runneth over with ideas for the non-academic, poetic and autobiographical books I would write: *The Anatomical Garden, The Seated Mask, Lost Profiles, the he and the she of it, Footnotes and Fetishes, Piglets and Ale,* and so on. It was a manic phase, full of beginnings with very little follow through, although I suppose traces of each of these inspirations survive in some way here.

I did finish one little fable, a *jeu d'esprit* called "Glove Story," which I illustrated by hand and bound as a chapbook for Carin, since it incorporated our atrocious puns on lost gloves and satirized our romantic aspirations. It was the surreal story of a man named Titt, who mistakes himself for an afghan hound in the reflection of a car window and falls in love with the fit of a glove. "An obsession is a hypothesis," he says. It occurs to me now that the story of those lost gloves separated from their mates was just another retelling of Aristophanes' account of the origin of desire in the Symposium, like our matching ashtrays, *un coup de dés*. But, as Mallarmé said, *"Un coup de dés jamais n'abolira le hasard."* And chance, I had found, has everything to do with love.[55]

---

[55] It occurs to me now, too, that the ineluctable impact that the Roger Heaton performance in Oxford had on me makes perfect sense in the context of Mallarmé's perception of chance and Boulez's recognition of the profound connections made in aleatoric music. The geometric staging of *Domaines* was nothing less than a performance of the chance encounters of my seemingly accidental and often atonal loves. Yet: "*Domaines* may be fragmentary music but it is not *pointilliste* in that there is always a sense of the larger structure, the way in which the player travels from material to material and from page to page giving a sense of expressive and coherent continuity." (https://www.rogerheaton.uk/boulez-domaines)

*   *   *

In the spring the dream of Carin and me wearing each other like garments seemed to go from a quaint romantic notion to a suffocating nightmare. We had lived so much in each other's orbit that soon we hardly took notice of the world around us. Each of us had become the other through a *dérèglement de tous les sens*. All around us worlds were coming into being and going extinct. Punks and 2 Tone Ska, Skinheads and New Romantics. Not that we cared about them. Flashes of fashion and musical movements were our stage setting and accompaniment, but we were each other's audience and main attraction. Our world had shrunk to the size of her Swiss Cottage attic. Or to the circumference of each other's skin.

As my infatuation began to fade, I began to look for a way out. The more she clung to me, the more I chafed. How did Ovid put it? "Casting off all her garments," Salmacis "holds him fast though he strives against her, steals reluctant kisses, fondles him, touches his unwilling breast, clings to him on this side and that." Yet I had to admit that I had started this struggle, throwing myself into this entanglement in the mistaken notion that it would relieve my essential aloneness while also helping me to escape my other entanglements back home. Still, here we were: "At length, as he tries his best to break away from her, she wraps him round with her embrace, as a serpent, when the king of birds has caught her and is bearing her on high; which, hanging from his claws, wraps her folds around his head and feet and entangles his flapping wings with her tail." Then the horror of the imagery is completed, since the trap cannot be escaped in air, or earth, or sea: "or as the ivy oft-times embraces great trunks of trees, or as the octopus holds its enemy caught beneath the sea, its tentacles embracing him on every side."[56] Thus Ovid captured the claustrophobia of the thoroughly consummated union. Our great desire, satisfied beyond our wildest dreams, too soon begins to cloy.

---

[56] Ovid's *Metamorphoses*, trans. Frank Justus Miller (Cambridge, MA: Loeb Classical Library, 1984).

* * *

At the end of April I went for a quick trip back to California to attend my little sister's wedding. It was a last-minute decision, since my sister, ten years younger, and I were never very close.[57] I did not intend to go, but when I found an irresistibly cheap flight on Laker Airways, I used it as an excuse to see my daughter after eight long months without her. When I showed up at the reception, instead of throwing herself into my arms, as I had imagined she would, Cyleste retreated to a stairwell and sat down as though I had betrayed her. "You're not supposed to be here," she said. It broke my heart, but maybe she was right.

My father looked uncomfortable in a rented tuxedo. The smell of aftershave only hovered above the acrid black grease under his fingernails that infused his usual blue coveralls or gray work pants. He was a practical man, a mechanic and ex-Marine, but between us there was none of the cliché of the father who tries to bully his bookish son into his own trade or, worse, into a profession. There was only a laconic distance between us, open to interpretation. As the youngest of his three sons, I escaped even the unspoken coercion of expectation. I once asked him why he never showed me how to fix cars. He said, "I didn't want you to become a mechanic like me." Barely literate himself, he never understood my love of literature, but he never underestimated where it might lead. He had a respect for learning not based on familiarity, although he was quick to point out the errors of "educated fools," especially those engineers who bowed down to theory over praxis. When I had left in September for London, he left me at the curb for Mnemosyne to drive me to the airport since it was on her way back to Irvine, retreating into the house before I could see him wiping the tears from his eyes on his sleeve as he went.

---

[57] My three older siblings were all born during the war years. If I, seven years later, was an afterthought, my sister, a decade behind me, was, according to my parents, an accident.

I adjusted the bow tie in his crooked collar and told him he looked very dapper.

"This is the last time they get me in a monkey suit," he vowed.

Everyone was appalled at my appearance. I had lost all color in my skin, as well as the beach highlights from the previous summer that had lightened my now darkening hair. Living on Guinness, the irregular sandwich, Lion bars and lovemaking, I now weighed just 135 pounds, spread pretty thinly over my six-foot skeleton, a wax museum facsimile of myself. I felt fine, though, and danced the night away—drawing on what I had learned at various clubs in London with Carin—first with my daughter, and then with her mother.

After the wedding in Los Angeles, I borrowed a car to drive to Irvine to see Mnemosyne. To prolong the prelude to seeing her, I stopped by Bob Peters's house in Huntington Beach. He was on sabbatical for the semester and deep into his Mad King Ludwig of Bavaria persona. (When *The Picnic in the Snow* was published, Bob scrawled a cryptic inscription in my copy: "You know of my deep feeling for you—*Ludwig* is a small testament of that.") He would later add to his portfolio of eccentric disguises the querulous Benjamin Robert Haydon (whose portraits have been called "consequential yet inept"[58]), as well as the Cornish vicar and sometimes mermaid Robert Hawker, but culminating in his transvestite tour de force, Elizabeth Bathory the Blood Countess of Hungary.[59] A few years later he would expand the *Ludwig* and *Blood Countess* Browningesque dramatic monologs into plays, which he himself would perform in outrageous costumes of royal purple and ermine robes, and crimson gowns. His lifetime companion, the poet Paul Trachtenberg, joined us briefly on his way to the cinema, where he said he spent his days immersed in the escapism of Hollywood movies. Paul was exploring

---

[58] Shirley Hazzard, *The Great Fire* (Farrar, Straus and Giroux, 2003), 6.

[59] See *The Picnic in the Snow: Ludwig of Bavaria* (St. Paul, MN: New Rivers Press, 1982) and *Ludwig of Bavaria: Poems and a Play*, revised edition (Cherry Valley, NY: Cherry Valley Editions, 1986). See also *Haydon* (Greensboro, NC: Unicorn Press, 1988); *Hawker* (Greensboro, NC: Unicorn Press, 1984); and *The Blood Countess* (Cherry Valley, NY: Cherry Valley Editions, 1987).

his own female persona in what would become *Short Changes for Loretta*. I filled Bob in on what I had—or rather had not—accomplished in London, minimizing my peregrinations and procrastinations. But I couldn't put off seeing Mnemosyne forever, and was soon on my way to the university to meet her in her office, which she was inhabiting in the absence of another professor who was on leave in France for the semester.

I intended to tell her that we should make a clean break of it now so that both of us could be free to live our lives at least for the rest of the time I would be away. I met her at her office on campus. Her reaction to seeing me was stoic, almost robotic. She handed me a copy of *Theatre Journal* in which my first piece of criticism had appeared while I was gone, an essay on Hegel's *Aesthetics* and Shakespeare's *Cymbeline* called "The Comic Dissolution of Art." It should have been a cause for celebration. She had, in my absence, shepherded it through the editing process, for which I thanked her warmly, but she was still cool to me. Then she took me outside (was she afraid I would cause a ruckus, break some furniture, weep and wail?) and I found out why her reception was so chilly. "I got married over the weekend." She said it with little or no emotion, as though she had broken a diet that she had not particularly wanted to be on anyway, and then looked away. I was reminded of the Caravaggio I had seen in the National Gallery, in which Salome, with the head of John the Baptist on a platter, looks away, a troubled but not repentant look on her face, almost as though she were thinking, "All right, that's done. What now?"

Her attitude did not really surprise me, I always expected from her the defensive posture of detachment. But my reaction did surprise me. It was simply relief. For eight months I had acted as though I were free, yet always with the shadow of guilt for my infidelities. Now, suddenly I was freed of all responsibility. All my infidelities had been amnestied by her marriage. Her anaconda embrace had finally relaxed, dropping this bird to fly away at liberty. I had not even realized that it was Mnemonsyne who had *entangled my flapping wings* more surely than Carin ever had. Had this release been what I wanted all along? Mnemosyne was very kind in how she let me go, pretending to want to continue our friendship, our intellectual bond. She declared in a later letter: "I keep you in my mind always as a kind of model for many things." It was a fitting flourish to end our relationship, formal, complimentary, civil and vague. As self-soothing and exclusionary as thumb-sucking. It had very little to do with me.

* * *

Back in London, Mariola informed me that Carin had gone through several stages emotionally during my absence. Crying, longing, lashing out, sighing, languishing, and refusing to talk about me at all, even though she stayed in my room for much of the time, which could not have helped her to cope. Having been celibate while away, although I had been tempted to sleep with my wife, I longed to hold Carin close again. When we got back together we spent several days in bed, with uneven results. Something had been broken. Some connection had been severed.

In May a graduation party for Carin and some of Mariola's friends followed the senior fashion show and ended with a group of us having a late-night breakfast at a restaurant somewhere in Knightsbridge. I flirted shamelessly with Charlotte the Swedish model, making a date with her for the following day, all in full view of Carin, who could not have missed our exchange of glances and phone numbers.

Charlotte and I met in Hyde Park the next afternoon and ambled around the duck ponds of St James Park and beyond. The waning light provided just the right overcast valedictory atmosphere. In a few hours she would leave for Stockholm for the summer, she said, her accent striking me as more French than Swedish. Our mood was desultory. I was hungover, but I took her lack of enthusiasm as disinterest. She always seemed entirely at her ease in her boredom, and therefore somewhat haughty, which gave our conversations a lack of urgency, a lack of passion, even when they were flirtatious. Charlotte's beauty, it turned out, was too perfect, too distant, too confident, too cold. To be candid, I was flattered to have been found *trevlig* by this classic beauty. Problem was, I was not deeply moved by the sort of photogenic austerity to be found in fashion magazines.

I let it fall that I might travel to Sweden in a few weeks, a sudden impulse due entirely to her, a little test to see her reaction. "You must visit me in Stockholm," she said with more animation than she had previously shown. "I simply will not hear of you not calling on me if you are there." Perhaps I had misread her. And so we parted amicably, polite kisses not quite landing on cheeks, with a vague promise of more to come.

Meanwhile, my dedication to Carin waned. Always hypersensitive, she felt my declining interest viscerally, which caused her to drink more, or at least to let herself become tipsy quicker, which in turn made her act more childish and lose control. She would cling to me and, in her own words, become "leechy." She hated herself at these times, she said, but she couldn't help it. What had become of the petulant toss of the head that I'd loved? The "idle intelligence" that had thrived independent of me and that I found so attractive in the beginning now became agitated, aggressive and attached. She had lost the very thing she was afraid she would lose, her freedom and independence, by being unable to keep herself from trying to deprive me of mine. I told myself that she was only nineteen, but this explanation could only take us so far, and she would be leaving soon, which did not help to calm her down.

Carin clung to me in desperation, and I recoiled. But now that she was really leaving, I became the desperate one. On our last night together, in a fury of urgency, I lay siege to her as though she were a castle, penetrating her defenses from every direction with a violence that was meant not just to violate her but to obliterate her, with a passion that had become cold-blooded, clear-headed, and mad. It was more like warfare than the end of a love affair. If I was a cannibal, I would have eaten her. But instead of obliterating her from my life, my violence incorporated her into my being. She impregnated me as oil impregnates bread. Yes, I was able to put her out of my mind consciously for a while, only to have her inform me from within, like a sibylline whisper, from the depths of my subconscious where she disappeared for a season like Persephone only to appear again in dreams. She would always be a part of me, lost, but sometimes found in the whiff of a British cigarette ad or the lyrics of a song.

* * *

A journal entry for 6 June 1981 tells me that there was supposed to be a "Dada Experience" in several *"actes"* in Hyde Park that day. I jogged by to see what this nostalgic attempt at a happening might be. There was only one *acte* going on. A couple of people, the *artistes*, I assumed, were rocking and nodding moronically in a wooden wagon under a tree. The posters had advertised it as "a reinvigoration of the *artes*." Dada being the caricature of Surrealism and an insult to and assault upon the so-called arts, if it had drawn a larger crowd and actually reinvigorated the artes, it would have been a total failure. As it was, it was a complete success because no one was there to witness it, except me, an anonymous jogger. Their secret was safe. I wouldn't tell a soul.

This demented bit of bad Dada somehow sums up the dark night of my spring.

I felt like a starveling at an empty banquet. Carin had given me everything she had, offering herself as a feast for the heart and body, an absurd sacrifice to love, and I had feasted selfishly to surfeit. Charlotte had offered an hors d'oeuvre in the form of a single kiss and a vague promise, a parody of seduction, and I panted after her like a love-starved puppy. It was all too much and none of it was enough. I felt desolate and defeated.

That Dada performance should be seen in tandem with another performance piece that I happened upon at the beginning of spring and which haunted me like an externalized nightmare for months.

I was walking home from Bloomsbury one evening when I glanced into a storefront and stopped at the window to take in a performance art installation. A naked man with a shaved head, his entire body covered in powdered pigments, was slowly making his way around the room in what appeared to be random paths. The lighting was dim. A roving spotlight overhead did not exactly follow his random path. His blue arms hung away from his body, and he leaned slightly forward, which must have been awkward in the short term and excruciating after not very long. There is no telling how long he had been at the task, nor how long it might go on. Most disturbing, though, and surely most excruciating, was this: his penis and scrotum, dusted deep red in the powdered pigment, were elongated by a cord tied around them and a weight suspended from them. This created a sort of paintbrush that swept the sawdust on the floor as it swung from side to side and back and forth between his legs like a pendulum in an observatory with each harrowing step of his absurd journey, mapping a temporary and utterly meaningless record of his movement. I turned away with something like fascination, amusement, horror, nausea, and (worst of all) recognition.

11 / The Ex-Beauty Queen's Daughter

> It was strange—it was distasteful; indeed, there was something in this indissolubility of bodies which was repugnant to her sense of decency and sanitation.
> —Virginia Woolf, *Orlando*

After a luncheon at the Fulbright Commission with Laury and his new cockney girlfriend Joan, she and I went back to Ashley Gardens, while Laury bought art supplies at Falkiner Fine Papers in Holborn. On the bus I was surprised to discover that she had read Henry Miller's two trilogies. I knew she could be funny ("The Queen's got some front, puttin' her mug on all the money, wot?") but I had underestimated her sophistication and I repented it. Aside from the visual arts, which might claim to find some freedom from ideology simply by being free of words (the eternal discussion among British painters in particular), we explored whether writers might somehow avoid ideology in their writing; whether it was possible to remain on the level of concrete description and narration, or whether by selection and emphasis they didn't intimate more in the way of ideology than they meant to. Wasn't ideology something only others could see, like toilet paper on one's shoe? Was essayism in the novel as inevitable as the taint of autobiography?[60]

---

[60] How different the path our conversation might have taken today when theoret-

These questions remained tantalizingly unanswered when we ran into Evelyn on the way into the building. She was just getting out of her car, a green Volvo with its ESCAPE TO WISCONSIN bumper sticker, with a couple of bags of groceries which we helped her with. On the way up in the lift, one of those wrought-iron bird-cages that rise up through the spiraling staircase, Evelyn invited us into her flat for coffee and conversation.

Evelyn was pleased to discover that Joan was Laury's friend and not one of my "constellation." This was one of her kinder words for what she at various times would call my "aggregation," "agglomeration," "compilation," or even, once, my "anthology" of love interests. Joan had soon extracted Evelyn's story, how she had lived in our flat with her American husband until they divorced and she took up with the neighbor across the hall, a distinguished older gentleman, a doctor and former MP (Labour, of course), who had once been a parliamentary under-secretary for the National Health Service and helped to legalize abortion.[61] An eloquent speaker, John was at one time seen to be the future leader of the party and was married to another Labour MP, the intrepid Gwyneth Dunwoody before they divorced in 1975. To put an additional glint of celebrity on him, he had also been Julie Christie's physician. When Evelyn moved in with John, she rented out her old flat to students like us, who became her hobby. She took great interest not only in the continually unfolding drama of our household, its romantic exploits and sexual shenanigans, but also in our intellectual and professional

---

ical questions strike me as beside the point as theological ones and only the nearness to the reality of actual experience—whether imagined or actualized, whether in fiction or memoir or some mixture of the two—is of vital interest. The authenticity of the writing as the voice of the writer being what is relevant, whether it's Henry Miller or Harriet Sohmers Zwerling.

[61] Ashley Gardens had from the first attracted the professional class, doctors and lawyers, as well as MPs, due to its central location and its proximity to the Houses of Parliament. The flats were spacious and included servants' quarters. See Valerie Kingman, "The World of the New: The First Ten Years," in *Ashley Gardens: Backward Glances* (London: Ashley Gardens Residents Association, 1990).

pursuits, and finally in our general welfare. Evelyn had all the qualities of a good house mother, therapist or, in another era, the hostess of a literary salon. She knew how to listen, exhibiting intelligent curiosity, sympathetic humor, and—what most inspired trust—a benevolent absent-mindedness. If you told her your innermost secrets, you felt sure that she would pretend to misplace the damning information just as she pretended to misplace everything else, from her keys and cash to her marijuana stash. The thing is, though, she never really misplaced anything. It was only temporarily elsewhere. Evelyn insisted that her own flat was growing uninhabitable because of all the accumulated scraps of information that crowded it—telephone books, cookbooks, statistical reports on the state of diabetes in Iran, letters, checks, and telephone messages. Here and there throughout the apartment, if you looked closely, you might discover a gem, like the small blue Emil Nolde painting that hung discreetly in the hall. Anyone else might have drowned in the deluge of disconnected facts. Evelyn had it all at her fingertips. Someone once mentioned in passing that they were thinking of redesigning their kitchen, and from one of the piles of nondescript documents under the coffee table, she pulled several brochures fresh from the showroom floor.

John and Evelyn were patient landlords to us always, and gracious hosts on more than one occasion. John once regaled us with tales of his motorcycle trip through Bulgaria to Greece just after the Second World War when he was a wild adventurous youth, not unlike those of us who passed through the London flat now, whom he tolerated for Evelyn's sake like the wise physician and statesman he was.[62]

When Laury arrived, we left Evelyn for Soho where we ate at a favorite Chinese restaurant called Man Lee Hong on Lisle Street, then had a drink at a packed Real Ale pub in Lamb's Conduit Street,

---

[62] During this time Dr. John Dunwoody (1929–2006) served as Chairman of the Kensington, Chelsea, and Westminster Area Health Authority (1977–82). He had married Evelyn Borner the previous year, 1979, and died in 2006 after an accident at their home in Béziers, France. He was awarded the CBE in 1986.

Holborn.[63] I recalled with some nostalgia my time with Concha, whom I had met at the immigration office nearby, and wondered what had become of her after I last saw her just before Christmas. Was she still seeing her Jewish boy who wanted her to wear skirts? Was she still playing Maria Poppins to the children of Thatcherite yuppies in St. John's Wood? I realized I had no way of contacting her, other than possibly hunting her down someday in her beloved Salamanca. But to what end? What if she, like the eighteenth-century Spanish nun Fernanda Fernández, should be found to have, after all, a small penis capable of emitting semen and changed her name to Mario? No, she was in some ways the ideal gynander but she was no hermaphrodite.

Still up for one last drink I dropped in at Rumours by myself. It was beginning to be my regular haunt, even if I could only at times afford a Guinness for "dinner." As I ordered my drink at the bar, I struck up a conversation with the tall blonde sitting there. Her strong profile was softened by a constellation of fine freckles strewn across the sharp bridge of her nose and around her eyes like the glitter of a subtle carnival mask. She was in short order generous with information about herself. Originally from Derby in the Midlands, she moved with her mother to St. John's Wood when she was just five. She would turn twenty-one in August. She worked as a hairstylist and her name was Stacie. "Very pleased to meet you, too."

We left the restaurant for a club, the Whiskey-a-go-go, not the one on Sunset Boulevard in Hollywood, of course, but a knock-off on Wardour Street in Soho. A real dive, or "tip" as Stacie called it. She ordered Pernod and lemonade, and I had a couple of Martell cognacs with a side of tonic. By 2:00 a.m. she had given me her home and work numbers, scrawled along with her name on the back of her card: Hebe[64] Hair Stylists, William IV St., Charing Cross. We

---

[63] Man Lee Hong closed sometime in the early 1980s.

[64] Hebe was the Greek goddess of youth, a cupbearer to the gods, serving nectar and ambrosia at the Café Olympus, until she tripped on her dress and was fired by Apollo for exposing her breasts. She was then replaced by Ganymede, Zeus's catamite.

agreed to see UB40 at the National Club in Kilburn near the end of the month. It was early June.

A few days later I called Stacie at her work. She was supposed to go to a Moody Blues concert that night, but she canceled so we could meet at Tutton's in Covent Garden, where we drank two bottles of wine over dinner. At 11:30 we returned to my flat for coffee and talked. We called for her a minicab at 1:00 a.m. and canceled it at 1:02 a.m. She continued to discourse on her extended family as we lay in bed. Her father died recently, at age forty-one, from stomach cancer. Her Great Aunt Madge had eloped on the eve of her marriage with a Canadian gentleman to Gretna Green in Scotland, but the husband turned out to be a faineant who allowed himself to be supported by his wife. "I thought that was the definition of a gentleman," I joked. We cuddled and caught an hour or two of sleep before she went directly back to work in the morning, to the teasing of her colleagues since she had not been home to change clothes after leaving work the day before.

* * *

Later that morning I met up with my cousin Dale Tannehill, who was visiting from Colorado. He was traveling with three other born-again Christian missionaries who wanted to visit Cambridge. He was in the "incipient frozen yogurt" business. So he said. On the train ride out, we spoke of family matters, mostly unremarkable news. I asked about his brother Harold. "I still hold out hope," said Dale, folding his hands and bowing his head as if in prayer, "that Harold will find his way to the Lord." Harold had always been a troublemaker. One of my first memories of him was hearing that he had been attacked in the Three Musketeers, a bar on the main drag of Orange Cove, California, with a broken beer bottle that someone shoved in his face. Dale had said at the time, "Harold probably asked for it." Now Harold was serving time in Chino State Prison for murdering his wife in front of his two daughters for sleeping with a Mexican farmworker.

In Cambridge I played tour guide as we punted on the Cam and visited the grounds of King's and Trinity Colleges. I told stories of Byron bathing naked in the Trinity fountain in winter and how he was rumored to have kept a pet bear who, he said, was helping him study. I also explained the plot of my favorite novel, *Zuleika Dobson*, in which the title character (a *seeker* not a *piker*, said Beerbohm, the author, to explain the pronunciation of her name), a femme fatale and prestidigitator, charms the entire student body of Oxford, including an otherwise impervious dandy, to such a fever pitch that they commit mass suicide in her honor, an event that she takes as only her due, and ends by examining the train schedule for a contemplated trip to Cambridge, since Oxford had recently become so boring without any undergraduates to admire her. But the dark and decadent humor was lost on my cousin and his wan missionaries.

The story I was tempted to tell but kept to myself was that of the two dons who were bathing naked on the banks of the Cam when some town girls happened by. One don quickly covered his face, while the other covered his genitals. Said the one to the other, "Why did you not cover your face?" Answered the other, "Well, I was afraid of being recognized!"

I wondered how these born-again missionaries might react to the story of my life in London. I wondered even more how Dale would react to the notion, uncovered in my research, that Christ's "dual nature" was not simply both divine and human but also both male and female. This was not simply a conceit of the alchemists, but philologists entered the debate, citing the *mastos* (breasts) on the Son of God who appears in Revelations 1:13

On the train home, Dale continued his monologue about his brother's prospects for salvation, recounting how he himself had been saved. He believed the Bible to be a sort of medico-legal text and that prayer was a form of legal argumentation. As Dale explained, in a voice of such a mild tone and modulation that no one could have imagined contradicting him, any more than they would any other madman: "By petitioning the Lord with prayer" (all I could think of was Jim Morrison: *You canNOT petition the Lord with prayer!*) "all we have to do is insist on His contract with us as already promised in the Bible; in consequence, He has no choice but to honor those promises. For example, we all have the right to insist on living to be at least seventy years old because, as promised in Psalms 90:10, 'the days of our years are three score and ten.'" (But what of my sister Wanda, cut off at one score and four? Or Harold's wife, shot in the face before one score and ten? All the old theodicy questions arose in my mind, with a new twist: why do bad things happen to good people *under seventy*?) Dale also believed that he had healed his mother of a blood clot. "It's true," he testified with a smile that I took for beatific. Dale the Healer, Harold the Killer: two sides of the coin of delusion, the Brothers Tannehill meet the Brothers Karamazov. "I healed myself of poison oak," he said, rolling up his shirt to show me the scars on his back. I asked him how he did it. He answered with a look of incredulity, as though it should be obvious to me by now. "By saying, 'I curse you, poison oak, in the name of Our Lord Jesus Christ!' of course."

I always felt that Harold the Murderer was in some way the smirk of Ironic Karma come to mock Granny Tannehill and her faith. Before she ascended to her dreaded heaven, she had lived to see any number of blows to her belief in a benevolent God, blows dealt always through her children or her children's children. First, he had taken her favorite son, the eldest, Cleo, whose skin was white as Ozark snow and whose hair was black as the baby snakes his wife Jewel kept in a jar in their rustic kitchen. When he died of a burst appendix at the age of twenty, Granny wailed for weeks. Her suffering never really let up, it only disguised itself as bitterness over the abominations of this world.[65]

Dale's father, Uncle Olin, was a mild-mannered man (like his father Jesse) who had married a feisty woman with one leg shorter than the other. (Dale's prayer, while effective against blood clots, could not cure his mother's congenital deformity, it seems. Even

---

[65] Cleo's story is told from his sister's (my mother's) point of view in a story I published, "A Jar of Baby Snakes," *Rosebud* 1:3 (Autumn/Winter 1994).

God's power had its limits.) Uncle Olin was known around Orange Cove as Tex, due to the Stetson he always wore, and had been mayor for a couple of terms. Just after he had divorced his crippled wife (a double disappointment for Granny Tannehill, first the disability, then the divorce), we visited him when he was living by himself, sleeping in a sad, sagging single bed in a narrow room off his electrical shop.

Doc and Emery, her two middle sons, both alcoholics, had each been "taken by The Cancer," an allegorical figure whose status in Granny's Pantheon of God's Punishments was just a little higher —and more deserving of her awe, being more malevolent—than Divorce and Disability.

Finally, her youngest son, Jay, had left his wife for a backwoods beauty by the unlikely name of Letha Goodnight, and with whom he lived in great poverty (and sin) in a drafty house outside of Ark City, giving her endless sets of twins with destinies as twisted as those of Leda and her unfortunate cygnets. It was Granny's cross, these Tannehill spawn who were almost (but not quite) as bad as Collinses. It had to be the bad blood of those Tannehill men and not that of her own Scottish clan, the Dugginses. While I certainly hoped that Dale's Christian magic reformed his fallen brother, I had not much faith in the efficacy of his incantations to reform the sons of—or the efficacy of his divine lawsuits to reverse the curse on—the legendary House of Tannehill.

As the train lumbered back into King's Cross station, Dale leaned forward and took my knee in his left hand and clapped his right hand to his forehead, saying, "Pray with me, Rick." The idea of prayer (*you cannot petition* . . .) was bad enough, but I had long ceased to be a Rick except to my family, and I had listened to my enthused cousin's diatribe long enough, so I ignored Dale's invitation, removed his hand from my knee, and left the carriage almost without another word.

* * *

The next day I dined with Stacie and her family in St. John's Wood. I met her mother and her mother's boyfriend, as well as her little brother and tragic Aunt Madge. The mother's boyfriend was a squat figure, a cross between Kaiser Wilhelm and Danny DeVito, whose profession was vague. I got the impression that he was a middle manager in the Jewish mafia of London. Her mother screamed at Stacie's brother for not making use of the ballet shoes she'd bought for him. Aunt Madge seemed deaf. They barely acknowledged my existence enacting their domestic dramas, which put me at ease.

No one would have mistaken Stacie for an heiress because she abhorred the thought of being taken for posh. When I first met her, I assumed she was from East or North London, but she was simply one of those well-off Londoners who disdain the BBC or Oxbridge accents as off-putting. She was a big-boned beauty and a little brash, Adele before her time. The spacious and dreary house in Cavendish Avenue, St. John's Wood, was a few doors down from Paul McCartney's, I was told. Its sitting room looked out on a neglected garden, the plants and statuary overgrown, the fences in disrepair.

Stacie and I went outside in the garden to smoke as soon as dinner was over. I asked if her mother was upset about something, such as my presence. "No," said Stacie, "she's always like that, on edge, halfway round the bend. Don't take it to heart."

Her mother was a model, a former Miss U.K., one of the faces of Oil of Olay. She had retained much of her former sex appeal but not without effort. In some ways she reminded me of the older woman who seduced me in the swimming pool, extroverted, unselfconscious, incurably flirtatious, somewhat mad. Almost Stacie's opposite in many ways, delicate-featured and brunette, she might have passed for Natalie Wood's sister until she opened her mouth. When she wasn't screaming at Stacie's little brother, she was criticizing Stacie's hair (bleached, with a slightly asymmetrical cut) or clothing (too trendy) or work (surely she could find something better than hairdressing). Mother and daughter shared a certain spontaneous vulgarity that the camera in the mother's case disguised, while Stacie's superior inner beauty, an almost infantile quality of trust and openness, no camera could capture.

Stacie's previous boyfriend was a white Jamaican who came to England to get his British passport. In spite of the fact that his parents were wealthy, Chris had carried five coffee cans of marijuana into the country. After a series of breaks in the connections after the cans arrived, he was named to the police by a friend of a friend. He spent three months in Reading Prison (Oscar Wilde's old haunt) before his trial and three months more after sentencing. He came out "introverted and bitter," said Stacie. He was working in an art studio when Stacie met him. He was not untalented. She convinced him to go to the States for art school, obtaining, filling out, and sending off the applications for him. Her mother footed the bill. Stacie was supposed to follow him there, but he never wrote to her. It turned out she was pregnant with his child, but since he absconded, she had an abortion. Her mother offered to support her and him and the baby while they got on their feet, "if he had only had the bollocks to marry her." After the abortion, while Stacie was in recovery and mourning at their country house in Surrey, the butler brought her dishes of strawberries. "Eat the bloody strawberries," her mother commanded. Stacie wasn't up to eating anything. "Don't be stupid, eat them!" The strawberries splattered the bed like a crime scene—or a delivery room. Stacie began to cry. Her mother locked her in an upstairs bedroom until she had stopped crying. Her mother burst into the room. "How can you stop crying when you've just killed your baby?" This from a woman who had done far worse things in her life as a model, things that she said she would never reveal to Stacie because she had done them for her, a sweep of her hand indicating that the fine house was the fruit of her secret sins. This from a woman who had written a note to her daughter's teacher at school which read: "Stacie hase bean ill." Stacie got the worst of that incident because the headmaster would not believe that such an illiterate note could have been written by a full-grown person, much less a rich and somewhat glamorous mother.

The morning after that lovely family dinner, Stacie took off from work without calling in, and we lay around in her bedroom giving each other massages, eating very little, cuddling, and finally getting around to making love for the first time that night. Her mother's boyfriend walked in on us while we were still half-naked and wanted to talk to me about writing.

"I've got a notion of writin' my memoirs," he said, sitting down at the foot of the bed. "I got tales to tell, I have. You're a writer. What do you think?"

I had mentioned at dinner that a screenplay I had written with Mnemosyne had been a semifinalist for a competition at UCLA, which led to our ghostwriting a treatment for a screenplay. Not wanting to offend the mother's boyfriend, I encouraged him, suggesting that, while I didn't know exactly what sort of tales he had to tell, a screenplay might be the best medium for what he had in mind. I could see Bob Hoskins in the starring role as the lovable mafioso.

"No, no," he protested, all blushes and modesty. "Bob Hoskins, really?" He licked his lips, clearly liking the idea. Then: "You really think so?" We made vague plans to meet to sketch out a film treatment.

The following Saturday morning Stacie and I took the train to her mother's country house in Surrey, where her mother would meet up with us at some point. Bob Hoskins had to stay in London to take care of some business. Stacie's mother ditched him soon afterward, so we never got around to writing the scenario.

Allerton Hill was built by the curator of Kew Gardens in 1896. It was one of those photogenic country estates surrounded by manicured gardens, a croquet lawn, a secluded swimming pool, tennis court, vegetable garden, animal pen, and a pine hurst where we stripped and made love on a bed of needles in those lazy June afternoons. There were half a dozen other people staying in the house, off and on, but with its several drawing rooms, billiards room, conservatory, and acreage, it was not crowded. One often wondered where everyone was. Off the kitchen was an antiquated communication system of porcelain bell-pulls that connected all the rooms upstairs to the servants downstairs so that anything the masters and mistresses needed could be obtained in short order. There were no live-in servants anymore, although there were part-time cooks, housekeepers, and gardeners.

During our stay in Surrey, Stacie asked me to live with her, which she said she had wanted to ask me since we first met, but she thought that might have been too forward of her. She even hinted at marriage. She seemed a bit desperate. Was it a sudden passion, love at first sight? I doubted it. We were comfortable with each other, but not madly in love. I felt like I was more of an escape hatch from her mother. ("Cor, she's gettin' on my tits!") Another chance at going to the States after her disappointment with the dope-dealing artist Chris.

When we got back to London, I was a little late one night meeting her, and Stacie was furious. She had drunk half a bottle of wine and worked herself into a dangerous state of mistrust and self-doubt. We had ended on a bad note, causing a scene in the midst of Covent Garden, and spent the night apart. The next morning she apologized, but the damage was done. She was only twenty, of course, and might well have grown out of this stage, but did I really want to involve myself with another woman who, like Mnemosyne, could cause such scenes, or who, like Carin, would cling like the ivy on the walls of the ex-beauty queen's estate?

What Stacie really wanted wasn't me but to get married to someone, anyone, and move to the States. I think she liked the idea of marrying a future professor, in spite of her ambivalence towards the more educated classes. As an American, I was exempt from any claim of class superiority. She and her mother were sensitive to class distinctions, having "come up" to London from the Midlands. The country house was part of the elaborate stage-set in which they enacted their ambivalent class statement, in a sort of reverse application of Childe Harold's Byronic stance, standing "[a]mong them, but not of them," them in this case being not the lowly "crowd" but rather the upper classes.[66]

---

[66]Under pressure from her Midlands family, who mocked the "country [i.e., posh] attitude" they felt the house gave her, the former beauty queen sold it in 1998 to

I have to admit I was tempted by the thought of marrying Stacie in part because of her picturesque family, and not least because of the dream house in Surrey, which would have made a comfortable getaway whenever her mother was absent. It was something out of a Trollope novel, where guests could come to stay for months on end and still avoid their hosts if they liked, and where financially embarrassed gentlemen (or even American) sons-in-law might "get on their feet." But I had no illusions of living in a Victorian novel and no intentions of marrying for money or living like Aunt Madge's ne'er-do-well Canadian off my hair stylist wife's model mother's and her live-in mafioso's money, even if we had been able to tease a film script out of his life of crime, charming as the house and all three of them were.

It reminded me of what Evelyn had said once about Debbie-from-Princeton, whose parents were entertainment industry royalty.

"She's rich," said Evelyn, hinting at greener pastures, "and I think she likes you."

"Two things that should disqualify her."

"Wouldn't you like to have a cold martini shaking for you at night when you come in the door?"

"I don't want Debbie shaking anything for me when I come in the door."

I was probably harder on Debbie than I should have been. It's lucky Debbie was getting an advanced degree at the London School of Economics before going on to Stanford because she was useless as a roommate. Pampered from birth to Princeton, she could not wield a sponge, much less a mop, nor could she make a sandwich. Not that I was looking for a drudge in a roommate or wife, far from it. But beyond conveying telephone messages accurately, which I admit she did with precision, and playing a passable game of squash, she had little to offer the household. It was not her fault. Her sheltered

---

Brian May of Queen, who called it Allerton Hill Studio. In 2020, the house was described as having 6 bedrooms, 6 baths, and 4 reception areas, and was valued at £2,900,000. May, however, has said it is "priceless."

upbringing gave her limited life experience to work with so it was a good thing she had a fat trust fund like a well stuffed mattress to fall back on. But that was not the life—or the wife—for me.

I could not have accepted Stacie's proposal of marriage in any case. There is no more effective prophylaxis against marriage than being married already, although it did not stop my incorrigible grandfather on the Irish side, Ephraim Adam "Ed" Collins, from committing bigamy, they say. Still, I intended to stay married for as long as possible since it was the only way of keeping me from some impulsive lifetime commitment. Contrary to what Stacie thought, it was not that I was unwilling to commit, it was that I, incurable romantic, was all too willing to commit on the strength of a marathon of erotic bliss. I might well have proposed to Carin, for example, in the midst of an erotic embrace that I hoped to perpetuate indefinitely, had I not been thwarted by that piece of paper. No, marriage to Stacie was out of the question.

In July, Stacie left for her holiday in Greece. Greece might have been the most inviting part of the whole marriage fantasy, since Stacie regularly vacationed there. I had not yet been to Greece, but I felt its attraction. Still, if Greece (or wealth) were the prize, I would have cynically courted Lena, Mariola's friend and heiress to a Greek shipping magnate. Lena was small, dark, and sturdy, and one could see on her upper lip the foreboding shadow of the Greek widow-to-be. Her vacations were spent at her father's resort in the Cyclades. With all the talk of marrying for money in the Victorian novels I'd read, one might think I would have considered it myself. And I did consider it, but not seriously and not for long, with Stacie for less than a month, with Lena for about a minute, and with Debbie-from-Princeton not at all. I suppose marriage was in the air, though, including the historic one that occurred a few blocks from our flat that summer at Buckingham Palace.

There is no mention in my journals of the Royal Wedding of Prince Charles and Lady Diana Spencer on July 29, 1981. It's odd, because I have some vivid impressions of the day, if not of the event, which of course obsessed and continues to obsess the world.

To view the fireworks display the night before the wedding, all of London seemed to flood into Hyde Park like a festive high tide and then afterwards to recede, pooling outside of the pubs as the giddy hordes sidled their way home like crabs. The next morning I caught a glimpse of the early festivities on television. As the bride and bridegroom's processions left Buckingham Palace around 10:00 a.m. I took the tube to the East End, passing underneath the carriages as they made their way to St Paul's Cathedral for the ceremony, which I missed.

Instead, I met Laury and his girlfriend Kathy, who had flown in from Connecticut, for an alternative reggae concert dubbed "Not the Royal Wedding."[67] Afterwards, stoned on the abundant free pot that was circulating in the crowd, the three of us made our way back to Hackney, stopping at an off-license for beer before climbing the wall to the public pool of the London Fields Lido to go swimming in the nude. Kathy too was a painter, her dark hair lush and dripping from that fine pubic goatee women used to wear at her cool white hips. She was studying at Yale, yet I was the one who had footed the bill for her trip, since Laury, who likewise had studied at pricey RISD, was never one to stint himself for food or painting supplies, including expensive art books, yet he always put on a show of great frugality as though he was constantly on the edge of starvation. In truth it was I who was always on the verge of pencelessness. While I was aware that she was here at my expense, we enjoyed each other's company, the three of us, that day more than I can say, even though their long-distance relationship did not last much longer and my largesse was never repaid.

Another major current event that I recall very little about was the election of Ronald Reagan which occurred the previous November,

---

[67] According to the *Hackney Gazette*, the official name of the free concert appears to have been "Funk the Wedding," an "anti-monarchist funk, rock, and reggae pop concert" attended by 3,000 people in Clissold Park, a little northwest of Hackney. It was organized by Rock Against Racism. "For most people, though, the music was the message—and they had probably all watched the royal event on TV earlier in the day anyway."

and even less about the inauguration in January. I only recall a poster from the *Daily Mail* that someone had nicked and put in our sitting room that showed the grinning POOR BOY FROM TAMPICO in a cowboy hat. Someone in the house hung a string of sausages around the Poor Boy's neck. (I kept a snapshot of this, I am perplexed to say, yet I have no photographs of Concha or Carin.) It was, of course, also during the reign of Margaret Thatcher, of which I remember next to nothing except that there was a popular satire about her husband staged at the Whitehall Theatre called *Anyone for Denis?* IRA bombings were still on everyone's mind, having occurred mostly in the 1970s, with one accidental bomb going off in Dunmurry near Belfast in early 1980. Riding the tube or attending a film in Leicester Square, we were constantly reminded to report stray packages or suspicious behavior, but this was a brief period of relative calm for IRA activity. None of this I mentioned in my journals, which shows how little I cared about the world of politics so completely was I immersed in my various researches.

* * *

My closing memory of Stacie is supported by a photograph of her in fancy dress for a party that I have no memory of. I'm sure we went to the party (or at least made an effort to go) because I recall in vivid detail the two of us, dressed uncannily alike, in black and white, sitting in a black London taxi somewhere near the Chelsea Bridge. I had picked up a morning coat (vintage 1890s, or so I imagined) in one of the street markets and put together a decent facsimile of formal wear considering my budget because I assumed "fancy dress" to mean something like "black tie." When my error was pointed out by our amused companions in the taxi, it was a little like stepping off the curb on the way to the immigration office and realizing that I had everything backwards. Fancy dress is one of those British expressions that is counterintuitive to the American ear, like going "up" to London from the North, or the oxymoron of a labor "action" meaning a strike, or the exclusive nature of a "public" school. I had unwittingly dressed "up" for a costume party, while Stacie had assumed a costume of male attire in the manner of Marlene Dietrich in her cutaway tux. As a result, we faced each other like twins in a mirror, or two grooms on their way to a gay marriage. She was handsome, I have to admit, with her blonde hair slicked back behind her ears, accentuating the strong profile that had so enchanted me on our first meeting at the bar at Rumours. But I found nothing provocative or erotic in her costume, unlike Concha's casual corduroys and oxfords that had set off in me such sparks of lust. Had I become inured to the attractions of transvestism? Or was I simply done with Stacie and her dreams of a hermaphroditic caricature of marriage?

Lamentations Around the Remains of Christ, c. late 1500s. Anonymous. Collection of the Museum of Notre-Dame à la Rose Hospital. Lessines, Belgium.

"... Christ's 'dual nature' was not simply both divine and human but also both male and female." (p. 148)

12 / The Garden of Edinburgh

> We live fixations, fixations of desire [sic].[68]
> —Gaston Bachelard, *The Poetics of Space*

With Carin having left for San Francisco to continue her college education, and Stacie away in Greece for her holiday, I was left alone to await the decision of the Fulbright Commission on my extension. I had applied for an additional year of support, even though I knew I could not stay past September, when I was expected to return to Irvine and resume my duties teaching Shakespeare and Homer to freshmen surfers with dried salt in their hair from their morning tumble in the waves at the Wedge in Newport Beach. My great hope was that they might connect with sailors washed up on Prospero's island or Nausicaa's shore. I was scheduled to teach a class called "Romance and Realism," but what did I really know about either of those incompatible terms? By trying to fuse them over the past nine

---

[68] This is a misquotation. But this is how I recalled and recorded it in my journal. The actual quotation is "We live fixations, fixations of happiness," a very different idea. Bachelard's happiness is a longing for the past, a nostalgia for vacated spaces. Desire, however, is a longing to occupy future spaces, a different kind of longing. I keep the misquotation, however, because it more accurately reveals my frame of mind at the time, which was fixated not on settling back into past haunts but invading the future with travel.

months, hadn't I utterly confused them? Surely another year in London would teach me all I needed to know—or so I told the Fulbright Commission and at times myself.

Mr. Herrington had early on encouraged me to request funds for any expenses incidental to my research, saying that they had extra money for me since, as an independent PhD candidate, my arrangement with Professor Fletcher did not require them to pay tuition. "Would a six-month extension be useful?" Herrington now asked, meeting me halfway. I said it would be "just the thing." I did not say that I only needed tiding over for the summer because this was the only way I could finance my planned European tour. Even if I had to return the money to the Commission later, I would have had my vacation and been on my way back to California. I could cut my extension short on short notice and worry about the hell-to-pay down the road.

I was not returning because of Mnemosyne. She was out of the picture, married even if temporarily and not happily, so it wasn't she who made me determined to return. Of her I was cured. It wasn't really my teaching duties, either. I just didn't think I would be able to stand another year away from my daughter. On the telephone the night before Thanksgiving, Cyleste had said, "Daddy, I love you more than you think." I only hoped that she loved me as much as she could, which was more than I had earned or deserved. If she ever stopped, I would not have been fit for human consumption. And then there was her anxious welcome when I surprised her at my sister's wedding, telling me I wasn't supposed to be there. I had never really stopped missing her since arriving in the land of Mary Poppins. I dedicated the novel I wrote at the time to her "to tickle her *serius ocius*" (sooner or later, although in my twisted Latin-lite mind I stubbornly thought it should also mean "serious bone," instead of funny bone). Not that *The Fop* (later called *Give a Dog a Bone*) would ever see the light of day. It was at once too weird, too derivative, too reminiscent of Ronald Firbank. It was, as Samuel Johnson is supposed to have said of someone's work, both good and original, but what was original was not good, and what was good was not original. Several otherwise encouraging responses from publishers both large and small agreed. The verdict: it was unpublishable.[69] Still, Rita Rosenkranz at Random House admitted that it "did have a tickling effect." Maybe farce was not my forte.

My argument to the Commission was based on the fact that I had "not exhausted the materials available in Britain on the fascinating and topical subject of hermaphroditism." It's true: I had hardly scratched the surface of sexual ambiguity in the available texts and artworks. But as was clear by now, the more urgent research I was conducting was the experience of my own life, which was not entirely unrelated to the topic, and that might well take at least another forty years to complete. This journal entry dated only "1981" glimpsed the truth:

> *At the Warburg Institute today, reading Rafael Lopez-Pedreza's* Hermes and His Children, *I realized what should have been obvious all along, that in researching the Hermaphrodite, I have really been researching myself.*
>
> *I am obsessed with sex, not so much with the mere sensual but more with the cerebral fascination of sex, the idea (but also the distinct sensuous sensation) of merging with her, becoming a hermaphrodite, she and I in the sexual act, the toy of double shape, a game that can be played a thousand times, each time for an eternal moment only, each time being enervated by the ecstatic union, by the symmetry, the exhaustion of completion, and in consequence longing again for the asymmetry of being myself alone.*
>
> *It is as though I am at one moment the nymph Salmacis, overcome by the beauty of my opposite, and at the next moment, having merged her with him, becoming at that moment Hermaphroditus, yet protective of my separateness, rejecting that part of myself that longs, that desires, that longed, that desired. I am conflicted. I need both impulses simultaneously, integrity and integration; both*

---

[69] "Our funny bones reacted appropriately, but I'm afraid common sense took over," wrote Pat Strachan of Farrar, Straus & Giroux. Less diplomatic, but in the spirit of the manuscript, was the reader at Fiction Collective: "If we were the publisher of individual lines, there'd be a hat-full here we could publish with joy."

drive me.

But isn't that the moral of that cautionary myth? Not to lose oneself in the union, not to become, like Paris with Helen, lazy and effeminate, emasculated from too much luxuriance in love, too much collision with the physics of even the most beautiful woman in the world, exchanging not just bodily fluids but the atomic particles of gender as the hammer becomes part of the nail, as sweat and blood and semen and saliva are licked, sucked, chewed and swallowed? To be careful of abandoning oneself entirely and becoming the other?

Exploring orgasms and origins, the odyssey continues.

* * *

To get a feel for the land of the Tannehill ancestors on my mother's side, I took a trip to Scotland. My mother was a gentle woman and kind, deliberately so, in part so that she would not turn into her mother, who was a self-righteous, God-fearing Southern "shout" Baptist from Missouri. My mother grew up as the only girl in a household with five brothers on a sharecropping farm in the Ozarks, and then during the Depression in the Central Valley of California, where she met my father. (Similarly, my father was true to my mother his whole life and strove not to become his father, Ed—gambler, rounder, bigamist, conman, and Irish cad—and "never missed a day's work if I was able, by God.") As a girl she had worked first on the stingy farm and then as a housemaid for rich California farmers. Later, when I was six or seven, I would accompany her in the evenings to her job cleaning empty offices in Upland. Between them my parents had just twelve years of schooling, and although she had never made it out of junior high, she had two years of education on my father, who rarely read anything but the occasional Louis L'Amour Western, an extrovert who stammered yet cussed in complex periodic sentences whenever he had to fill out a form or write anything longer than his name.[70]

---

[70] "The name on his birth certificate is Alvie Corder Collins. He changed his first name, in Old English meaning "friend of the elves," to Alva (as in Edison) but pre-

I got my verbal abilities from my mother, who was keeper of the family lore, a prolific letter writer who would play Scrabble until the sun came up if you let her, even though she seldom won. She was attracted not to my father's mind but to his shyness and his stutter, and most of all to the idea of a marriage that would take her out of the house of her disapproving mother, Allie Tannehill, née Duggins. In the early years her parents had fought like cats, the battles always beginning, it seems, at night in the bedroom. Her father, Jesse, had long ago found the formula for domestic peace: he would pick up his Stetson and go into the yard and sit in his chair under the shade of the elm tree to watch the leaves fall. My grandmother criticized my mother for marrying into "that Collins bunch" of heathens and would treat all of us children with disdain, me especially, calling me a "sneaky little Collins outfit." "Why does he never talk?" she'd say, with narrowed eyes behind her rimless glasses. Jesse would gently intercede: "Now, Allie, the boy's listening. That's how he learns." She was not convinced: "I don't trust someone who never talks. He's hiding something."[71] What she really meant, I think, was that she knew I was listening to her, watching her, and hearing the hypocrisy in her fear of a child's judgment.

In Scotland I wandered from town to town with no particular itinerary, as far north as Inverness, stopping at Loch Ness without attempting to see the loch or the Ness. What with the pissing rain and the pissant tourists at Inverness, I continued even farther north but turned back as soon as I arrived at the desolate little hamlet of Brora. The forbidding landscape was scenic without being inviting. Like my mother's side of the family, the countryside was handsome and severe, with chiseled features like the Tannehill men, and not

---

ferred to be called Corder (which my mother misunderstood as Corner) until he shortened his first name even further to Al.

[71] Granny Tannehill, aka the Candy Granny, always had sweets on her coffee table in a glass hen shaped like herself. Ironically, Granny Collins, who resembled Geronimo, was the sweeter of the two, although she was called the Biting Granny, for her penchant of grabbing little children, lifting us up as we passed and gobbling our tender parts, like Rubens' *Saturn*.

without their stony charm like the glittering granite of my next stop, Aberdeen.[72]

Britain was enjoying an oil boom that began with the discovery of oil fields in the North Sea in 1970. As a result, accommodations in Aberdeen were scarce, so I ended up sharing a room with several offshore oil rig workers whose accents were impossible to understand. From what I could tell, at least one of them was from around Glasgow, but as for the rest, they could have been speaking Icelandic, for all I knew. The lodgers in some of the other rooms were more easily understood, as I discovered at breakfast.

"Would you care for a knife?" asked the landlady's plump daughter with a curtsy, as she tended hand and foot to the roughly handsome quiet man across from me.

"I can butter me toast wi' me finger if ye like," he replied, not unpleasantly. At which she blushed most unnecessarily.

Meanwhile the loud and unselfconfident youth in a nylon training suit next to him looked up from his book and down on the prospect of his day with dismay, rousing himself to action: "Up! Ya bastid fairy! Aar, I've got a dee todee, I do. I'm off to see my wife, the bastid!" Then he slumped back into his chair, returning to his breakfast-table reading material, *Khrushchev Remembers*. He kept several other books stacked by his bed, all politics and history, which may have accounted for his jaundiced look on life.

A fair blond boy who must have been a student kept his red tie tucked into his soft gray shirt and his mouth shut. Listening, learning, hiding, or judging, it was hard to tell.

When I first got to my crowded room, there was only one fellow there, asleep, a sort of voluble Ancient Mariner, it turned out.

---

[72] I was reading Scott's *Waverley* on the train. His description of the Scottish character seemed to be taking dictation from my mind: "Yet the physiognomy of the people, when more closely examined, was far from exhibiting the indifference of stupidity; their features were rough, but remarkably intelligent; grave, but the very reverse of stupid; and from among the young women, an artist might have chosen more than one model, whose features and form resembled those of Minerva" (Chapter 8).

When he woke up, he was blurry but friendly, using each of my brief remarks as a launchpad for one of his endless monologs.

"To Edinburgh you're going, is it? Yes, Edinburgh. I've spent time myself in two of the youth hostels there. There's one in the center and another in the south, much nicer. You know them, maybe. And you're from . . . California? Now that's a long way, innit? They haven't anything like this, do they, in California, eh? Granite cities, I mean."

At breakfast he continued where he left off. "California's where that David Hockney fella's gone, painting swimming pools and such."

No one at the table responded to this comment, and I felt no need to either. His accent was English, not Scottish, not the north of England either, although, like my roommate Eric practicing dialects, he seemed to waver between accents, making it difficult to pin down where he was from exactly. His eyes were slightly askant, like a modern alabaster imitation of a primitive mask. A seated mask. But talkative, babbling like a mechanical sybil spouting empty prophecies but without conviction. Apropos of nothing, he added: "I'm not going to any more of them *frustrating* establishments, those *third* establishments."

No one seemed to know what he was referring to, and no one asked. It was a reticent crew, men of few words, like the Tannehills, like my grandfather Jesse. Clearly they didn't care about this gypsy scholar's rambling travelog. Either that or they had heard enough of it in the past.

To mollify him as much as to test the limits of the others' forbearance, I asked where a good place to eat could be found.

"Well, you must be selective about the fish-and-chips shops round here, but there's one down this way which will feed you for about 70p, and then there's another shop further down which serves Chinese takeaway and haggis . . ."

The quiet roughly handsome man raised his coffee cup, as if in a toast, as he broke in: "You know, yair a brilliant convairsationalist; do you nevair bore yairself silly?" This to the delight of the admiring girl of the house, his willing personal servant, who giggled as she jumped to refill his cup and again blushed and curtsied.

*   *   *

It felt odd descending into Edinburgh from the north. The city had always seemed like Ultima Thule, as far north as I ever would like to go. And Aberdeen had in my mind always been to the south of it, the way to me as a child all dogs seemed male and all cats female, all evidence to the contrary be damned. Maps were arbitrary mental constructions, of course, like the genders of nouns in certain languages.[73] There was no up or down in geographical reality. Just one of those things: like the way people in the north would say they were going "up" to London. But I could not shake the sensation that I was ascending into Edinburgh from the south.

Unlike the cold shoulder of Aberdeen, Edinburgh welcomed me with open arms. I felt comfortable there immediately. The cobbled winding streets with their scowling buildings of quarried ancient stone blackened by long dark winters and greened with moss seemed eerily familiar. Some cities are like that. One enters them almost with a sense of deja vu, as though one once called the place home in another life. With this difference: these places are more home than home. I've felt this way in only a few places: of all cities only Edinburgh, Copenhagen, and New Orleans; of all countries only Greece. Thomas Wolfe was right: you can't go home again. But you can sometimes go home for the first time *as though* it were again.

Once I arrived in Edinburgh, a well-dressed man on the bus, who may well have been doing an impression of Sean Connery, asked if I was traveling. I informed him that I was visiting Scotland but had been living in London for the past year. His response was

---

[73] Casanova's "first literary exploit" came at the age of eleven when he gave a precociously witty response to the question (in Latin) of why cunnus was masculine and mentula feminine: "because the slave always bears the name of the master." *The Story of My Life.* Trans. Stephen Sarterelli and Sophie Hawkes (New York: Penguin, 2000), 31.

unequivocal: "Ah, laddie, I *rregrret* it for ye. I lived in London for two longest yairs. The best thing *evairrrr* to come out of London was the *trrrain to Edinburrrgh*." By the time I left this gentleman's beloved Auld Reekie, I was inclined to agree with him.

* * *

"Sometimes like a light—sometimes like a windin-sheet—sometimes like the body that's to dee, gaen mad—an' sometimes like a coffin made o' moonlight."
"Was it in the evening you saw this apparition?"
"It was a little after midnight."
—James Hogg, *The Brownie of Bodsbeck*

Hogg's vocabulary shows how impoverished the English language is compared to what it might have been had it embraced Scottish dialect. We would do well to lament the lack of ways to say some things that must be said. Like "ugsome" for loathsome. Or "yestreen" for last night. *How gude to whommel a sonsy quean or kimmel in bed with a steelrife ramstamphishness!*[74]

* * *

It was summer in Scotland, so the sun went down for a wee nap about the time the pubs closed. At a lively pub I fell into conversation with three French sailors, who spoke no English, from Brittany, Cannes and Paris. They were trying to pick up three Scottish girls, all from Edinburgh. I mediated with my broken French, trying to keep up (*plus lentement s'il vous plaît!*) with the most talkative one's Breton idioms, but after a while they had no need of me. As I was leaving near closing time, sunset glowing on the blackened rooftops, I met a woman named Caroline, who asked, "How do you find

---

[74]*Gude*: good. *Whommel*: to turn upside down. *Sonsy*: comely, buxom. *Quean*: a young woman. *Kimmel*: gossip, girl, or married woman. *Steelrife*: relentless. *Ramstamphish*: heedless, devil-may-care attitude.

the females of Edinburgh?" This use of the word female for women or girls enchanted me for some reason. "My mother is a wonderful female," she said. "Works in a pub. She's forty-five. Aye, a wonderful female she is."

Caroline turned out to be a wonderful female herself, very open, very candid, very direct. "I wish it was Friday, I could say let's go back to my place but I can't. I'm a very direct person. You'll always know where you stand with me." Until 2:00 a.m. we talked and parted with a kiss and a promise to meet again the following evening. "If you don't remember anything else," she said, "remember that I said your face has character. I actually thought you were Scottish. I thought you'd come up to me and say 'How's it *gooin*?'"

By the time I got back to my room and wrote down my first impressions of Caroline and her Edinburgh, it was 3:00 a.m. and already getting light out.

The next night when I met up with Caroline at a pub called Oliver's she seemed a little reticent, a little nervous. She said it was because she had not been very "active" since her recent divorce and that she had a "wee man" at home that she'd like me to meet. She took me home to her highrise flat in a scheme called Wester Hailes where I met her "wee man" Lloyd. I spent several nights with her, this frank and honest single mother and her boisterous and affectionate "laddie." We got along famously in the evenings, while I made the most of the long summer days by taking in the literary sites (the houses of Burns and Scott and Stevenson, Hogg and Hume, among them) and lingering among the stocky sinuous women of Henry Moore, voluptuous raw bronze abstractions reclining on the lawns of the Scottish National Gallery overlooking the romantic cityscape.

A day trip to Glasgow confirmed my suspicion that while the great city to the west was thriving and its *art nouveau* architectural heritage well-deserved, Edinburgh was where my heart beat sincerely. The Glaswegian accent was impossible to process, and the city had a mercantile if not mercenary feel. I returned thinking that maybe the best thing ever to come out of Glasgow was the *trrrain* to Edinburgh. But then I had Caroline and her "wee pal" to get back to.

* * *

8 July 1981, Pencil Cottage Tea Garden, Shanklin Chine, Isle of Wight
In Brighton I came upon a black plastic garbage sack, secured by a maroon necktie with horse-head designs. Later, on the train, a young man in a maroon suit, shiny black nylon shirt, white socks, and black scuffed loafers.

The tables in this tea garden are made of cast-iron Singer treadle sewing-machine stands, the kind my mother used to make my shirts.

An old woman sitting near me is stuffing her mouth with strawberry compote and clotted cream. Apropos of nothing, she leans over and comments to me, "At your age when you're alone for five minutes, it seems like an hour. At my age it's the other way round." She wipes her lips on a napkin, lips that were once made for love and now kiss only scones.

A quick swim in the calm and clear warm waters of the Channel before heading back to the station.

My Britrail pass allowed me unlimited travel for a month, so I took every opportunity to head off in all directions during July, taking in Brighton and the Isle of Wight for a day, then Edinburgh for a few, then south to London to check on my mail and Stacie, before reversing direction and going to Devon with a stopover in Exeter and Plymouth on a whim. And then because I was nearby, I decided on a visit to Totnes where an American friend was teaching at Dartington College of Arts.

On a visit to London Donna had told me to come down anytime I wanted, with these directions and the key to her cottage: "Totnes, Devon. Harbertonford. 3-4 miles from station up road to Kingsbridge. Red Lion Cottage. Enter village, take left on old road by Maltsters Arms (Hungry Horse on right). Cottage on left, about 4-5 doors up." Her thatched hunchback of a house was a study in Bloomsbury-style rural bohemian living, with its low-slung ceiling, damp whitewashed walls and wide smoky hearth. Its name, Red

Lion Cottage, was aspirational; Quasimodo Cottage would have been descriptive. Harbertonford was a quaint village where everyone in the Maltsters Arms pub seemed to be deformed or mentally defective. "Inbreeding," said Donna simply. The college's grounds were enchanting, but her colleagues there were insufferable snobs, but maybe it was I who was the snob. It's entirely possible. In fact, now that I think of it, I'm sure it was I. The argument was about English humor, sparked by my lack of appreciation for *The Hitchhiker's Guide to the Galaxy*, but it was its contemporaneity that insulted me, as though the *serious* humor, the *meaningful* humor of Max Beerbohm, Firbank and Ackerley were being slighted by such obvious stuff. The truth was: I was tired of England generally (and more particularly English people) as well as its and their cutting, exclusive humor. The truth was: I longed instead for the direct, embracing honesty of Scotland. In other words, for Caroline.

Donna and I spent my final afternoon hiking over the green hills and taking Devon cream tea with scones and the most excellent clotted cream in the yard of what seemed to be a private house. Afterward, Donna and I wandered some more over the hills whose chartreuse and emerald shades changed constantly with the clouds playing hide-and-seek with the sun.

Manchester and Birmingham and Liverpool all offered their lavish art museums built by Victorian industrialists whose profits had filled the galleries a hundred years previously with romantic representations of the natural landscapes (and supernatural themes) that their own science and industry had ravaged. I stopped in York, which spawned Guy Fawkes, the country's most famous domestic terrorist (alas, poor Jórvik!), and took in the Shambles and an ancient free house pub or two to drink to Yorick of Jórvik, Sterne's religious mouthpiece in Tristram Shandy, first published here at Hildyard's bookshop in Stonegate, and which I had read in Folkenflik's novel seminar.[75] Then came Carlyle, Inverness, and Kyle. I was like a tennis

---

[75] See Anaclara Castro Santana, "Yorick of Jorvik: Sophisticated Provinciality in Sterne's *Tristram Shandy*." *ANQ* 28:1 (2015), 29-33.

ball on a grass court map of England, or a cue ball colliding with its geometric fate over the felt of an organically shaped billiard table. *Free to be geometric*, I had jotted somewhere.

> **23 July 1981. Manchester City Gallery of Art.**
> *The much-reproduced painting by J. W. Waterhouse,* Hylas and the Water Nymphs *(1896). Hylas was a young traveling companion and lover of the wanderer Hercules on the whale-road with the Argonauts. On the coast of Troad, Hylas was sent in search of water. The (count them: seven!) nymphs lured him into the depths.*
> *This really is an eerie painting, much more disturbing than its facile ("pretty") surfaces would allow. The duplication of the same face among the naiads with only a hint of variation for individuality is nightmarish. Hylas is being lured to his death, sucked to the bottom of the pools of—and by—the eyes of these identical septuplets. And to think that he willingly surrounds himself with—and surrenders himself to—these beauties brings the theme home to me. Their nascent breasts are perfection, though, so what's to be done?*[76]

At Stirling I stayed at a bed and breakfast near the castle. I met there a woman from Toronto who told me over eggs with baked beans, grilled tomato slices, rashers and kippers that she truly believed that musicians were prophets who talked directly to Jesus, from whom they get their best lyrics, and to aliens from outer space, whose language comes to us verbatim in the form of instrumental music, thanks to musicians who are actually mediums who pluck harmonies like radio waves from the atmosphere. We talked for a couple of hours after breakfast over endless pots of tea and her gold-filtered

---

[76] In 2018 this perennially popular painting was removed from the gallery in an attempt to change the narrative around depictions of women, the museum explaining: "We'd like this gallery to tell a different story in 2018, rather than being about the 'Pursuit of Beauty' with a binary tale about how women are either femmes fatale or passive bodies for male consumption." The website concludes: "Let's challenge this Victorian fantasy!' One wonders what the campaigning curators might make of that strange landscape of fallen females, *Diana of Ephesus and the Slaves* (1899) by Giulio Aristide Sartorio in the National Gallery in Rome, a far more disturbing array of flesh and fantasy.

pastel Sobranies. She was loony but probably more interesting than the thirteen historic castles of Stirling.

The endless train trips up and down the country kept me in motion, which seemed to be the point, since I had no particular destination. I felt compelled, if only for form's sake, to touch down in London to see Stacie, home from her holidays in the Cyclades.

She looked healthy and refreshed, thanks to the Greek sun, but she was even more coercive than usual, trying to get me to take her with me to my next destination, which was to be Cornwall. Mariola found Stacie loud and crass, warning me not to let her expect anything more from me. But even as I vowed to break it off, I still appreciated Stacie's good heart. She was a wounded soul; all she really wanted was a little loyalty, a little respect, and a bit of happiness, even if her methods of asking for these made her seem desperate. She seemed to be aware that I had something going on in Scotland, but she allowed herself to be deceived. She may have realized that Cornwall was a decoy to deflect attention from my real interest in Edinburgh in the opposite direction. She did not press me for details, even when she felt the long scratches on my back from Caroline's nails. Maybe they really were from my backpack, why not. She did not press me for proof. But how I longed to be free of this clingy posh trendy Londoner so that I might return to my independent working-class Scottish divorcée!

I returned to Edinburgh to attend a party at Oscar's for a friend of Caroline's. On the way to her flat I stopped for lunch at Henderson's Salad Table, a vegetarian restaurant in a basement at 94 Hanover Street.[77] It turned out to be a fateful detour. Propped next to me at the picnic-style communal table was the forest green North Face backpack that Mnemosyne had left behind when she moved out of our apartment for the last of many times. And atop that was Jesse Tannehill's beat-up, sweat-stained Stetson, the one he wore under the elm tree in the yard. I cut a romantic figure, or so I was told later by one young woman who invited me to share with her companions

---

[77] Henderson's closed the doors of its three locations due to the pandemic in 2020 after sixty-three years in business.

—her sister and her Dutch boyfriend Ben—the carafe of wine she set down on the table between us. We talked about California and Steinbeck, London and Edinburgh, Africa and Amsterdam. About cities as lovers, intimate or cold, and books as countries unto themselves with their own customs, karma, and dialects.

Her blue eyes were lively and full of light, her forehead intelligent beneath a short fringe of bright flaxen hair. She was a doctor and would soon complete her medical studies and residency. What then? She wasn't sure, but she thought she might return to Africa, where she and her sister were born and had spent many years as children with their parents, who both died there, where her father had been a missionary doctor, so the connection ran deep.

"Come stay with us when you return for the Festival," she said when they got up at last to leave. "We live nearby in Marchmont." She wrote her name, address, and phone number in the back of my journal. "I'm Mhairi. Don't forget."

This diversion made me more than an hour late for my date with Caroline, but she wasn't in the least upset. No brainyell[78] from Caroline. We had drinks at the pub, got lost in conversation until after eleven, then went to a party at a townhouse somewhere, danced, drank Famous Grouse and ale, and caught a taxi for Wester Hailes at dawn, which was about 3:00 a.m. When we got up the next afternoon, it was time to say goodbye again. Caroline did not try to keep me but told me to come back when I could, to call her when I would.

"Aye," the word you hear most in Scotland. The confidence of assent.

* * *

When I returned for the Edinburgh Festival, instead of letting Caroline know I was in town, I took a room in a bed and breakfast on Spring Gardens with a stunning view of Arthur's Seat. In those days you didn't need room reservations months in advance of the

---

[78]*Brainyell:* an outburst or uproar.

Festival. I didn't end up spending the night there though. When I called Mhairi, she let me know that she was on duty all night as part of her residency at the Women's Hospital, "but you're welcome to come visit me there. I'll need to do my rounds in the wards. I have a small apartment on the campus, and we can be alone when I'm not needed by the patients. It's very private," she added. And then, thinking perhaps that this was too forward, added, "we can talk."

After she took me to bed, we did talk—all through the night. She had grown up in Zambia, where her father had established a women's hospital. Now she was on her way to Zimbabwe, following in his footsteps, just as soon as her residency was completed. A guitar was beside the bed. She took it up without getting dressed and sang several traditional Scottish ballads, as well as a few songs of her own. She was surprised at herself, she said, for following the bold impulse to pick me up when she saw me in the restaurant.

"I don't usually do things like that," she confessed, as she nestled in my arms. "I have been so focused on my education and my work for so long. I think it must have been the hat," she laughed. "It made you seem romantic, some sort of gypsy man. I just wanted to claim you for my own."

"It is my grandfather's hat," I explained. "His name was Jesse Tannehill."

"Oh, a very Scottish name."

She stroked my cheek. I breathed her in, first her neck, shoulders, and armpits (soft wisps of cottonsilk fragrance); then her waist, where a string of red and white African beads like stitches encircled the slim isthmus connecting the lower half of her body, her sexuality, I mused, with the upper half, her spirituality—not that these two were separate, on the contrary, they seemed fused so that sex and spirit were one, each, like an alloy, making the other stronger.[79] I

---

[79] "An Orphic poet could not doubt that the monstrousness of Aristophanes' fable was a sign that it concealed a sacred mystery ... the Aristophanic man can attend to the upper and lower worlds simultaneously." Edgar Wind, *Pagan Mysteries in the Renaissance* (London: Faber, 1980), 202.

inhaled her warm scent like a drug deep into my lungs and into my sinus cavities, where they hit me like a headrush of future memory. I turned her over and breathed in the scent of her velvety spine, kissing each dimpled vertebra, down to the mound at the small of her back, where a hidden thermal spring generated heat.

"I love this part of your body," I said, my palm resting on this sacred mound. "It's so hot! Literally. Feel!"

"That? You mean the sacral lumbar region?" she said over her shoulder, her cheek resting on her forearm. "That's where the *os sacrum*, the 'sacred bone' is located."

"That's kind of a perfect name," I said.

"It's called that because it was the bone that was offered as a sacrifice in ancient Greek temples."

"To Aphrodite, I assume." How effortlessly she merged mythology with her medical training. I turned her over and traced with my fingertips the red and white beads around her waist. "And these?"

"These were a gift—a souvenir from Africa."

I drew a line from her navel downward. "And here is the omphalos, the center of the cosmos, the world's body, navel and umbilicus."[80]

"The Chinese call it the *tantien*," she said, "the Japanese call it the *hara*, where the body's consciousness is located. Not up here in the brain but down here, where all the important stuff happens."

"The root that connects us to our birth and thus to our destiny. In your case to your African past—and future."

"Do you believe in destiny?" she asked, after a pause.

"It's hard not to—tonight. If you mean as in 'character is destiny,' yes. Heraclitus was right. We make our own destiny. Or break it. Sometimes consciously, sometimes unconsciously. Or we don't live up to it, exactly. We compose it, with courage and determination,

---

[80] "The name of *Omphale* denotes the *centre* of the human body, the intersection of two axes, the *root* of life, the cord which binds the child to its mother and which represents the destiny of each one of us. This constellation of metaphors will perhaps provide us with a key for the deciphering of her legend." Marie Delcourt, *Hermaphrodite: Myths and Rites of the Bisexual Figure in Classical Antiquity*, Trans. Jennifer Nicholson (London: Studio Books, 1961), 24.

like a work of art, or we make a mess of it. Or we let destiny determine our character, who we are, letting it compose us, passively, like someone else's clay—the worst way. Most works of art, like most lives, though, are failures."

"Like a song," she added, ignoring my pessimistic conclusion, following analogies to her own art form. "Sometimes it rhymes, naturally, sometimes not. Sometimes it doesn't need to, if the meaning resonates. Even when it doesn't rhyme there are patterns and rhythms that make sense anyway, even if we can't say how. Surely our lives are like that too. We inherit the forms, but we improvise as best we can."

I tried to press the point, to take it further. "Maybe we don't always live up to what we are capable of because we are afraid to embrace our own boldness."

She gave this some thought. "There are different kinds of boldness," she decided, showing her superior wisdom. It wouldn't be the last time. She no doubt sensed that what I had said was self-serving. I wanted her to be bold with me, to keep being bold with me, as she had begun, to take what she wanted on a whim. I wanted the rational doctor, the anatomist, the scientist, the humanitarian even, to break character and run away with me, to be selfish, to run wild, to lose her mind in abandonment to her body's impulse. I wanted, in other words, this night not to end, to stop time, to merge with her conclusively.

Every hour or so she would disentangle our entwined limbs (and our interwoven minds) to get out of bed to do her rounds. In addition to these interruptions she might also be called away to care for one or another of the patients, most of whom were somewhere on the spectrum of pregnancy, either about to have a baby, or had just had one, or would never have one again. Her realm was here at the center of the world—I thought of Courbet's scandalous painting *L'Origine du monde* in the Musée d'Orsay—the women's hospital as Omphalos under the sign of the sacred bone, where women gave birth, suffered, died . . . and made love. Here for a brief moment though, together, we claimed a space of timeless grace. No babies were born there that night, none conceived, and not one woman died. Mhairi did, however, tend to a woman dying of cancer and several women on the verge of childbirth. It was as though the clock of birth and death and rebirth had paused for us. Each time she returned to bed, she would give me a brief report on the cases, and then she would throw off her doctor's role with her white jacket and stethoscope, and we would take up where we left off, getting to know each other's bodies thoroughly since we could only scratch the surface of our minds. We told our life stories in brief to one another with an urgency that was inexplicable and startled us both; stories that should have taken hundreds of hours to tell, like novels, were condensed into scenes and synopses that were like free verse poems and songs. How could we have located each other on this spinning earth at this moment without trying, not knowing what we were looking for? Each of us had found in the other someone who understood instantly, completely, instinctively. Not only the pace of the hunger of our desire, but also the exact pressure of touch, the firmness of holding the other without grasping. It was as though we knew we would have only this one night of "destiny," and we had to make the most of it. And we did. Magically, we lingered in our constantly interrupted night of lovemaking as though we had all the time in the world.

Hylas and the Water Nymphs (detail), 1896.
John William Waterhouse. Manchester Art Gallery.

"The duplication of the same face among the naiads with only a hint of variation for individuality is nightmarish." (p. 173)

13 / Decadent Interludes

> If it has happened, by the will of fate, that in your life the erotic element has not played the dominant part that it has in mine, you are at once luckier than I have been and less lucky! You have escaped a great deal of grotesque tragicomedy, but you have been deprived of many thrilling and rapturous expectations and perhaps also a few paradisic fulfillments.
> —John Cowper Powys, *Autobiography*

Back in London, I wrote to Mhairi, eager to see her again. I wrote a song or two for her, and she sent me tape recordings of her singing them, as well as the songs she had sung that night and morning. By early August, I was still fixated on her and only her. She wrote to say that she planned to be in London in a week to consult with the Zimbabwean Consulate. That gave me something to look forward to. But having tasted paradise, I was hungry for more, and that made me dangerous.

Feeling restless, I went to Rumours intending to meet Mike, an American who was taking his post-graduation European tour before entering law school at UC San Diego. As I waited, I ordered a drink. In a desultory mood, I talked to no one. A pair of exotic looking women came in. One wore white flounces on top that revealed her even whiter shoulders and a black patent leather miniskirt that hugged her hips like cellophane. She smiled at me but I could not bring myself to peel myself away from the bar and thoughts of Mhairi. Her friend, in a black angora sweater and bright green miniskirt with a pert flare, cast an attractive pall of ennui: she was a visual embodiment of my mood. They looked dangerous, each in a different way, with their jet-black hair and long, long legs. All of a sudden I wanted to catch the attention of the one in the chartreuse skirt with the exhausted look of a half-starved vampire, my shadow. Maybe she could put me out of my misery. Temporarily. Or eternally.

Her black hair was the exact color (or lack of color) as her black sweater; the translucent pallor of her face, in lost profile, a halfmoon hovering in a pitmirk sky. Her ivory skin was set off by the sheen of her hair, which threw sparks like the silica of broken coal, shining out like "shook foil," gathering to "a greatness, like the ooze of oil." The sheer unique beauty of some women has always given me the closest glimpse I've known of what Hopkins called the Grandeur of God, especially if there was something sinful about them.

She looked painfully thin and bored. As though she had already seen it all and there could be no next time. Yet there was a smolder there among the ashes that I took as a challenge for me to become the next time. If only the cinders were prodded in the right way, I sensed that her fire could be brought back to life and her limbs might come thrashingly alive.

Mike arrived just before closing time. It was only 10:30 but Rumours closed early on Sunday. The two intriguing women left, and we happened to follow them in the direction of the Piazza. "Let's take a little detour," I said. "Which might turn into a long detour," Mike added.

The women were talking to a couple of guys on the street. We passed them and considered going into Tutton's, but then, seeing that they were free again, followed them into Maxwell's. I wanted something to eat anyway.

Ms. Ennui was at the door, waiting to be seated.

"Everything all right?" I asked her.

"Now," she said. "Once we escaped those jackals."

"You should have let out a yell. We would've rescued you."

"Would you have done?"

"Don't you see my shining armor? Next time, just shout. Or wave."

"What if I'm *not waving but drowning*?" I got the reference. First she had put me in mind of Hopkins and now she was quoting Stevie Smith. So she was a reader, and I could use some intelligent conversation.

Just then the hostess seated her and her flouncy friend at the bar.

Mike and I were shown to a table and ordered beers and club sandwiches. Mike considered the merits of our waitress Maria. Well-rounded, with round eyes and abundant curves, she was a fine foil to the lean and leggy specimens who had been seated behind us at the bar. They were being chatted up by several different men in turn, it being late, and desperate men assumed women out at this time were as desperate as they. Mike and I ate our sandwiches and bided our time. Then a pair of men, drunk and weird-eyed, began to hover over them, too close for comfort. They looked generically foreign— Middle Eastern or Arab or from one of the lesser Soviet Republics— with their misconceived American knockoff items of clothing, nylon track suits and baseball caps at midnight.

"Have you ever had a woman with such long legs?" asked Mike. "A friend of mine never settles for anything less. He says he likes their knees instead of their ankles around his ears. More padding. And for the wrapping action and digging in."

I imagined a praying mantis with its angular limbs spread out for just the right balance to sustain the leverage for slow preternatural insect love. It must have been the color of Ms. Ennui's skirt, the electric green of chameleons in bright spring grass. I followed that thought, saying aloud:

"Did you know that there are lizards that change their gender?"

"Like chameleons?"

"Yes, but not their color, their sex. And not to blend in for protection but to reproduce. Parthenogenetic species that have no need of the opposite sex. They are completely self-propagating."

"Like the Virgin Mary?"

"Lizards. You gotta love 'em."

At that moment Ms. Ennui looked over the shoulder of one of the men. Her eyes, smokey with black and blue haloes, caught mine and held them. She mouthed something that made her lips touch twice. I assumed it was the *p* and the *m* of "Help . . . me." It was not a shout or a wave, and she was not exactly drowning, but it would serve as a signal. It was a good mouth, wide, and the lips were pale pink, a little chapped from chewing, no lipstick, and full.

"That's your signal," said Mike. "Damsel in distress."

After a reasonable lag, I waited for one of the men to vacate his seat, then got up and slid into his place. I began by speaking to Yvonne, the cellophane-wrapped flouncy one, while Mike nudged the second drunk guy to one side to speak with Ms. Ennui. Mike had played basketball in college and cast a healthy shadow. When the other fellow came back from the loo, we switched. The two fellows swayed for a moment, woozy with uncertainty, then seeing that we were Americans, left the field having decided not to compete.

Ms. Ennui was Irish, from Donegal, and her name was Eileen. After studying physics for two years at university, she quit because of speed and a "sudden undermining" of all her values, those she had been taught as well as those she had picked up along the way. She had been sitting at a café with friends and suddenly realized that she had no interest in anything they were saying. It was as though she (or they) were from another planet.

"Since then I've become a degenerate," she said with a dryness belied by her Irish irony. "It's my only ambition. I also operate computers."

Before stopping out of university, she had been reading Sartre's *Le Chemin de la liberté* in which Matthew tries to decide if he is free.

"Sartre was no degenerate, though," I said. She seemed disappointed by this. "Only an intellectual degenerate. He believed in stuff. Existentialism was just a phase. Or a pose. It doesn't matter, though. I still think *Being and Nothingness* is brilliant, and right, even though he went from a pretty interesting phenomenological ontology to a pretty uninspired communism later on." I asked if she had read *La Nausée* as well because it sounded like that crisis was what she was going through.

"I've decided against suicide," she said, adding, "for now. Now I'm just looking for a good time."

Maxwell's closed and we were treated to free pints by the manager, Sally, who, it turned out, shared a flat with Yvonne and Eileen in Stockwell, near Brixton, south of the Thames. As she prepared to close up, the waitress Maria seemed interested and we exchanged lingering looks. I filed her away for future reference. Or maybe it was Mike she was interested in, and I was her decoy, just as Yvonne had been mine to approach Eileen; it was hard to tell.

Eileen got down off her barstool, stole a friendly kiss from my cheek, just a quick brush of her pale pink chapped lips, which might almost have been mistaken for an accident, and asked for my phone number. Luckily there was no pen to be found immediately at hand. Not that we looked very hard.

"What are you doing tonight then?" she asked.

"This is it."

"Why don't you come home with me in that case? Sally's driving."

As we stepped outside, Yvonne asked Eileen, "Are you going home with this young man then?"

"Taking him home with me, yes," said Eileen, turning to me: "if he doesn't mind."

Yvonne yawned, "Well I'm hot for sleep and have to get up for work in the morning." And then to Mike: "Sorry."

Sally dropped off Mike near Victoria Station.

Their flat was a three-room affair in a dilapidated building not far from where the Brixton Uprising had occurred in April, which was why they had it so cheap. Each of them paid £2.50 a week but would soon have to move or pay an extra £428 per month, or so they said. We had to go through Sally's room to get to the kitchen for coffee.

Eileen suddenly opened up, like a burst dam, and she talked and talked. She seemed starved for an ear that might comprehend the extent of her traumas and how they had developed into existential crises. Her Catholic upbringing had stifled her at a young age, but she wanted to love the world. Then, recently, she had been raped by a black guy in the neighborhood. He had a knife. She took it the only way she could to survive. "As though I'd just been fucked by someone I didn't want to fuck me, which was about right. But I didn't want him to kill me." There had been no excess violence because she managed to talk her way out of that, asking him, "Why didn't you just come up and ask me out? I might've said yes." I said that I imagined that might be humiliating to someone who fancied himself a hardcore rapist.

Every subject we touched on quickly turned into a discussion of another guy she had known. Her most recent sometimes live-in boyfriend was a vinyl junkie who had been strung out on her pretty badly but all he knew anything about was music and she couldn't take it anymore. He had left her with a first-rate sound system and the record collection we were listening to at the moment.

"Have you ever been in love? I haven't. At least I don't think so. Isn't that unnatural? Maybe there's something wrong with me. I think there's something wrong with me."

Then there was the Australian who only called her for sex. "A well-built brute, but good fun, a real beastie. I would go see him and come back destroyed. He would treat me like a piece of meat, and I loved it. I suppose that sounds terrible." She craved the rough sex but she was afraid that it might kill her in the end. I laughed, but she was serious. "I suppose I just want to be loved and not have to love in return. Is that common? I suppose that sounds sick but if it's true, it's true." She wanted to play the cynical tart, but there were always undertones of the little Catholic girl from Donegal who was not the tough bickie she portrayed herself to be.

"My friends always hold it against me that men tell them I'm stunningly beautiful."

"It's because you look unapproachable. Men tell your friends because they're afraid of you. They trust that your friends will relay the message."

"You might have noticed Yvonne tonight. She fancied you and then you took me. I'm not stunning, though. I look okay. It's unfair. Like being blamed for something I didn't do."

In bed she seemed to lack confidence.

"Why aren't I exciting you?" she said.

"But you are. I'm taking it slow, enjoying you. Doesn't your Aussie take his time?"

"Ha! He takes a lot of things, but not his time."

"Aren't you excited?"

"I'm excited." She took my hand and slipped it where I could feel the proof for myself, like a spoon through warm honey.

We pooled our excitement, the one slipping inside the other, hers warmed up and swollen, mine stiffened and growing, slowly at first and then suddenly. The interpenetration of Being and Nothingness; what was the difference? Which was which? I watched her eyes grow as she melted below even as her lower body bowed upward. I had the odd sensation that I was pumping her up from inside, causing her eyes to widen, her hips to arch, and her jaw to unhinge. We were caught, clenched, contorted and coiled, No Exit. We followed some of the syncopated rhythms of the excellent sound system, (thanks to her vinyl junkie), slowing and building, almost stopping, which frustrated her, then building the tempo again. I buried my face in her neck to keep from coming. She grabbed my face and pulled it in front of her, gasping, "*Look* at me! Look at me! Look at *me!*" It was a good idea, an inspired idea. I'd taken on the role of the male mantis with a good view of her grimace and groan before he is devoured.

Our metamorphosis gradually reversed and we took human form again.

"You are so thin," I commented, running my hands along the barely fleshed bones of her hips. Her breasts were perfect mouthfuls (*des amuses bouches*), small enough in proportion to her lean body. And her compact ass, like a couple of hard-boiled eggs, was a perfect handful. I could almost get them both in one palm, like a juggler. "I'm almost afraid I'll break you."

"Maybe you have a touch of the pedo in ya," she said, lighting a cigarette, and then flicking a tiny ember from her naked breast.

"I may have all sorts of paraphilias, but that's not one of them. Your eyes are not a child's. Your mouth is not a child's. And your— . . . definitely not a child's."

With the hour and the lighting, the tired British sun just rising, subtle greenish-blue undertones began to appear under her translucent ivory mask like the subdermal coagulations of a corpse. No, not a pedo, but with a nod to Praz and old Busst, maybe necrophilia was more my line. (Or entomophilia?) I shuddered. Her hair, however, as they say it does in the grave, retained all of its original sparkle and magic, *a bracelet of bright (black) hair about the bone*, and my reverence for her godless grandeur remained unaltered. Newly aroused, we went at it again.

Perhaps she was too thin. Maybe she lacked confidence but she certainly enjoyed herself in bed, with sudden seizures, and whimpers like those ejaculated from a squeeze toy. She expressed her satisfaction immediately afterward, no basking in the afterglow, and yet kept it understated: "That was *very* nice." I asked if it wasn't rough enough for her, and she said it was a welcome change of pace. Maybe she didn't have to be destroyed to be undone.

For all her ennui, which was not all feigned, she was affectionate, even if it was awkwardly expressed, as though she were not—but wouldn't mind getting—used to tenderness.

"I'm liable to become reliant upon one man, I warn you," she said with the same ironic disdain as when we met. "Not because of my moral training so much, but because I'm lazy."

When Sally dropped me off at almost noon at the bridge near Westminster Abbey and the Houses of Parliament, Eileen got out long enough to bump up against me for a quick kiss, another feigned accidental brush of her now very chapped and chewed lips almost on my lips, and climbed back in the car without a backward glance.

* * *

A few days later Mike called and asked if I wanted to go to the

Playboy Club. He had been given a key for graduation and wanted to break it in. We had to borrow jackets at the door. Ties were optional. The Bunnies were friendly, but the fantasy seemed infantile and overpriced, although the beers were cheap enough. It was basically a fancy bar with waitresses in minimal animal costumes. Our Bunny was Claire from Kent who had a waist like no other I'd ever seen, except on wasps. She could have balanced a tray on her hip. She wanted to tell us (in a whisper) all about the London Playboy Club scandal and her trip to Florida, which for her meant Disney World. We weren't interested in gambling and the place was full of rich Arabs, anyway, angling for all the blonde Bunnies, so we left after only two beers.

We went back to Maxwell's. Maria, the waitress who watched us pick up Yvonne and Eileen a few nights before, now watched as Mike tried (and was succeeding) in picking up a new waitress named Mandy from Birmingham. Maria put a stop to that by taking Mandy aside. When she returned, Mandy would not only not look at us, but also refused to serve us. I asked Maria if she was all right. She said she was furious, which seemed a bit drastic. What had Mike done to her? After all, he had been dropped at Victoria Station. The minor mysteries of Marias and Mandys at Maxwell's.

We ended up going to a pub and picking up a couple of stray kittens who were not ready to go home at closing time. They knew of a club near King's Cross where we could continue to drink and get to know one another not at all. It was one of those after-hours clubs that charged a 50p "membership" for a single night's entrance, appropriate for a one-night stand. Such was capitalism. This holdover from the time of the exclusive men clubs that allowed those with means to circumvent the licensing laws aimed at improving the lowly hoi-polloi who drank in pubs. In the same way, publishers of Victorian erotica like Edward Avery and Leonard Smithers briefly circumvented obscenity laws by printing scandalous books through "private subscription." Two wars and bohemian ingenuity, though, had democratized the club scene so that artists' clubs sprouted up in imitation and defiance of elitism. The postwar years of Carnaby Street and Abbey Road further eroded the elitism of the gentlemen's club scene so that by the 1970s these sketchy but inclusive after-hours venues could offer "exclusive" 50p memberships to all comers, drunks and insomniacs alike. Yet the Victorian licensing laws, designed to save the working class from the curse of alcohol, remained unchanged, with arbitrary closing times occurring in the afternoon and at 11:00 p.m. Nothing much had changed in Eliot's Wasteland.

HURRY UP PLEASE IT'S TIME
HURRY UP PLEASE IT'S TIME
Goonight Bill. Goonight Lou. Goonight May. Goonight.
Ta ta. Goonight. Goonight.
Good night, ladies, good night, sweet ladies, good night, good night.

Those in the know, though, could always find a way to thwart those who would tone down the frivolity of jolly old England. Nevertheless, at 3:00 a.m. we released the kittens, properly petted but unviolated, back into the wild.

* * *

Believe it or not, I had not forgotten the great mystery of Mhairi. Everything I read referenced her, every poem echoed my sense memories of her (like this: "je voudrais être ton aisselle", even better expressed in English: "I want to be your armpit"[81]). I spent the next day in St James Park reading Denis Hills's *The Last Days of White Rhodesia* and fantasizing about applying for a teaching job in Zimbabwe to be close to her. Oddly enough, the book in some perverse performance of biblio divination seemed to keep telling me to reconsider. Certain lines, taken out of context, read like fortune cookie forebodings: "The risk ought not to be taken. Yet heightened

---

[81] "Alain Bosquet, "Lèvre en exil." *Quatre Testaments et autres poèmes* (Paris: Gallimard, 1967).

alertness is enjoyable, and perhaps therapeutic. Man is not a vegetable." Of course Hills was not thinking of my personal problems nor even affairs of love generally. Yet sometimes a random book can read our minds if not our futures. Later, the book told me, in a rather stertorous tone: "People who are not free (whatever that means) are maimed."[82] Mhairi remained my prison and my place of worship: "partout / l'odeur qui me résume / car je suis entre nuque et nombril / ton insecte sacré."[83]

From the park I went to Covent Garden and had a drink at Punch and Judy's, then grabbed something to eat at Tutton's. A trio of blondes from Dallas—Kelly and Kathy and Kerry—were there. I had met them on the train from Dundee to Edinburgh where they spent a weekend after their summer at Oxford. At Oliver's, the pub in Edinburgh, they had drawn quite a crowd of Scotsmen, as one might expect six (there had been six of them then) tall blonde Texans in a smoky bar room would. I was recruited to attest that I was Kelly's (or was it Kerry's) fiancé to protect them from this onslaught of admirers. Now they were debating whether Kelly should hire a Rolls for her father when he visited. Kathy (or was it Kerry) had just found out that her father had remarried, this time to a third-grade teacher, and Kerry (or was it Kathy) shrieked, "You mean Lucky finally hooked himself a schoolmarm, ha!" They discussed their sorority rush (TriDelta, of course) at SMU and other things Texan, like country two-stepping in Tyler. I was bored. "Can you imagine having this one for a professor?" Kelly said (or was it Kerry). *"I was a little drunk last night, Doc, could I type up my paper for you tomorrow, pleeez?"* This faux flirtation was so superficial, so bubbly, that it seemed, in contrast to my recent experience, entirely sexless; like playing with Barbie dolls.

I shared a taxi with them to Victoria where they dropped me at

---

[82] Denis Hills, *The Last Days of White Rhodesia* (London: Chatto & Windus, 1981).

[83] "everywhere / the scent that sums me up / because I am between your nape and navel / your sacred insect." Alain Bosquet, "Tu as." *Quatre Testaments et autres poèmes* (Paris: Gallimard, 1967).

my flat on the way to renting a Rolls (or was it a Bentley) for Lucky and his schoolmarm bride. I grabbed a skimpy meal of raw carrots, brie, English cheddar, bread and butter. Then I took a quick shower, dressed, put on my Mariola jazz saddle oxfords, and was off to a nearby music club, the Venue in Victoria Street.[84] I had skipped going there the night before and (unwisely) missed seeing Kate and Anna McGarrigle in favor of the Playboy Club.

As usual I felt awkward and out of place until there entered a *female* (I could with fondness hear Caroline's pronunciation in my head) who might have been Eileen's physical, intellectual, and spiritual polar opposite. She was short and curvy, with clipped blonde hair and bright eyes. She wore her flowery low-cut blouse with a denim miniskirt and white boots, and her knees were plushly dimpled. I followed her to the bar and having overheard her name asked her if her name was Roxanne. "How did you know?" she asked brightly, eyes shining. I came clean: "I overheard your friends. I just want to say you look smashing." It might very well have gone no further. I began to walk away but she stopped me and we ended up talking for the rest of the evening.

Like many other English people I'd met, oddly enough, she had never been to a funeral—until her grandfather's death a week earlier. The week had been doubly devastating for her because she had recently worked—temporarily—as a prostitute. I didn't ask how exactly the two were related. "Just two weeks to pay off my bank overdraft, that's all I needed, just two weeks," she added. "I only made it through a week though." She told the last man she just couldn't go through with it. "You know what he did? He wrote out a cheque for £100 over and above the usual £25 agency escort fee and told me he was glad I was going straight." Predictably, he wanted to see her again "off duty" but she said she couldn't. "He was nice enough, but it had to do with what I'd been doing before and I didn't want to be reminded."

"My roommate Rosie did it once on a lark, that's how I got into

---

[84]The Venue closed in 1984, the building demolished in 2013.

it," she continued, pointing out her friend on the dance floor. "A day or two ago I was supposed to go to Nigeria for four days." She shuddered. "I might have been there now. I'd have made £1500 but I just couldn't go through with it. My grandfather and all. You understand." (I didn't.) "And there were no flights, it seems. My luck. My flatmates were all supportive of my decision not to go. I have to move out of my flat in a couple of weeks, though, whether I have the money or no, but I have a deal with a businessman to do secretarial work in return for a three-bedroom maisonette."

"I have to leave my flat soon, too. For other reasons."

"Why don't you come live with me! I'm joking, what a disaster I'd be with you so serious and scholarly and all, but really, you should. Seriously. It's almost like fate. Let's do it."

After she went onto the dance floor with her friends, she came back and sat herself on my lap, tipping her Singapore Sling into my mouth to sip. Her friends were ready to go.

"I'd like to see you again," she said, holding one of my hands in both of hers and pressing it between her breasts in a gesture of great sincerity. "Just say where. And when."

"Covent Garden?" I cursed myself for falling back on familiar patterns, but it was territory I knew. "Maxwell's. No. Tutton's. Two o'clock. Tomorrow."

"Okay! It was great talking to you." It was true: she had done most of the talking—and to me rather than with me. "I really enjoyed it," she added as she danced out the door in her go-go boots.

It rained all the next morning. Violent thunderstorms. I half expected Roxanne not to make it. Had she reconsidered Nigeria? £1500 was a lot of money. Or maybe she went to Maxwell's by mistake. But she was on time, sans go-go boots, looking very respectable in a skirt and jumper. When she arrived, she seemed preoccupied.

"I haven't felt this way in ages," she said, lighting a cigarette and then immediately stubbing it out. "I'm so nervous."

I asked why. I thought she was referring to our date, as though she had discovered in herself a newfound modesty. But she was thinking about her work.

"Tomorrow I'm supposed to see a toady little man about doing a film, a three-minute striptease act with a couple of 'high-class' leggy blondes. I don't really want to do it, but I need the money. I was counting on Nigeria."

By the end of lunch, though, she had talked herself out of doing the movie. We went to my flat so she could call to cancel the appointment before she changed her mind again. When we passed some adult bookshops, I suggested we stop in to see if we could find any of her photos in the current issues of the men's magazines she had posed for, like *Rustler*, *Rapier*, and *Men Only*. She almost shrieked, "No! It'll put you off me!" Reminding her that I used to work in a porn shop in Hollywood, I said, "I'm not that easily put off." It was touching to see that this twenty-three-year-old who had modeled for nude magazines and worked as a prostitute (for a week) was still shy and schoolgirlish. One moment she seemed much older than me and jaded beyond repair; another she seemed half my age and fresh as a bowl of clotted cream. When we got to my flat, she took one look at my bed, which was just a single mattress on the floor, and said, "You really must move in with me! Seriously. Anyway, you must come to our removal party."

That night Roxanne confided something to me I have never forgotten. However nightmarish her life got to be in London, she never had bad dreams there. She barely dreamed in London at all. It was only when she went home to her parents' middle-class house outside of Swindon and slept in her childhood bedroom—surrounded by the smothering sensations of familiar furnishings and memories and the lulling hum of security—that she had nightmares. It was only when she let her guard down that the panic of her life streamed in upon her like floodwaters filling a lift.

* * *

Roxanne's moving-out party promised to be fun but turned out to be a fiasco. Frustrations and coincidences abounded. Roxanne's would have been the last place I expected to see Eileen again, her polar opposite, but there she was, as friendly and open and morbid as she was on that first night. Like all vast cosmopolitan cities, London contracts perhaps even more than others into a number of overlapping small villages, according to the lifestyle of its tribes. Even decadent opposites attract.

In a flash Eileen had wrapped her long limbs around me, asking, "Do I still seem as naive as ever and as affectionate?" I think Roxanne was a little put out to find us in the doorway of her bedroom making out, but Eileen was amused by Roxanne's angry reaction, all of which I found endearing in both of them, Eileen's unfounded affection as much as Roxanne's unjustified jealousy.

The party was a reflection of Roxanne's confusion. It embodied her state of mind. There was too much going on, too many histories, too many options. Too many people, too many cigarettes, too much to drink (I didn't get too drunk but she did), too much tangible sex in the air. I was torn (almost literally) between these gentle bacchantes, Roxanne and Eileen, but I was also drawn to someone named Vanessa (who looked nothing like her name) and another woman named Maz (in part or mainly because this was short for Mhairi, of all things—yes, I was still obsessed). I spent most of my time, though, with Eileen. Roxanne was busy playing hostess to her party, but the real reason was that Eileen was the most intelligent thing in the room and thus (not discounting the arousing effect of her pink lips and pale legs) the sexiest.

Eileen was saying that since she had been with me she had slept with one guy, "*only* one guy," she emphasized, as though this were unusual and significant. I suddenly realized that I hadn't slept with anyone since I had slept with her, not even Roxanne, and I told her so, adding that I remembered her luscious mouth and pale pink chapped lips and thighs, also her hard body and supple mind. "I've meant to call you," she said, "but I've been in an odd mood and spending a lot of time by myself. Reading, reading, reading. I'll call you this week, I promise. I enjoyed myself the other night with you."

"Not as much as I enjoyed yourself, I'll bet."

"Well, there's no way to measure that, now is there?"

This got us onto the ancient philosophical question of whether, in general, men or women enjoyed sex more. As for most enduring and unanswerable questions, the Greeks had a myth for that. I told her about my research, and how the blind seer Tiresias had been changed into a woman after seeing two snakes copulating. Seven years later he saw two snakes copulating again, and was turned back into a man.

"Because of his unique experience, he had fucked and been fucked—"

"Haven't we all!" interjected Eileen.

"—so he knew what most of us never will. When Zeus and Hera were arguing about the question, they decided to consult Tiresias. Hera said the man had the greater enjoyment, Zeus contended that it was the woman. Tiresias confirmed that the woman enjoyed sex more, and not just by a little bit but *ninety percent to a man's ten percent!* Enraged, Hera blinded poor old Tiresias, and Zeus, feeling bad for him, gave him the dubious gift of prophecy. Just goes to show you, you should never weigh in on a domestic argument."[85]

---

[85] This was according to Hesiod and other early writers. That Hera gouged out Tiresias's eyes is a telling detail. Eyes, like testicles, are an erotic site. The promiscuity of the glance appears in many other stories, including those of Susanna and the Elders and Actaeon. In another version of the Tiresias myth (according to Callimachus) Tiresias is blinded (but not eviscerated) by Athena when he sees her bathing in a pool when he was still a pubescent adolescent like Hermaphroditus. His evisceration, a symbolic castration, mirrors the emasculation of other adolescents at other nymphs' pools. Emasculation and blindness make eyes and testicles close cousins if not equivalents. In Georges Bataille's erotic masterpiece, *The Story of the Eye*, this equivalency is explicit, with eggs and buttocks added to the mix of permutations of roundness, or wholeness, like the first beings in Aristophanes' creation myth. The evisceration motif as punishment for sexual transgression is repeated in Sophocles when Tiresias tells Oedipus what he does not want to see: that he has copulated with his mother, and when Oedipus realizes it is true, he gouges out his own eyes with the brooches from his hanged mother's dress. Thus the motif of dual sexuality continues to play itself out, since incest is essentially a forbidden return to the wholeness of undifferentiated or dual sexuality, the male inside the mother's womb, and thus monstrous. (Think Satan's incest with his daughter, Sin, and how their offspring, Death, reenters his mother's womb to devour her from within in Milton's terrifying allegory.)

We were still standing in the doorway of Roxanne's bedroom when our hostess joined us. She seemed drunk and jealous, a perilous combination.

"What are you talking about now?"

"Whether the man or the woman enjoys sex more," said Eileen, matter-of-factly, as though she were genuinely interested in Roxanne's opinion. "What do you think?"

"That's easy, no question," said Roxanne as she dragged me by the arm into the bedroom, spilling my drink, and slamming the door. To Eileen, as I was borne away, I shrugged and whispered, waving and drowning, "Call me."

Roxanne wanted to talk, but not about Hera and Zeus.

People kept coming in and interrupting us, though, leaving the door ajar. Eileen would glance in occasionally and smile, seeing that we were sitting on the bed and not lying in it. It seemed to amuse her. Roxanne explained that she was suffering from guilt over her relationship with Steve, who lived in the house, and with whom she had been sleeping on and off. It was he who had invited Eileen to the party on impulse, having met her and Yvonne and Sally the night before at the Embassy Club. Steve kept coming in unannounced to borrow money for more booze and drugs—"Don't mind me, carry on!"—taking five-pound notes from a box on Roxanne's dresser and waving them in the air as though in salute or to cover his eyes.

"Does he always do that?"

"What? Come into my room?"

"No, take money from you without asking."

"Oh, it doesn't matter. I don't mind him poncing a quid here and there. That's money I made that week. He knows I don't like to use it, myself."

"So he relieves you of your burden."

"I suppose so."

Roxanne kept dragging me onto the bed, pinning me down, then getting up for a cigarette or to close the door or to clean her teeth. Once she fell asleep, dropping like a stone in a pool, and I went out into the party, but she woke up and took me away from Maz, with whom I was having a pleasant conversation about my lack of musical taste, and back to bed. Another time I got dressed and, since she was talking seriously to Steve, I waited in another room and smoked, watching the dawn through the window. Finally, I said goodbye but realized I needed to be let out since the door was locked from the inside and Roxanne had pocketed the key. Roxanne got between me and the lock and wouldn't let me go.

"I'm confused," she said. "I want to sleep with you, I really do." Back in bed, she threw off all her clothes and promptly fell asleep after doing the cigarette bit again. When I began to get up, she sprang erect, saying, "Do you just want to screw me or what? Because if you do, you can just go right now because I don't need that. There are ten or twenty men out there I can get that from." And so on.

"Look, Roxanne," I explained, trying to be reasonable for once through my frustration. "If that's what I wanted I certainly wouldn't be here because there's damn little chance of that happening with you in this zoo. You've been talking yourself in circles. You're drunk *and* dizzy. You won't give yourself a chance to enjoy anyone's company, much less anyone else having a chance to enjoy yours. If we screw, we screw; if not, fine. I suggest that since you're so mixed up, we go to bed and go to sleep."

She was stunned, frozen in some no man's land between tears and rage.

"So you don't fancy me! If you fancied me, you'd want to screw me! You'd want to be with me. You'd want to be inside me. *You'd want to be me.*"

"I can *fancy* someone without 'screwing' them, my dear."

"Well I can't. I know if I sleep with you I'll screw you. I'll want you to screw me. I'll want you to come all through me. And then where will I be?"

By the time she shut up, we were both exhausted. I didn't sleep well. At that point I certainly didn't "fancy" her at all, nor did I feel like "screwing" her, the repetition of these words having rendered them even more absurd than usual, the former evoking Coleridge's distinction between fantasy and the imagination, and the latter sounding like a garage mechanic's fetish or Concha's nightmare of mechanical reproduction. In the morning, she virtually ignored me except to let me out of the locked door, like a dog whimpering for a piss.

*   *   *

Returning to the flat that morning, I found Evelyn and my roommate Eric in the living room, talking about me over coffee.

"We've been trying to decide," she said, playful, "do you think you are immoral or amoral?"

It was a fair question, but I was offended more than their curiosity called for. What could I say? I had a bad night.

"The essence of literature is Evil," I said, pompously, avoiding their either/or. "And life, like literature, demands a hypermorality."[86]

I suppose this was not the first time someone had asked the question, but to Evelyn's credit, this time not behind my back. The terms, though, struck me as irrelevant. Scientists and social scientists of course have their Institutional Review Boards (IRBs) to weigh in on the ethics of their research and how it might affect their subjects. There is no such board in the humanities, nor in this, our human life. We undertake our personal quests without oversight. We don't wait for an IRB's seal of approval before falling in or out of bed or love, often our most earnest experiments. But if we pay attention to the hypotheses, the processes, and the results, we might learn something.

I sipped my coffee and offered them a number of quaint and archaic literary terms that they might like to consider: *cad, rogue, rake, gay blade, Casanova, Don Juan, womanizer, bounder, picaro, Lothario, libertine,* even *lady-killer.* Only the slightest sarcasm clouded my assistance with their search for le mot juste to brand me

---

[86] I was paraphrasing Georges Bataille in his preface to his study of Brontë, Blake, Baudelaire, Sade, Swinburne, Proust and Genet, among others. *Literature and Evil*, trans. Alastair Hamilton (London: Calder & Boyars, 1973).

with.

"How about *philanderer*?" offered Evelyn brightly. "Did you know that Shaw set his play by that name in one of these flats, while they were brand new in 1893? Maybe they were still being built, although he spelt it Ashly Gardens without the *e*. Shaw was famously a stickler for simplified spelling."

Philanderer was as good as any, I supposed, although at the moment I felt that none of these terms applied, torn as I was between being dismissed by Roxanne and ignored by Mhairi. I felt a willowy nostalgia suddenly for the uncomplicated lust of Eileen, the interpenetrating erotics of Concha. Had I been using women? In some cases, I was pretty sure they were using me.

In my room I found an unopened letter from Mhairi. The contrast between Roxanne's mad, incoherent rants and Mhairi's measured prose, like a diagnosis, was stark. The one had no idea what she wanted; the other knew exactly what she didn't want: me.

> *I nearly took the train to you this morning. One of these days maybe*[87] *I will. One of these days I'll be on your doorstep! This is a powerful drug and I'm not sure if it's good for us. The withdrawal symptoms are hard to cope with—insomnia, restlessness, irritability, dreams, being over-critical of others, etc. etc. Could be talking about heroin.*

I could sense her backing away from me, withdrawing into the mist, for "our own good." Next day came another letter, the death blow in the form of a velvet bludgeon.

> *You see, you have become a kind of 'god of love'—a warm, strong, wise, all-knowing being. You were there at the right moment and you gave me something that I needed very much. So when that need wells up again I think of you. You are an inspiration, a wonderful dream, a kind of opium. By not knowing a great deal about you, I have surrounded you with a mystique and made a saint of*

---

[87] "*Maybe* may be the cruelest adverb in the language," Carin had said.

> you (you're the 'holy man' . . . as well as all the others . . . in my song—enclosed.)
> Perhaps you've done the same sort of thing to me by seeing in me the kind of things you were looking for.
> The thing is that you can't survive on a dream, and I'm not altogether the creature that you may think I am. It wouldn't take very long for that to become obvious. So it's better to remember the dream for what it was—just a dream.
> Now I kiss you goodbye, although we are bound to meet again—if only in thought and dream.

It was over. I remembered that morning in Edinburgh, how I got out of bed and dressed and went out for a walk on the grounds of the hospital, drinking in the fresh air, smelling her body on every part of my body. When I returned, she had showered, put on a simple cotton kimono, and written a song. She sang for me, holding the guitar instead of me. Now all I had left was the echo of the song, the lyrics on a sheet of paper in her handwriting, and a cassette tape with her voice and guitar.

> I once loved a gypsy man
> I own his eyes were brown.
> I once loved a wanderer
> He roamed from town to town.
> > And it's worth all the trouble
> > And it's worth all the pain
> > There'll be when I call for you in vain.
>
> And I once loved a holy-man
> His thoughts were pure
> And I once loved a little boy
> He wasn't always sure.
> > [chorus]
>
> I once loved a rebel
> He didn't care what people said.
> I once loved a playboy

He was very good in bed.
[chorus]
And I loved the playboy by night
And the holy-man by day
But I love the gypsy-man best
Because his eyes are brown.
   And it's worth all the trouble
   And it's worth all the pain
   There'll be when I call for you in vain.

I would have to add these roles to the list of quaint caricatures I had provided to Evelyn and Eric—*gypsy, wanderer, playboy, rebel, little boy,* and *holy-man*—for weren't these romantic stereotypes the dangerous reflections I saw in Mhairi's eyes, eyes in which I had drowned as surely as Narcissus drowned in the seduction of his own reflection, deaf to the true meaning of Echo's song? Maybe getting over Mhairi would really mean getting over myself, the me of whom I saw reflections everywhere and had grown weary. I wrote:

She held him, kissed him, rocked him to sleep,
Wrapped him in her future like a winding-sheet.

Wasn't this the unadorned truth: that I had lost myself in her as surely as Salmacis was lost in Hermaphroditus?

*   *   *

Once it became clear that Mhairi would leave for Zimbabwe without seeing me, I dropped the dead-end distractions I had sought out with Roxanne (who might have gone back to being a call girl) and Eileen (who probably went back on her promise anyway to call me) by taking off for the continent. I was wounded by Mhairi's greater wisdom in not allowing us to become disillusioned with each other, or ruining our intimacy with intrusiveness. I remained replete with the experience of her. And yet I was—in every other sense—free.

Bacchanal of Satyrs and Cupids, c. 1640-42. Gerard van Opstal.
Rijksmuseum, Amsterdam.

"I wondered whether this orgy in ivory might be a
representation of the polymorphous perversity
of my past, or a prophecy of my future." (p. 206)

Maria Magdalene, 1480. Carlo Crivelli. Rijksmuseum, Amsterdam.

"The wrists are as fleshy as slim hips, but the hands and fingers are freakishly long and thin, delicate but expert and exact, like a surgeon's tools or ivory chopsticks, articulate and poised, as if they have a consciousness of their own and would speak if they could." (p. 209)

14 / *Lysglimt*

> I once had a girl
> Or should I say she once had me.
> —John Lennon, "Norwegian Wood"

Soon I was on my way to Amsterdam, for the ridiculous reason that that was where, before leaving for Zimbabwe, Mhairi said she was headed, followed by Norway and Sweden, for a month's holiday with her sister Joan and Ben, the Dutch fellow I had met at lunch that first day at Henderson's Salad Table in the garden of Edinburgh and who was, she now admitted, her lover. She had told him about us and he was less jealous than intrigued, which allowed her to luxuriate in the memory of us. Yes, Mhairi was complicated. Aren't we all, more or less, in reality even more complicated than our dreams.

The easygoing festivity on the ferry to Vlissengen did not affect my watchfulness. Hoping against hope to run into her, I imagined I saw Mhairi everywhere. That must be her at the railings about to be sick with the lurching of the deck, or at one of the boat's many bars buying a drink, or laying a bet at one of the gambling tables, or disembarking among the holiday hordes, or disappearing down the long and crowded corridors of the train to Amsterdam. Each time I thought I had found her she managed to evade me because of course it was never her—never would be her.

Arriving in the city, I took a cheap dormitory room with seven other travelers in the heart of the red-light district in the Hotel Kabul, Woermstraat. Life having played me for a fool, I retreated as soon as I could to the welcoming arms of Art. Taking refuge in the museums, I admired the painterly textures of the Adolphe Monticelli paintings (maligned, it seems, by all but Van Gogh himself) and a print of the actor Nakamura Shikan in the female role of Ohatsu by Utagawa Kuniyoshi (1707–1861), which had belonged to Van Gogh. When I came upon the *Bacchanal of Satyrs and Cupids* by Gerard van Opstal (1594–1668), with its parade of cherubs lining up to suckle the breast of a satyress, I wondered whether this orgy in ivory might be a representation of the polymorphous perversity of my past, or a prophecy of my future.[88]

At the Stedelijk Museum I gravitated to the weird Bosch-like hermaphroditic hallucinations of Melle (1908–1976). His *Schoorsteenstuk* (c. 1972) might as well have been an illustration from Payne Knight's *Worship of Priapus*.[89] A favorite motif of Melle's is a personified penis with feminine characteristics, sprouting breasts or splitting open ripe with vaginas, or turning into a crowned pig. A homely reclining hermaphrodite gazes out at the viewer, like Goya's *La Maja desnuda*, somewhat apologetically, with drooping penises for breasts. Disembodied, unidentifiable castrated things are in perpetual motion. A foot with a wound like Christ's stigmata takes the form of a vagina. Another painting features my old friend Aubrey Beardsley presiding over a landscape of pigs and penises humping one another, his arm draped over a monstrous bright pink erection, eyes wide with the hypnotic visions of the paraphiliac.[90] *Onvoltooid I* shows a horse-headed breasted figure with an erection which turns

---

[88] The female satyr, or satyress, is a modern European invention; ancient Greek and Roman satyrs were all male, accompanied by nymphs

[89] Richard Payne Knight, *A Discourse on the Worship of Priapus and Its Connection with the Mystic Theology of the Ancients* (London, 1786).

[90] Ezra Pound in the *Cantos* (80) tells how when Yeats asked Beardsley why he always drew grotesques and "horrors," Beardsley said, "Beauty is difficult." Here it seems especially so.

out—in the manner of Chinese boxes within boxes—to be a mask within a mask within a mask—until the female within is revealed in an infinitely diminishing series. A double-headed dildo, like a double-headed fish or Janus, is reminiscent of Ourobouros, the snake that swallows its own tail, or a fleshy Japanese enso. Several hermaphroditic women clutch their own erections in a bliss of autonomy, sufficient unto themselves, while another wields her dick nonchalantly as she pisses a triumphant golden arc. Finally, *Witte Rat* (1971) holds its nose proudly in the air with various naked sexual characteristics exposed below, humanoid scrotum and penis dragging the ground, rows of breasts, but also an engorged anus and clitoris, and a spread vagina out of which emerges a hand tossing a butterfly into the air.

Needless to say, Melle spoke to my current state of mind.

The first person who spoke to me in Amsterdam was a Scottish woman (not Mhairi) asking directions. In Leidseplein Square a guitarist stood up and yelled, "Help!" Then, after a pause, continued with "I need somebody. Help! Not just anybody," finishing the Beatles song with far less drama and an accent full of vees. I listened to the lyrics all the way through. They spoke to me.

My eyes met those of a tall short-haired blonde in the street; we exchanged frank, interested glances, bemused smiles between two strangers, and passed on; I saw her again a few streets away and we nodded in recognition but did not stop to speak to one another. If a third chance encounter offered itself, I vowed to bow to the inevitable.

A small dark child circulated with a shoebox covered in opaque plastic illuminating a peepshow inside. For only a guilder you could take a look. I was almost certain of what was inside; I imagined that he had one of Melle's polymorphous nightmares displayed there.

The last person who spoke to me on the first day in Amsterdam was a prostitute who bore a faint resemblance to Mhairi. It was, of course, why I chose her. It was in Trompetter Straat, the smallest, darkest, narrowest, reddest passage in the red-light district, as though the street itself was a welcoming walk-in vagina. On this summer night she was sitting, half-dressed, in the window display with a small but quiet dog on her silken lap. I was shopping for experience, this time with every intention of buying, unlike in the rue Saint-Denis in Paris, where I was only window-shopping like on my walks with Concha in Bond Street (*I like this; I don't like that*). The animated item for sale, my chosen Mhairi stand-in, was slim and fragrant and tan, and her hair smelled good. She wore a chain around her neck with a locket dangling the letter L in silver. It was not an M, but close enough. "Does it stand for Lucia?" I asked, once I entered what might be called her inner office or examining room. "As you like," she answered, amused without smiling. Her breasts were smooth and firm, her hands precise like calipers and scalpels. She was friendly in a businesslike way and efficient, directing her lapdog to get under the bed before she washed me and attended to my wayward desire, which was short-lived in spite of my efforts to forestall it. When I paused like a stubborn mule in the midst of our ride, she asked if anything was wrong and then, expert muleteer that she was, knew just how to spur me forward to bring my heavy load to its destination. I came out of her lair fifteen minutes older, fifty guilders poorer, and very thirsty. I drank a beer and slept soundly amidst my snoring dorm mates, other travelers with their own baggage to dream about.

Among the 750,000 inhabitants of Amsterdam it is not surprising that I have not found Mhairi. Back at the Rijksmuseum the next morning I am reminded of last night's adventure by a bronze relief called *Bacchus vindt Ariadne op Naxos*. Like so many depictions of satyrs revealing sleeping hermaphrodites, a satyr assists the god of wine in uncovering the sleeping Ariadne, while beneath the bed hides an impish Cupid with his pet Owl. *Post coitum*, said Galen, *omne animal triste est, sive gallus et mulier*. Whether it was true of the goose, it was certainly true of the gander. But then Galen described everyone's sexuality as falling on a spectrum of masculine and feminine, the ideal being the golden alloy of intersex. Thus sexual congress, while inferior and something of a caricature, was the best we could do in achieving the perfection of balance, and any separation would seem an occasion for sadness rather than the afterglow of good coital completion and release, followed by the freedom to go at it again.

And then, like a revelation, she appeared there in the gallery. It was not Mhairi but her surrogate from the night before. Carlo Crivelli's *Maria Magdalene* (c. 1480). The wrists are as fleshy as slim hips, but the hands and fingers are freakishly long and thin, delicate but expert and exact, like a surgeon's tools or ivory chopsticks, articulate and poised, as if they have a consciousness of their own and would speak if they could. What would they say? Would they reveal her intimacy with me? She gazes outside the frame of the picture downward at the viewer's crotch (mine) and holds up her labia-red skirt in front with thumb and forefinger, a scarlet advertisement of her underskirt. And what's in that golden tankard that she balances on her freakish palm? She is all sex for sale this one, here in the middle of the Rijksmuseum instead of in Tompetter Straat. Ah Crivelli! How I admire your decorative indiscretion! Yet so subtle.

In Amsterdam one walks with one's head just above water, as in a dream. The streets are full of dreamers, revenants in the midst of reveries, canals full of drowned dreams, tragic illusions, Ophelias floating just below the surface, lips poised for a mirrored kiss. These Lotos-Eaters don't follow fashion, not high fashion at least. This is not Paris or Milan. It's all too seductive.

I am glad to get out of Amsterdam if only for a day-trip to the Hague and then Haarlem, planning to return by eight in the evening in time to board the train for Copenhagen. At the Frans Hals Museum I admire an erotic painting by the artist Jan Sluijters (1881–1957) called *La Chemise verte* (c. 1930). The dark-haired woman wears, in a manner of speaking, a green chemise that slips off one small breast (its slight nod to gravity more erotic than any pert perfection). She gazes off into the distance in weary self-accusation, heavy green pearls encircling her neck.[91] I am tempted to stay in Haarlem overnight if only to see the Frans Hals by candlelight.

As I am trying to decide, I see the short-haired blonde from

---

[91] This painting was sold at auction 19 April 2021.

Leidseplein Square sitting at a café. We greet each other here in this distant city for the third time, as though we are old friends. One must respect such insistent serendipity. I join her at her sidewalk café and order a genever on ice. A drunk at a nearby table takes up most of our time intruding on our conversation. She is a teacher of children's theater. She asks if I will agree to eat with her. "I must go home to first get some money. I live with my boyfriend, a painter, but he is away." I am trying to decipher this invitation, I almost offer to pay, but I can't decide what exactly she is inviting me to do and why exactly she is taking me home—to get money, or for some other purpose?

Their attic room with the slanted and timbered ceiling overlooks the rusty rooftops of Haarlem. She is very conscious of the condition of the town's buildings and searches for the right word to describe them. She is looking for "run-down" but can only come up with their needing to be "built up." Time is running out if I am to make it back to Amsterdam in time for the train to Copenhagen, which for some reason has taken on the aspect of an appointment not to be missed, in spite of this lovely, ambiguous blonde distraction. No Frans Hals by candlelight for me. No beautiful Dutch children's theater teacher with an out-of-town painter boyfriend either. "I really must go," I say. At the door of her apartment, she kisses me four times on the cheeks and says, "Well, I suspect we will meet again!"

"I don't know. Thrice was magic. Four times might be demonic."

"We will meet again," she said knowingly.

I made a mental note to return if possible via Haarlem, but failed to get her name or her address. Was I tired? Jaded? Depressed? Perhaps we really would meet on the street again, perhaps even in another city, who knows, maybe another lifetime. I made it back to Amsterdam in time to catch the train to Copenhagen on my way to Stockholm and a vague fantasy of melting the icy Charlotte. I slept through Germany like a Lutheran sermon, waking only as the train boarded the ferry to Denmark before dawn.

* * *

When I arrived in Copenhagen I didn't expect to stay long. It was raining and cold, and the area around the central station was not beautiful. I would stay one night, at the most two, and see what happened. I inquired at the Huset (Use-It) information office about cheap accommodations. They suggested I try the Sleep-In at Per Henrik Ling Alle. It was a temporary youth hostel in an auditorium with partitions in the center that held dozens of bunkbeds. There were hardly any restrictions (except No Smoking) and hot showers and fresh linens were provided. All very civilized. I showered, dressed, stowed my green backpack in a locker, put on my grandfather's lucky hat, and went out with no expectations.

I wandered into FaelledParken where I stumbled into a Land og Folk Festival, a music and propaganda fest put on by the DKP (the Danish Communist Party). There were tents and bands of all sorts, food and drink and lots of soft-core propaganda for the Eastern bloc and against the demon America.

Soon I met the eyes of a handsome young woman in front of a music stage. It was her open smile that hooked me, and the asymmetry of her clear blue eyes. Later, we saw each other again as if in recognition. The first time I saw her, I knew I wanted to talk to her; the second time I saw her I asked if she spoke English. She did, a little. (How far I had come from those awkward advances of indirection and overthinking, dishonest because they were meant to cover up my naked sexual attraction to Concha, at the Immigration Office in Lamb's Conduit Street, Holborn.)

Her name was Marianne, the vowels pronounced not nasally in the American "Mary Ann," nor musically well back in the mouth as the Scottish "Mhairi" (thank god) with suggestions of Robin Hood's Maid Marian, but with the first "a" hard and long, the second "a" soft and warm, and the final "e" an imperceptible sigh that was less an "ah" than an involuntary release of air as the tip of the tongue left the upper palate's doubled "n." I noted this distinct pronunciation as if to differentiate in my mind once and for all the superficial similarity of the two women's names, since the only thing they otherwise had in common was their beauty, each very different and unique, and the location of their city, each again very different and unique, but both just above the fifty-fifth parallel north.

Marianne was tall and angular, in a loose button-down light blue shirt and beige slacks. I had trouble taking my eyes off her smile, and she seemed to have the same problem with mine. (Later she told me that there was a Danish word for the spark in that look: *lysglimt*.) For me, it was her eyes, the blue of the now-and-then clear sky over Copenhagen on that particular partly cloudy day, that captivated me. Her widely spaced, asymmetrical eyes lit up her ready and reachable smile, which seemed somehow engagingly askew, framed by hair the color of cappuccino and caramel and swept back from her broad and tan forehead, as though the wind were always blowing through it.

We were soon exploring the festival together, eating ice cream in freshly pressed and fragrant waffle cones, and sheltering from the occasional rainshower under the border of trees. She was a young communist, recently returned from a trip to Cuba. Thus the cinnamon tan. Alone at first, she soon introduced me to her friends at the Danish-Latino band's stage, where we all drank Tuborg beer together, Claus and Peder and Tina, and Hennig, who was as new to the group as I was. As the sun began to set, the group of us went to Claus's simply furnished apartment and ate smørrebrød with fish and tomatoes, eggs and salami. We drank more of the mild red and green Tuborg beer, punctuated with shots of an excellent Polish vodka and Danish *snaps* in small two-finger glasses.

Peder (who went by Pedro) and his girlfriend Tina invited everyone to Hand i Handke, a pub-café offering folk music on Sundays. I had planned to go there that evening anyway, having seen a poster for it or read about it in my *Let's Go* guidebook. As we entered the café, the first thing we saw was someone who had literally drunk himself under the table. "Here you have it," said Hennig. "Copenhagen by night!"

Tina objected to this caricature of her city. "This is not typical Denmark! I can't believe this is your first day in the country," she added to me as an aside. "Indeed it is not normal to have such good luck. A festival, a meal and a party in a Danish home, and a beautiful lady companion, too!"

I assured her that I felt very lucky indeed and tipped my hat.

We moved on to someone else's apartment, where we sang folk songs and communist worker chants to records while drinking more *snaps* and akvavit. A German arrived with a Che Guevara scarf at his neck and wearing a black leather vest. Two Finnish girls had come for the festival from Helsinki and even further north. A little German was spoken, but the Finns objected to this and asked that it be banned from our little party as "ideologically inappropriate." So everyone tried to get along in English, not just for my benefit, although Danish was resorted to more and more as the party went on and the alcohol took effect. Now and then I would be excluded from the conversation but I welcomed the pause for the chance to observe the festivities, to appreciate the male and female beauty of these northern faces, especially Marianne's, and to savor my good luck, as Tina had pointed out.

Marianne's apartment was just around the corner from Hand i Handke. Hennig, too drunk to make his way back to his lodging on the other side of the city, came back with us. He was not sleepy, however, so Marianne gave him a key so that he could go out again and return without disturbing us. She was very trusting, having just met him that day as well. Hennig seemed like a good soul, though, and sometime in the middle of the night he found his way back and onto the couch without making too much noise. He had been drinking for several days, it seems, and at breakfast his hands shook.

Marianne and I gazed into each other's eyes over the breakfast table, which amused Hennig. "Get a roooom!" he said, having heard this in some American movie. "Oh wait. You already have a room. It is I who have no room."

"So, Harald Bluetooth, you had a good sleep?"

"Tak," he said, and then, "I mean yes, we will speak English. A baby sleep."

"Why Harald Bluetooth?" I asked. "I thought your name was Hennig Dahl."

"It is because he is Christian," Marianne explained. "Bluetooth was first Christian King of Danemark. That is what we was laughing about all last night at Hand i Handke and I could not explain you why we was laughing so hard. He is a drunken Christian who sleeps in the house of a communist."

Harald shrugged and grinned good-naturedly. He seemed to be good-natured about everything: his nickname, his drunkenness, his religion, even his place of birth, the backwoods island of Bornholm, a chip off the old block of Denmark, which he said had floated eastward almost out of sight around the lower tip of Sweden, like a prodigal son. He even had one transparent blue tooth the color of skim milk, which made the nickname even more apt.

When Hennig finally wandered off after breakfast to find another day's ration of alcohol and God, Marianne kissed his forehead and tidied his collar as a big sister would and told him to behave himself "for Gott's sake."

Marianne went to work, giving me the only other key to her apartment, and trusting me to return at the end of her shift. I went out, first to fetch my backpack from the locker in the hostel and bring it back to the apartment, before wandering to get my bearings in this new and beguiling city.

Marianne had trained as a dental assistant but hated the job. Now she worked at a theater-café-bookstore called Klaptraeit in Kultorvet, one of the main squares. In the fall she planned to study music for six months, but for now she loved her job. It was stimulating intellectually and undemanding, leaving her plenty of free time to enjoy life and to think. I found the city beautiful for the same traits I found beautiful in Marianne: both were open and unpretentious, unadorned and authentic, with a casual intelligence that seemed spontaneous and natural. Students lounged in the squares drinking beer and having what I assumed were deep discussions, judging by their subdued tones of voice. In contrast to the colorful circus of crowded and crumbling Amsterdam, the atmosphere of Copenhagen's spacious squares was muted and almost monochromatic, except for the green and gilded rooftops overlooking parks full of flowers and stands of trees everywhere.

Their citizens were a contrast, as well. Compared to the rigid burghers and carefree dreamers of Amsterdam, the natives of Copenhagen seemed to express their modest aspirations with an unstudied understatement with little regard for what might be in vogue. Seeing a young man with a blue streak in his long blonde hair, I thought how in London this subtle touch would have become a full-blown costume, from the rainbow mohawk to the chained combat boots. One young man's checkerboard hairdo (perhaps he had just come from London) drew bemused stares and good-natured un-selfrighteous smiles. It was not unusual in London to see someone who had gone to such lengths to be different that they met themselves full circle in this way. But here, even the youth, who thrive on excess everywhere, seemed to be obsessed neither with fleeing from the past nor with chasing the flash of the future. They lived in their own present. This was at least my first impression.

This matter-of-factness extended to their attitude to their bodies. At the festival it was unremarkable to see men, women, and children standing or squatting to pee under the trees without taking special care to remove themselves from the view of others. Marianne felt free to stroll through the apartment naked, or at least in only her white cotton panties, even though Hennig was there, whom she'd known for only a day or two. He seemed to take no special notice either. There was no shame on her part, which is just the wicked stepsister of coquetry, after all. There was no hint of either in Marianne.

Marianne said that it was nice to hear Americans speak Danish because they always tried to sing it. I liked to hear her speak English because she gave fresh meaning to stale patterns of speech, like Hennig's direct "baby sleep" instead of the stale simile. When she was trying to find the word for spices, Marianne said, "You know, what you put on your foot to make it smell bedder." Her d's sounded like t's and vice versa, so death became debt, but vegetables somehow became "wenchtables." I loved picking up the stray Danish word that somehow worked as well or better than its English equivalent, such as *upsada* for upsy-daisy, or *kaelen* for cuddle, which we used a lot in our time together as an invitation.

These smatterings of local color, however, do not explain the feeling of wellbeing I had in Copenhagen and in Marianne's company. It was something more profound than this and simpler. The simplicity of the sensual experience made me feel a clarity inside, something uncomplicated and real. That's what Marianne did to me, made me feel clear to the point of being empty, empty of all and everything, even her.

The rain gave us a good excuse to stay in for a day or two, going out only to forage for smørrebrød fixings and Tuborg. One evening we ventured out for jazz at La Fontaine. In the morning Peder and Tina came for breakfast and we went on an outing to Sophienholm where we strolled around Lyngby Lake and went shopping. I bought a pair of black leather and wooden clogs (Mariola would not have approved, I'm sure), which I found to be surprisingly comfortable. Peder joked about his one month of military experience. "When they had a job for two and a half men, they would send me as the half-man." After dinner we watched a slideshow of Marianne's trip to Cuba (she refused to call it a holiday).

We came home and made love standing at the window. When we had recovered, Marianne said, "Now we make a party." She brought out milk and bread and butter and sugar. "Don't tell your dentist!"

Next morning I woke up to her staring at me, a frown on her broad forehead, a hand thrust in her hair.

"Are you worried about something?" I asked.

"Sometimes when I am with someone for many days all at once," she said, "I get tired of being together and I want to be alone. There was an Italian boy, he stayed with me for three months. I told him go. But with you, no. I don't think so."

"And that worries you?"

"Worries me, yes. Bothers me. Makes angry me, a little."

"It's not three months yet," I pointed out. "Maybe you don't want me to go because you know I'm going away tomorrow. It's different when you don't want to be alone yet."

"Yes, maybe."

Later, she said: "Sometimes I wish I can speak English so we can make discussions. But sometimes I don't szink zo. Maybe it is bedder we can't discuss things. Maybe I like you bedder. Sometimes, you know, people say something you don't like. Little things. And you don't like them so much then."

I knew exactly what she meant.

"Maybe this way we find out that there are more important things than what can be said."

We made plans to go to Paris or London when I returned from my trip. I was still intent on keeping my date with Charlotte in Stockholm and then going south to glimpse France and Italy, even though the thought of leaving Copenhagen was beginning to sound stupid. In case she needed to rent a car in my absence, I left my driver's license with Marianne, but I kept my passport of course. I also gave her one of my shirts, a striped one that she liked to put on when getting out of bed "because it smells like you."

One night we went to another cinema, not the one where she worked, with some of her friends to see Jimmy Cliff's *The Harder They Come*. We got into the cinema for free because Marianne had made a deal with the guy at the desk. In return, he could see movies at Klaptraeit. The Jamaican dialogue and the Danish subtitles made me feel adrift and in between as I had in Glasgow. But the weed we smoked beforehand in the spirit of the film helped me to understand without understanding. After the film, we said goodbye to her friends and walked together in the light rain and drank cappuccinos.

"I'll miss you, you know," I said.

"Yes, okay, miss me," she said. "But only here," pointing to my heart. "Not here," pointing to my head. She was right, of course. To miss someone with your head is to drive yourself crazy. I did that with Mhairi, and it was a mistake. I drew castles in the clouds and fell from them like a cartoon character who runs out into midair and only falls when he realizes the mistake he has made: that there is no foundation on which to stand in the clouds. I did that with Mnemosyne as well. I badly wanted our intellectualized passion to be a success—in my head. In love we all blow things out of proportion and distort the reality of our life. Then, when we get back to where we started from, we can't believe we went gaga over *that*. But when you miss someone with your heart, you "forget" about them; you keep them clear and close, so clear and close that they become a part of you, your heart, and when you are with them again, you take up where you left off, as though there had never been an interruption in your connection. Reunited, you are simply ecstatic—outside yourself, at least your thinking self—and truly with them outside of time, unconsciously. In that case, leaving is not heartbreaking; coming back is beautiful.

15 / Life Is as a Tribe of Birds

> The phoenix riddle hath more wit
> By us: we two being one, are it.
> So, to one neutral thing both sexes fit.
> We die and rise the same, and prove
> Mysterious by this love.
> —John Donne, "The Canonization"

Stockholm
What to say about the standing Hermaphrodite in the National Museum with a basket of fruit on her head? The Carmen Miranda Hermaphrodite is all come-hither-and-go-to-hell, offering abundance of pleasure and yet warding off any and all approach, the gesture of *anasyrma* below, revealing her male genitals, her legs fused together in the square herm-like pillar, making her inviolate, although her feet are human enough, though powerless. Her gift reveals her secret power: an invitation or a curse?[92]

---

[92] "In Jean Cocteau's film *Le Sang d'un Poète*, the poet has a rendezvous with a hermaphrodite which illustrates the nature of the viewer's activity, partly indicated by the text which opens the film: 'Every poem is a coat of arms. It must be deciphered.' In the first episode the poet discovers a mouth in the palm of a hand; with it he brings a statue of a woman to life—echoes of Pygmalion. She encourages him to enter a mirrored doorway (which is, significantly, actually a pool of water). Once inside the mirror, the poet explores an imaginative space in which the distinction

I kept my date with the classically beautiful Charlotte, only to have my suspicion confirmed that our attraction was something less than passionate. I found her in the department store where she worked. She looked good there, immobile, like a manikin or a work of art. She asked what I was doing in Stockholm when I could be traveling in France or Italy. I said I came to see her. She was flattered, but she still thought I was a fool. I could tell that she had lost respect for me, going out of my way to see her instead of the Midi. What I felt for her smooth features and her perfect body rose only to the sort of admiration I would feel for an academic painting, like those of Alma-Tadema or Frederic Leighton, or the polished perfection of a Hellenistic marble. We had a pleasant evening, dinner and a nightclub, with a visit to her parents' respectable flat afterwards, where she offered me an apple tart.

There is yet another *Sleeping Hermaphrodite* here in Stockholm, an eighteenth-century reproduction in a decadent pink marble and bronze with the usual *trompe l'oeil* tufted mattress. A mere seventeen inches or so in length. Inviting, but cold to the touch, I have no doubt. Ah, Charlotte, good-bye and good luck.

Copenhagen
Rolled back into Copenhagen early morning, intending to stay

---

between material reality and the metaphoric world of art is blurred. Finding himself in a corridor of the Hôtel des Folies-Dramatiques, he begins to look through several keyholes. The author's voice intervenes to tell us that 'the desperate meetings of the Hermaphrodite took place in room 19.' As he looks through the keyhole of room 19, limb by limb the hermaphrodite assembles itself before his (and our) eyes: 'A head, masked in white, appears . . . A chalk drawing appears—torso of an outstretched woman. . . . A real male leg and a real male arm, up to the shoulder, appear.' The poet is directed to arch his back: 'The image should be sensual.' He does not perceive the hermaphrodite all at once, as a whole, but fragment by fragment, in double-takes. 'More limbs and another torso appear.' And then: '*Le main de l'Hermaphrodite soulève une étoffe à la place du sexe et dévoile une pancarte sur laquelle est écrit: Danger de mort.*' The hermaphrodite has winked at him! And at us, revealing the identity of eros and thanatos." Richard Collins, "A Toy of Double Shape": The Hermaphrodite as Art and Literature. University of California Irvine. PhD dissertation. 1984. 65–7.

for the day with Marianne and leave by the night train. But after breakfast and bed and Tivoli, I took Marianne to work at the cinema in Klaptraeit, where I stayed to watch the matinee showing of *Farvel, min elskede* (*Farewell, My Lovely*) on the big screen with Robert Mitchum and a sizzling Charlotte Rampling whose resemblance to Marianne was remarkable. After the movie, she asked me across the lobby, "Do you really have to take a train tonight?" What could I do? After I picked her up from work, we had a drink at Hand i Handke, and then it was back to bed. In the morning, breakfast. For lunch she showed me how to make an open-faced sandwich with wedges of fried Camembert smeared with tart cherry compote. When pressed, the crispy wedges oozed fragrant cheese over the bed of lettuce and toast. Then back to her bed for the afternoon siesta, followed by a much-needed espresso. Then dinner at Tokanten and warm embraces on the station platform before finally boarding the night train.

"What kind of human are you," said Marianne, her blue eyes bright with dew, "that you make me feel this way?"

Hamburg

As the ferry landed in Germany I looked back to find a rainbow over Denmark. I tried to think of the French word for rainbow without success. I could only remember Marianne telling me that first day in FaelledParken, a day of sun and showers, the Danish word, so similar to the English and yet full of a breathy beauty and a cunning pursing of the lips: *regnbue*. Could it be then that I fell in love with her?

Outside the train station a drunk sprawled across a bench, his head hanging over a puddle of vomit, chin dripping. Not far away, two more drunks—or addicts—in a parody of a fistfight, a kind of birdlike dance with hopping and elaborate hand gestures, doing no damage to one another. Two strolling high-white-helmeted Polizisten, meanwhile, cut in to continue the dance in a wholly different style.

Munich
I feel uncomfortable in Germany. In the Alte Pinakothek, a painting by G. Von Max (1840–1915), *Der Anatom* (1869) sums up my feeling for this country, a purgatory between two heavens, north and south. A scientist gazes with morbid sensuality on a beautiful corpse whose pallid breasts glow in the solitude of his study. He has her all to himself, an all-too-human dragon, and I want to play St George, slay him and save her, but it is clearly too late. Time to board the train for Italy.

Arezzo
I had meant to get off in Florence to visit Browning's old house, but the train was just pulling away from the station as I awoke, so I got off in Arezzo instead, recalling that it was the setting for *The Ring and the Book*, the poet's Renaissance murder novel-in-verse, told from several perspectives, like *Rashomon*.

I climbed the hill to the park overlooking the city. I was soon joined on the bench by a middle-aged man who when he discovered I was American said, "You look like a cowboy, lean, muscular. You work out, yes?" When he was just a small boy in Napoli he overheard the GIs saying "fick-fick," and he wondered if I knew what that meant. Some of them would ask him if he wanted to "fick-fick." He abruptly changed the subject to discourse on the prostitutes of Arezzo for some time before asking if I would like to go with him and get a girl together. I pretended not to understand Italian, nor just exactly what he was getting at.

In addition to the bordellos of Arezzo, I would have to miss seeing Santa Maria della Pieve, the church of Giuseppe Caponsacchi, Browning's conflicted hero. The handsome young priest is torn between the calls of the victimized girl-bride Pompilia and the call of his church, who, weirdly personifying herself as his true Bride, claims him as her property. As his Betrothed, the disembodied voice of Santa Maria della Pieve demands that the priest forsake for her all mere "fleshly" women because, as she says, "thou art pulseless now."

> Now, from the stone lungs sighed the scrannel voice
> "Leave that live passion, come be dead with me!"
> Browning, *The Ring and the Book* (VI. 1000–01)

And Caponsacchi obeyed, although reluctantly, in wholly another spirit than John Donne, who defined the clergyman as "a blest Hermaphrodite" who brings "man to heaven, and heaven again to man."[95]

Florence

The simple pleasures are the best. I like the prismatic effect of allusion and collage. I light a Danish cigarette with a Spanish match, drink French wine with Italian bread and cheese on the banks of the Arno. I have a cold, but having taken an American aspirin, I am feeling a little better in the sunshine.

The Pitti Palace is a mess, a disgusting monument to garishness and bad taste. There are exceptions. A very different sort of mess than the Victoria and Albert Museum, that unrivaled warehouse of hoarded gewgaws, knick-knacks, curiosities, odds and ends, almost crowding out a few works of art, like jewels in a trash bin. There is, for example, a striking painting of *Judith with the Head of Holofernes* by Cristofano Allori, in which the artist himself is Holofernes' dangling head and his mistress Mazzafira, richly attired in Florentine textiles, is the beautiful, unbefuddled beheader.

At the Palazzo Vecchio I pause at Donatello's very different towering bronze statue of *Judith with the Head of Holofernes*. On the pedestal directly below the head of the god-killing general is a hermaphrodite. What could be the meaning of this? Other androgynous creatures abound on the pedestal frieze, but they are probably just run-of-the-mill bacchanals.

An exposition of Paul Klee at the old Wool Merchants Hall with a Hermaphrodite (*Mannweib aus einen verschollenen Roman, or Ermafrodito, da un Romanzo perduto,* or *Man-woman from a lost romance*) from 1939, reminiscent of early Beardsley.

---

[93] Donne, "To Mr Tilman after he had taken orders."

Ronta

The prettiest little train station in Italy (maybe in all Europe). High in the mountains, it stands open, protected only by the well-manicured hedges, topped with pines and palms, and splashed with bursts of pink popcorn balls, potted geraniums, and cacti. The walls of this little cubic masterpiece are mottled avorio with the characteristic Tuscan greenish turquoise shutters and red tile roof. A brief stop, Ronta behind the glass and metal frame of a train compartment. And then we are in motion again.

I don't think of Mhairi much now. *That was just a dream.* Maybe that's what happens when you don't renew the dream, when you replace fantasy with flesh and blood, your ideal with what is real, Edinburgh with Copenhagen, Mhairi with Marianne. Or am I simply fooling myself with endless decoys of denials and displacements of desire?

Ravenna

Another festival, the Italian version of the communist folk festival in Copenhagen. These European communists are not the dour, cement-faced Slavs of the Eastern bloc but romantic idealists with a vision of an artistic and practical communism that does not put itself in opposition to color, vivacity, variety, and life.

Trieste

On the train to Venice, gazing out on hilly Trieste, Joyce's home away from home, or at least where the polyglot preached in the church of Berlitz, I'm reading another Irishman, Desmond Hogan, for whom the old dead Dubliner is prematurely judged passé, "out of favour . . . too punctual, too ordinary." Hogan, among his spare jottings and awkward austerities, sometimes hits moments of grace, like this:

> *"I met Picasso in Paris," she told me in Limerick mental hospital. "I wanted to tell him about us, you and me, Liam and Sarah. There were paper carnations on the table. It was at an American wom-*

an's house. Gerry was with me. He began quoting poems by Eoghan Ruadh Ó Súilleabháin and I spoke eventually to myself, under the Irish of Eoghan Ruadh Ó Súilleabháin, I said, 'Life is as a tribe of birds, some of whom hit the sun, others who fail, fail utterly.' She was quite clear saying this, clear as though her madness was feigned but when I looked closer at her I saw her pupils had separated somehow from her eyes and were planets in space.[94]

Which birds are we? The ones who almost hit the sun, or the ones who fail, fail utterly? Too soon to tell.

I'm wondering now why I've never felt the same urgency to visit Ireland, the supposed land of my father's tribe, as I felt toward Scotland where my mother's family is from. How could I not think fondly of Eileen with her angst and her posturing, and her praying mantis positions, and her endearing squeaks and whimpers? Have I been repressing the Eileen in me (my twin sister, the degenerate, the irrational philosopher, the tolerant hedonist, the easy lay looking

---

[94] *The Leaves on Gray* (London: Hamish Hamilton, 1980), 85–6. Reading this novel in its entirety recently, only this paragraph looks familiar, and only because I copied it out in my journal, for what reason I don't recall. I believe I must have read the excerpt, "Southern Birds," in *Granta 3: The End of the English Novel* (1 October 1980). I would have been drawn in by the provocative title of the issue, which I vaguely recall picking up at the Institute of Contemporary Arts on The Mall. I pretty much had to pass the ICA to get to anywhere in central London on foot, and stopped in frequently to drink a coffee and shatter my budget in the bookstore. The more popular young writers did not tempt me. Martin Amis, who had been around awhile but had not quite yet caught fire, was never to my taste. (I've never really gone in for smartass humor disguised as style.) Julian Barnes—in any case and by any measure by far the better writer—had not yet written the books of his much more interesting oeuvre. These two, who were seen as the inevitable up-and-coming literary sparks, were absent from the ICA shelves in any case, which were filled with art books, poetry, radical socio-political pamphlets, and small press offerings of experimental prose. I avoided them both in favor of the seemingly edgier Desmond Hogan. I might have been drawn to Hogan for his age, less than two years older than I was (although only a year younger than Amis and a few years younger than Barnes). A rising star of the avant-garde then, Hogan is currently reduced by the omniscient but not omnisapient Wikipedia to "Irish writer and sex offender (born 1950)." In the future we may perhaps all look forward to being summed up with one accomplishment and one crime.

for a good time, to be destroyed in bed by beasties) while aspiring to the Mhairi in me (my unrequited aspirational ideal, the rational, the practical, the spiritual pragmatist, the healer, the cruel-to-be-kind)? These national parallels are hard to resist. I've never really gone in for genealogy, preferring to explore the hard facts of geography and the soft geometry of the body. Who knows who slept with whom yesterday, much less a hundred, a thousand years ago? And who cares? The only thing I'm fairly certain of is that I've inherited in my bloodlines an inevitable taint of incest (we all share it) and a promiscuity that comes naturally, my Irish forebears almost certainly having taken on all manner of men and mistresses if not husbands and wives in the American South and the wilds of Oklahoma, according to family legend. A tribe of birds indeed. Let the genealogists, geneticists, and linguists sort it out. I'm busy flying south for the summer.

Venice

Dreamy above, nightmarish below. Silent city of cradled passageways, sudden squares, every face a drama, every sound human, even the cries of the startled pigeons. Footsteps over stone bridges that sigh.

Postcard to Mhairi: "You were right. Cities are rich, generous, and inexorable. After your green and golden city of crag and castle came Amsterdam where wanderers can lose their reflection in the yellow petals of a canal or in the raw meat glow of a fifty-guilder note. Memory extends like a wound from Edinburgh to Copenhagen, where the wound is cauterized in the heat of the moment."

I didn't mention to her of course getting off by mistake at the Venice-Mestre station and opting to hike the six long miles in the heat of the day over the lagoons to Venice proper. Some of the journey's details (and detours) must be left out of every romantic quest— to preserve the romance. The gods of love need to keep up their images.

Nice

The beach weather—baking with cool breezes off the sea—

reminds me of California. Except that here the motif of mounded sand is echoed by the women's exposed breasts and bare buttocks. An eroticized sculptural sandscape by Maillol. A girl sitting in front of me reminds me so much of Marianne that I am having trouble deciding whether to get up, eat lunch, mail my package, get a hotel room, continue on to Antibes, or call Marianne. The only problem with this girl on the beach is that she is not as beautiful as Marianne—simply because she is not Marianne.

Cap d'Antibes

A good feeling of camaraderie here in the youth hostel in Antibes. In the evenings we gather and drink wine around a table under the tall trees with the ocean susurrus in the background.

Dinner last night at a fancy restaurant on the harbor, tête-à-tête with Toria, an English woman obsessed with Tantric Buddhism. She got very excited explaining to me that in Tantric Hinduism all of us, every man and woman, are made up of both male and female, a reflection not only of our parents' physiology but also of the gods' and goddesses' spiritual energy. In sexual congress, she said, we can meet ourselves and discover what it is to be whole. It is not so much a sexual or gender issue, not a matter of fleshy parts and chemistry, but rather a matter of whether we will embrace the balance of our androgynous characteristics to become creative beings instead of falling into imbalance and becoming passive and "effeminate" or aggressive and "macho." It is this Eastern wisdom that she thinks Plato was touching on in the *Symposium*'s comic twist, love and desire being our motivating force. "It's the alpha and the omega," she concluded. "It's what gets us out of bed in the morning, and puts us to bed in the evening, and sometimes makes us go to bed together in the middle of the fucking day!" This morning she and I had breakfast together and said an awkward goodbye through the window of the hostel. She gave me her address and invited me to visit when I was back in England: Sunflower Cottage, The Orchards, Darlings Lane, Pinkneys Green, Maidenhead. I suspect with an address like that she was having me on. (She was not.)

Impossible not to trip over the ghosts of Gerald and Sara Murphy on the beach here in Antibes and Juan-les-Pins.

Visited the austere Picasso museum overlooking the coastline at Juan-les-Pins with Jarod from Mill Valley before heading to the Matisse museum in Nice, where I managed to get through by telephone to Marianne. Her voice was like cool balm from the north. She had more difficulty understanding me than usual without our physical presence to convey our meanings. The bad connection didn't help. She finally cut me off, telling me simply to come back to her soon. Our plans are still up in the air, whether to drive to Paris or London together, or to break the bank and fly. We shall probably end up doing neither.

I turned twenty-nine today. A baguette—with a line of wooden matches like soldiers with flaming heads for candles—was brought in on a platter (like the Baptist's phallic head) by twenty hostelers from around the world, Brits and Irish, Americans and Norwegians, ubiquitous Germans of course, Aussies and even some French. No Danish, I checked. I told on myself the story of my mistaking baguettes for French dicks at the London bakery, which went over well with everyone who could understand it. One said, "Well, your name is Richard, isn't it?" (Yes, but I have never accepted the phallic nickname, preferring Rick before one day I suddenly became forever Richard.) And then some wit said for the benefit of the French men present, "Il voudrait que c'est comme ça!"

Anne, the proper youngish woman from upstate New York, got drunk at my little birthday party, weeping nostalgia for Cooperstown and her Quaker roots. While Jennifer and I were talking on the rocks in the dark, she came down and said that she was becoming inarticulate. "I am becoming inarticulate," she said pretty clearly. She had been trying to talk to Jarod about the ethics of baseball but without any luck. Jennifer and I had to help her find her way back from the beach to the hostel, assuring her that as long as she could pronounce inarticulate she was not becoming that. This morning she came out and apologized profusely and unnecessarily. She was on her way, by herself, to visit Cannes and the monastery on the Île Saint-Honorat.

Daniel, the music teacher from Bristol, who was on his way to the Caribbean to research steel drum compositions, captured Anne by her arms on her way out and danced her about, intoning this little speech as a Gregorian chant: "Yea, hast thou remembered to floss thy beautiful orthodontized teeth, Ah-ah-ah-Anne? And brushed them as best as thou ca-a-a-a-an? Dental cleanliness is next to godliness, as thou well knowest, Ah-ah-ah-Anne." She answered by giving him the exaggerated version of a toothy grin. He answered with: "Thou didst a fine job if a little sloppy for being so hungover but not too ba-a-a-a-ad." She punched his arm, hid a shamefaced giggle, and bounded off down the road in her sandals, trying to conceal her overripe and still (so she claimed) unplucked sexuality.

The rest of us tried to figure out where we were going next. I am torn. On the one hand I am enjoying my new health and wellbeing in the enticing sunshine of the Riviera. Early to bed and early to rise, a bottle or two of wine, grapes from Italy, olives from Greece, nectarines and apples and peaches, light from the heavens, and hot chocolate in the morning. Swimming in the Mediterranean, warm and easy bliss. Paris is still on the itinerary and it is a long way to Copenhagen and Marianne. Only nine days until I am back in London and ten until I'm back in the United Bluff, as Marianne calls it.

Paris

I'm not sure why I'm here except that it is one step closer to Marianne. When I woke up on the train from Marseilles, these words popped into my head: "Les façades de tous les immeubles de Toulon sont étranges. Avec des formes de poissons roses et des hommes qui se gardent comme des dauphins. Et la couleur de tous les bâtiments est rose, la couleur saumon, une couleur profonde et sensuelle."[95] I wanted to tell the woman, elegant and gray, in the seat across from me "que mon rêve était très bizarre. Laissez-moi vous

---

[95] "The façades of all the buildings in Toulon are strange (or foreign). In the shapes of pink fish and men guarding each other like so many dolphins. And the color of all the buildings is pink, the color of salmon, a color deep and sensual."

le dire, madame. . . ." But I held my tongue. *J'ai tenu ma langue.* She looked up from her laminated Livre de Poche, a French translation of Suetonius, and asked, out of the blue: "London?" I nodded, not knowing exactly what she was asking. She said, in a perfectly posh accent, "A wicked thought," and then returned to the wicked history in her livre de poche. "I lived there once upon a time," she added, without looking up. "You should try Toulon."

At the Gare du Nord bar, I ordered a sandwich and espresso. A ragged man, dripping blood from his fingers, came in and demanded a glass of water. After an argument with the barman he got the water and drank it down in a long gulp. Another man at the bar, in a light blue suit, moved away, but the bleeding man edged closer, gesticulating as he raved, casting droplets of red. In spite of his avoidance, the man's sky-blue suit was soon spattered with blood and he began to curse. When the bleeding man stumbled back out into the ill-lit station, the barman wiped the blood from the bar and gingerly with his fingertips picked up the glass the man had left behind, his left nostril flaring with disgust. Thrusting the bloody glass into the sink under the bar, he washed it thoroughly and then hung it to dry for the next customer.

Yesterday I met up with Linda, a friend from graduate school who is making a short visit to Paris to examine some manuscripts in the Bibliothèque Nationale for her research on fetishism, feminism, and femmes fatales. Linda is friends with Mnemosyne, so she filled me in on how the honeymoon was going.

"Her husband is definitely a safe harbor for her, unlike you. He drinks beer and watches football. She's hoping it will last long enough for her to finish her dissertation. That's what she's concentrating on. That and forgetting about you. What did you do to her, anyway?"

We went to Beaubourg and visited the ectoskeletal Pompidou, climbing around it like ants on the abandoned carcass of a glass and steel cicada. We watched a street mime die of love, repeatedly, on the bridge to the Île Saint-Louis.

I am left with a disturbing impression of Brâncuși's atelier, which he donated in his will to France to be preserved as he left it. It became an obsession with him, the arrangement of his studio, a kind of memory palace, an enclosed space where geometry, surface and mass, could interact without contact with the outside world, a creative simulacrum of his mind, not only as a work of art but as a museum within a museum. The only thing missing is the human element, the passion, the artist himself and his models, the flesh before it became merely art, geometric. An obsession, it seems, can also aspire to an apotheosis.

I have never been to Toulon.

Somewhere North of Paris

No matter how educational or entertaining, our travel teaches us one thing above all others. That we don't have to go far for its benefits, no matter how many stones you might leave unturned. Mencius and Huysmans could have told me that. And after a certain amount of travel, all travel becomes the same journey repeated over again. Another Sunday at Hyde Park Corner, another weekend in Paris, another day in Paradise. Is it the same with the people we meet? It is difficult to tell whether the pleasures of travel are due to the comfort of this repetition or to the minor shocks of slight variations on the familiar theme. Relics and derelicts are everywhere. Or is travel simply a metaphor for sex? Exploring new territories, penetrating sensuous places until now only imagined, communing with the natives, becoming one with the Other, casting off one's self. A displacement both literal and figurative, mental as well as physical, not to mention spiritual.

The Timid Proud One, 1957. Asger Jorn. Tate St. Ives.
"... we bathed as if naked in the joyous aura of his art." (p. 240)

16 / The Timid Proud One

> The purpose of art is life.
> —Asger Jorn

After my quick trip north to Stockholm to see Charlotte and then south to drink a *beaker full of the warm south* in Italy and France, I headed pretty much directly from Cap d'Antibes to Copenhagen, with only a brief stopover in Paris, to say a long goodbye to Marianne. None of our elaborate plans to hire a car and drive to London or Paris panned out, so we spent my last week in Europe together seeing Denmark.

We visited the anarchist commune of Freetown Christiania, an autonomous district of Copenhagen that was attempting to put into practice the hippie ideals of a previous decade, a policeless state of legal drugs, environmental sustainability, and free love. It was an interesting experiment, which may still be going on, but it was only possible in a small, liberal, affluent, and fairly homogenous country like Denmark. It was reminiscent of Haight-Ashbury in the sixties even as it reached the tipping point of descending from spontaneity into seedy chaos. Marianne, more communist than anarchist, did not think it would last long.

We strolled among the tie-dyed and graffitied buildings, picking our way through the chaos of discarded furniture and barefoot hippie children, trying to make sense of our accidental love, or at least to see the boundaries of this irrational expansiveness we both felt as the result of this magical intersection of our lives.

"Do you have a girlfriend in the United Bluff?"

I told her all about Mnemosyne, how suited we were intellectually and even sexually, yet how we turned each other into monsters, and how, thank Gott, she had married someone else recently. I told her about my daughter, how I missed her and was returning for her sake, and about her mother, to whom I was still married legally if no longer in any real sense but still loved more deeply than any friend. None of this phased Marianne. She was not the sort to be threatened by competition. Still, I did not tell her about Mhairi or Stacie or Carin or Concha. She was not really listening anyway. Her mind was on other concerns. Her conflict was not with the other women in my life, but with herself.

"I don't like wanting you to stay here," she said, her hand placed lightly on my chest. "And I am wondering when you go."

"I can go today, if you like."

"No, I don't like, but I want you."

"To go?" It was all very confusing, emotionally even more than linguistically.

"Yes. I want you. To go." Then, shaking her head: "And to stay."

"Why do you want me to go?"

"Because I spend every day with you and I am not tired. Not tired of you. I don't go to communist meeting last night to tell my comrades about Cuba. And I don't care because I want to be with you. And so I want you to go. Soon. So I have my life back. Not now. But soon."

Friends of hers offered us the loan of their country house in Lolleland, and another friend loaned us a car to drive there. The house turned out to be a charming whitewashed cottage in the midst of endless flat fields, the soil so rich it was black.[96] The colorful collage

---

[96]A photograph informs me that my memory is an incurable romantic. The cottage was actually a rather unremarkable stucco house, not whitewashed but the color of

for the senses that had awakened my senses first in summery Copenhagen and then in Italy and the South of France not so long ago now faded to the black-and-white setting of a Bergman film, reflecting the transition from the bright beginning of our relationship to what we knew was making its way to its bleak autumnal conclusion.

I could feel Marianne kiss my eyelids and climb out of the tumult of plum-colored sheets. As she passed over me, like a sleek deer hurtling a hedge in slow motion, I let my hands glide along her slim flanks, still smooth and dark from what she called her Cuban tan. I had told her I could taste the cinnamon of her browned shoulders and flat belly and thighs. "But aren't you a little afraid," she teased, "you American, of this communist tan?"

"Come back to bed," I said.

She lit two cigarettes instead. She gave one to me, then smoked hers standing naked at the window deep in thought. I studied her figure against the light of the dormer window, the sharp shoulders and pelvis and the profile of a pointed breast, altogether a slender silhouette.

"It is making rain," she observed.

"Come back to bed," I repeated. "I want to feel you next to me, you and your Cuban tan, which I think I might eat, you look so scrumptious."

"Oh don't talk so fast, I can't understand you!"

"It doesn't matter."

"Ha! Do you know what you just said? It's funny. *Et dusin mad.* A dozen food. Are you so hungry? Me too. Let's eat. You're not hungry? Well then I will eat myself. Why do you laugh? Did I say something stoopit?"

We had intended to spend more time visiting the surrounding area, but we ended up spending most of our time in the cottage,

---

tanned flesh after the summer is over. Nor is it standing alone in a fertile field but simply crouched between two others, the small red car, a beat-up subcompact, in the driveway. There were such houses in such fields, but perhaps we simply drove past them and I projected us into them as a more appropriate setting for our love story.

playing chess and drinking Aalborg akvavit, and deciphering each other's approximations of translating what we felt and thought into each other's tongue, when we were not up in the attic bedroom with its bird's eye view of the stoic if fertile landscape.

On our last night together, playing chess, in the middle of the game Marianne began to get testy. She took every opportunity to provoke me into an argument, insulting the capitalism of America, its materialism, its acquisitiveness. I simply agreed with her at every turn, until she tried to make me out to be a cultural imperialist, more insidious than Harald Bluetooth who invited the Christians into Denmark in the tenth century. But what I offered was not a challenge to the mirage of her bright communist future but a reversion to the dark pagan past, pure hedonism, heartfelt sensuality. I refused to take the bait. I knew what this was about. She was putting up a brave defense, trying to turn me against her so that she could turn against me and be free. She finally made her gambit explicit by implying that to me she was just another capitalist conquest, cultural imperialism in the form of love. "You make me fall in love with you, you American!" At which she tipped over her queen in surrender and burst into tears that immediately turned to tears of laughter at herself and how ridiculous her comrades would find her right now. Like a long-building but short-lived thunderstorm, her outburst cleared the air and her eyes were sunny again.

It ended of course with us going to bed for the last time. We made love under the naked rafters of the sloped ceiling with the violence of desperation, forcing each other into distorted positions, bending an arm or lifting a leg and spreading or pushing limbs aside, like fallen angels, immortals who could not be killed wrestling to the death, rolling and twisting and sliding, biting and scratching each other to rip an entry into flesh where we might slide and forever reside, writhing like snakes coupling, as though we might trick ourselves into thinking we would be able to exhaust all possible permutations while we still had the present moment. Spent, we slept fitfully with the same sort of ambivalence, waking to examine each other in the dark by the light of the moon or the ember of a cigarette as if to engrave the image of this impossibility in the form of a person deeply in our memory.

In the morning I picked up her toppled queen and put away the chess pieces of the unfinished game, stowed the remaining supplies we had brought in the cupboards, and packed my bag. It had been a good European vacation, a good finale to a good year. It was coming to an end, but I was ready to do it all again. Except that I knew that I could never return. It was over, and I knew deep inside that I would not soon, if ever, be as happy as I was right now. Happy, though, was not the right word: better would be *replete*. Which is a much different state than *complete*.

I regretted not a single minute or month of the past year, for all its missteps and mistakes, mistaken identities and missed opportunities. All my regret had to do with the fact that this moment, this year, this week with Marianne above all, would never happen again.

13 September 1981. Vester Tirsted, Denmark.

He got up the morning of their last day together as though nothing had been or ever could be different than it had been during the last week. After he laid out their breakfast while she still slept, warm and fragrant in the clean sheets upstairs, he made himself a cup of coffee, lit a cigarette, and began to read, lingering.

That was when he realized that everything was different.

He named each item of food in Danish, as though that would give them the reality they would soon lack, as though he were Adam (entire with Eve) in the first days in the garden instead of himself (looking ahead to such lack) on the last. Brød, smør, honning, hytteost, mælk, appelsinjuice, emmentaler, skinke, tomat, kaffe.

It occurred to him that this is how a lifetime should end, over a meal set out and uneaten, untouched, with the Beloved exhausted overhead in a warm bed, looking out over the fertile countryside, on a Sunday morning, the spire of a country kirke modest in the distance, ringing bells to signify neither marriage nor birth nor death, but only the beginning of a long indolence built for a day.

The sun came in through the blowing mosaic of bamboo leaves at the kitchen window. The water began to boil. Her footsteps clocked the wooden stairs.

To pass the time before Marianne descended nude down the staircase, I idly obsessed on the M's in my life, Mnemosyne and all the variations of Mary—Mhairi, Marianne, and even Concha (née María de la Concepción), who I associated with the transvestism of Mademoiselle de Maupin, and with the possible model of Velázquez's *Lady with a Fan*, Marie de Rohan. I had to include that other au pair or rather governess Mary Poppins (*l'opposé de moi, mais c'est moi!*), with whom my London journey began, and Ann-Margret (Swedish, like Charlotte) whose hermaphrodite-in-the-hayloft dream haunted me from an early age, until I arrived all the way back to La Primara Maria, my first-grade (and, I suppose, my first real) "sexual" dalliance in the bushes after her mamacita's aphrodisiac spicy cookies and chocolate milk.

Wistfully, I recalled Donne's elegiac lines from "The Relic":

> *First, we lov'd well and faithfully,*
> *Yet knew not what we lov'd, nor why;*
> *Difference of sex no more we knew*
> *Than our guardian angels do.*

How far I'd come from the shapelessness of that first innocence.

But it was the lyrics of Marty Robbins's "El Paso," a song contemporary with my time with Maria, that I began to hum and then to sing aloud, to Marianne's amusement, who from upstairs heard me crooning:

> *Blacker than night were the eyes of Marianne*
> *Wicked and evil while casting her spell.*
> *My love was deep for this communist maiden*
> *I was in love, but in vain, I could tell.*

I substituted *communist* for *Mexican* maiden, and *Marianne* for *Feleena*, but who would know? Never mind that Marianne's eyes were not black but bluer than the Danish sky.

"What crazy thing do you sing?" she said, beaming as she came down the stairs not naked but in my striped shirt, her legs as long as they could be.

The time for my departure loomed. It had cast a shadow on our bright affair ever since I had come back. Our time together would forever exist in two parts: the brilliant beginning, all music festivals and akvavit and warm waffle cones; and this overcast farewell, full of foreboding for the loss of a future together that never could exist. My travels north and south had severed those two halves and set them in stark opposition, the lightheartedness of the early stage as far from this bittersweet latter stage as Denmark was from the United Bluff.

The cottage was a retreat from reality; we clung to it like denial. As long as we stayed inside, the world's grip on us loosened, and her comrades in Copenhagen and my college students back in California would have to wait. This morning, however, we finally acknowledged we would have to leave the cottage after all, and be on our way to the harbor at Rødbyhavn where the evening ferry would be waiting to take me across the bay to Puttgarden and beyond.

We began with a stop in the quaint fishing village of Dragør. Her father had begun as an auto mechanic, like mine, but then he became a harbor traffic controller in Dragør harbor. Now he had his own boat and went fishing on his days off, taking other men from the village with him. Brightly painted houses topped with roofs of thatch or fulvous tile looked out on the bobbing boats in the harbor. Marianne took me to visit her aunt, who gave us pastries in the kitchen, where the walls were embellished with Danish sayings, words of welcome and folk wisdom. Later, we talked with a man who was painting the soffits of his house long before they were in need of it, and we played with children in the street. In a surviving photograph we look happy, she with a plum sweater draped around her neck, smiling at the camera, I in a black shirt with epaulets, smiling at her, one of the children of the village grinning between us.

Afterwards we made our way to the obligatory literary tourist stop, Hamlet's Helsingør. As we stared out over the leaden water from the bleak coastline, I couldn't blame the famous Dane for being so melancholy.

More eye-opening to me than the setting of *Hamlet* was the

Asger Jorn Museum in Silkeborg.[97] I had seen one or two of his works in London at the Tate, *The Timid Proud One*, for example. I had always considered him a lesser Dubuffet. Seeing the collection he had put together, not only of his own work but that of the artists who had influenced him and that he had worked with, was a revelation. Here was an artist who had been the driving force in spontaneous-abstract painting and was a key member of the Situationist movement. But it was his affinity to artists like Otto Dix, and Emil Nolde, and especially Dubuffet, that resonated with me. Jorn's infectious dark playfulness raised our spirits that day when we most needed them raised. Even though we were on our way to the port where my ferry was waiting, marching to the scaffold so to speak, we bathed as if naked in the joyous aura of his art. I still had to return to London before continuing on to the States, but this goodbye was the true close to the chapter of my bounteous year abroad.

I had begun the year by stating to myself, like a jaded Mary Poppins, in Piccadilly, "the myth is defiled by my presence." Jorn gave the purity of myth back to me in his belief that "the image is prior to the myth." These images of experience and memory that I have recorded here, which include the images of all the senses and not just sight, are after all the raw materials of the mythologies we create through art like a destiny, a destiny we create like art. In this way we fix experience like a photograph so that our personal mythology has more clarity than memory but less than life itself. Myth is an attempt to account for the impression of the image, a story to animate or reanimate it, to remind us of the magic of life as it was lived.

As Jorn put it, life is the purpose of art. Wilde, I'm sure, would have disagreed; for him, it was just the opposite: art was the purpose of life. As a working hypothesis, Jorn's view now struck me as far

---

[97] This last day's itinerary does not make sense on any map of Denmark, either in the order of the visits or the distances traveled. It is probable that I am telescoping events or even confusing the last day with the previous days in Copenhagen before leaving for Vester Tirsted. But this is the impression I have of that final day, that we crisscrossed Denmark in an attempt to swallow it whole, just as we attempted to do with each other.

more interesting. Jorn's art-for-life philosophy was roomy enough to contain all contradictions, all paradoxes, all polar opposites, whereas Wilde's life-for-art was only good for paraphrasing life's paradoxes in the form of provocative *bons mots*, little mirrors in which to posture and pose. Like Blake, Jorn realized that opposition is true friendship: "Tension in a work of art is negative-positive: repulsive-attractive, ugly-beautiful. If one of these poles is removed, only boredom is left." This was the secret of the hermaphrodite's fascination. How many scenes from my year abroad might be summarized in those few words?

I had cut my further travels in Europe short to come back to stay awhile longer with Marianne, a strategy meant to ease the pain of separation. They say the men of the Aran Islands don't learn to swim because it only makes the drowning death slower. We almost regretted having spent so much time bathing in the warm presence of each other because it made our goodbye more painful.

I boarded the ferry to Germany at Rødbyhavn with a profound sense of loss. With not just one but two recent women in my heart and two cities (both at the fifty-fifth parallel north) in mind, these lines from Elizabeth Bishop's "One Art" came to me:

> *I lost two cities, lovely ones. And, vaster,*
> *some realms I owned, two rivers, a continent.*
> *I miss them, but it wasn't a disaster.*

On deck standing near the smokestack to borrow some of its warmth, I looked back at the Danish coastline as it receded. I could still see Marianne, who would always be Denmark for me, until she shrank to a speck on the horizon. I allowed one or two of the few Danish phrases I had learned to bubble on my lips: *Farvel, min elskede. Jeg elsker dig. Lysglimt i øjet.*

Then, in its wake and the boat's, like froth, a joke at my own expense, several more lines from the Marty Robbins's song welled up:

> *I saddled up and away I did go*
> *Riding alone in the da-ah-ah-ah-ark.*

> *Maybe tomorrow a bullet may find me*
> *Tonight nothing's worse than this pain in my heart.*

I smiled at the maudlin sentimentality of the song, tempering the end of this romance with a comic pathos. One thing Mnemosyne taught me: sometimes country music gets the emotion right. Sometimes life is maudlin. But as Mary Poppins claimed to her parrot umbrella before departing on a wind "blowing dead on from the west," "Practically perfect people never permit sentiment to muddle their thinking." Tomorrow, I would be cynical again and guarded, but tonight I was tender and raw.

Why was I always falling in love and always leaving? Each woman I met in the past year was a forking path, a possibility, a road not taken. How many "destinies" had I almost embarked upon and abandoned except in my imagination? I recalled Mhairi's question. *Is there such a thing as destiny?* Free will complicates destiny, as improvisation complicates yet completes form, giving flesh to abstraction. (Why do I hear the echo of that little girl's voice now, as she breezed past Uccello's *Battle of San Romano* in the National Gallery, "I don't like the frame of that picture at all, *at all!*"?) Weakness or blindness frustrates freedom, a lack of boldness holding the art of life hostage. Does boldness halt, or spur our destiny? Are we just *wee timorous beasties*, trapped when we aren't exposed? And what kind of boldness does freedom require? Can there be such a thing as a "missed" destiny?

Or is there only one destiny, one path, the one actually taken, the others mere dreams, myths in the mist, lies, self-deceptions, fantasies, fictions never written, stories never told (the saddest kind), mirages in the desert, illusions on the horizon, abandoned in the fog of what we think of as reality?

17 / Retrospective

> One is always at home in one's past.
> —Vladimir Nabokov, *Speak, Memory*

I leave off this floating fragment of memoir with a young man I hardly recognize adrift between Denmark and dry land, between romance and the onset of cynicism, asking more questions than he has answered. When he landed at Heathrow a year earlier, he had only just turned twenty-eight; when his *aeroplane* lifted off to take him back again, he was less than a fortnight into twenty-nine.[98] The

---

[98] In the interim he had become used to a number of British spellings (like *aeroplane*) and locutions that he now fell into more or less inadvertently ("French stick," however, was not one of them). He had lived in the present long enough—having previously been exiled among the pre-aeronautical Victorians, those grounded fledglings restricted to flights of fancy—that his brother's *aeroplane* no longer seemed strange. Indeed, he was tempted to make it his preferred spelling, if that hadn't seemed too uppish, since *aero* in Greek took on mythic resonance: the name of the princess Aero of Chios, daughter of a king and a willow nymph, aptly means to raise or lift up. When the drunken Orion was about to rape Aero in her sleep, her father put out the brute's eyes with a hot poker. That her heroic father Oenopion (whose name means "wine-drinker") was himself the son of Dionysus says much about the virtues of moderation and the vices of excess. Apropos, we mustn't forget that Dionysus himself, born of a father-mother after his incubation in Zeus's thigh, was raised female for a time and has always been ambiguous, androgynous, and nonbinary in terms of gender.

twelve months in between those two flights had been a Technicolor hallucination for all the senses, a yearlong dream from which he was thereafter never quite sure he had ever fully awakened.[99] It might have helped to have known from the outset that, as Anthony Cronin put it, "where the taking of London is concerned confidence is a great factor."[100] For he had been upon arrival as bereft of confidence as he was of a good wool coat or a decent pair of shoes.

Yet the time had been packed with experiences that should have boosted his confidence, some of which demystified and demythologized his most intimate illusions about art and love and life. As he said to himself early on, entering for the first time an electrified Piccadilly Circus (and not *with a poppy or a lily in his medieval hand*), "the myth is defiled by my presence." At the time he had meant simply that it wasn't Oscar Wilde's London anymore. He had not yet grasped the full meaning of the phrase. It was then simply a pretty epigram that he suspected might be profound, like one of Wilde's. It turned out to be prophetic. The mythical London he had imagined no longer existed. (Had it ever?) What he found wasn't Wilde's London, but a new myth that in time morphed into his own. Indeed, the myth became his own metamorphosis.

For a year he had made a stab at living the "hard, gem-like flame" that Walter Pater offered to the world in his 1873 Conclusion to the *History of the Renaissance,* even if the flame had often gone cold and tasted of ash.[101] A little over a century after Pater's man-

---

[99] Of course his momentous year abroad, while unique in its details, is recognizable in its outline as a postwar rite of passage, not unlike the Grand Tour of earlier scholars. The experience of young women abroad in their twenties, for example in Paris, can be discovered in Alice Kaplan's *French Lessons: A Memoir* (Chicago: U of Chicago P, 1993) and *Dreaming in French: The Paris Years of Jacqueline Bouvier Kennedy, Susan Sontag, and Angela Davis* (Chicago: U of Chicago P, 2012), as well as Harriet Sohmers Zwerling's record of her bohemian decade *Abroad: An Expatriate's Diaries 1950–1959* (New York: Spuyten Duyvil, 2014).

[100] *Dead as Doornails* (London: Calder & Boyars, 1976), 167.

[101] "To burn always with this hard, gem-like flame, to maintain this ecstasy, is success in life." Walter Pater, *The Renaissance: Studies in Art and Poetry.* The 1893 Text. Ed. Donald L. Hill (Berkeley, Los Angeles, London: U of California P, 1980), 189.

ifesto for aestheticism, this young man had come from America to write a dissertation on the figure of the hermaphrodite in late nineteenth-century art and literature, with Pater's philosophy at the center of his reflections, however primed by Georges Bataille's darker eroticism. At times he felt he neglected his research because he had not spent all his waking hours in the British Library or the Warburg and Courtauld Institutes. Little did he know, although deep down he suspected, that he was researching the hermaphrodite in the best way he knew how: by discovering in the bars and bedrooms of Britain and Europe how he was himself a "toy of double shape."

"The highest, as the lowest, form of criticism is a mode of autobiography," wrote Wilde in the Preface to *The Picture of Dorian Gray*. This young scholar certainly did not transcend Oscar's truism, just as he had not avoided Pater's cliché, nor some of Dorian's milder debaucheries, none of which his friend Laury, in his role as the portraitist Basil Hallward, really captured in the black and white charcoal portrait he drew with such focused energy in a frigid warehouse space in Hackney. Laury had caught a diabolical glint in one eye (but not the idealism latent in the other) and the general sense of tortured gloom on the brow that his friend brought to each sitting (but not the wry incurable optimism around the mouth). In the end all of the emotion in the drawing was only selection, a projection of the artist's own consuming concerns and limitations. No one escapes the truism, it seems, for the highest, as the lowest, form of art, too, is a mode of autobiography.

There is a Gahan Wilson cartoon (master of comic monsters) somewhere (in the *New Yorker*? *Playboy*?—or did he imagine this too?) captioned something like "The Passport Photo of Dorian Gray." The cartoon depicts a suspicious customs agent comparing the passport photo revealing Dorian's grotesquely decadent soul with the flawless young dandy in front of him. The thrust of Wilde's brilliant trope was that in reality the reverse occurs—art is only a snapshot

---

Pater removed the Conclusion from early editions due to charges of its "immoral" effects on the youth of the time.

in time, a preservative like formaldehyde to a corpse; it is the body, and especially the face, that records the soul's wasting disport—and Wilson's brilliant parry and riposte was to acknowledge the logical outcome given Wilde's premise. Although our traveler was sure no one could tell the difference between his own passport photo (now only a year out of date) and his transformed returning self, he knew that he had changed enough within that he could hardly recognize his own fresh-faced photo.[102] Wilde said he had only his genius to declare when he landed in America; this young man had only his experience to declare, although he did not declare it. He kept his experience close to his chest like a trove of smuggled riches he hardly knew how he might squander, or like drugs to transport him back to another, more vivid time in the long horizon of years to come.

* * *

On his return to the States and his PhD studies, which now consisted mostly of teaching literature to sophomores and trying to complete the dissertation, he felt the need to process his personal experiences abroad by turning them into a narrative that would parallel the dissertation but tell the real story, the living flesh and breath behind the dry scholarly quest. Julian Barnes has claimed that we all have "one story" to tell: this was his. He knew it at the time; perhaps one always senses that it is the one story when it is happening.[103]

He made endless beginnings, with a number of different approaches and tentative titles for his one story. But he could never shed the impulse to romanticize the experience, or to distort his impressions in an attempt to create an acceptable persona with a sufficient mix of the amicable and the peccable to be not just believable but

---

[102] The same might be said of the young man depicted in these pages and the aging version of himself who writes. In painting his own portrait, he has perhaps played Basil Hallward to his own younger Dorian; whether the narrative has captured his innocence or exposed his decadence, the reader can decide.

[103] With this proviso: that some of us have more than one "one story."

also true to the lived events, both objectively factual and subjectively actual. Would his molten experience pour smoothly into the novelistic mold, shapely with the artifice of meaning? Or would it amount simply to a picaresque romp, a bag of shiny but unrelated episodes, like glass beads in a game with no unifying thread to link them? Whatever he tried, the result always fell short, like the repellent fake selfies posted on social media through "improving" filters. He had a corollary tendency to overwrite, suspecting that his unadorned life was not good enough, just as he had once aspired to the stylistic pretensions of a Dahlberg, thrown up like a prickly palisade of self-defense, instead of the unsheltered truths of a Bowles.[104] The mistake, he realized at last, was to try to turn his life into art. That's not what Asger Jorn meant at all by "the purpose of art is life." Life was not meant to be a sacrifice on the altar of some aesthetic deity; art should enhance and *enlighten* life, not as we would like it to be, but as it is and was.[105]

Back in the house on Balboa Island that he once shared with Mnemosyne and others, he now had new roommates, including the goth Morticia, a deep-voiced grad student from Portland, Oregon, who wore elbow-length black gloves (even to bed) and drove a vintage Chrysler with bench seats. She read his notes on his remembrances—without his permission but with fascination and deepening horror, but hers was a moral repulsion, not aesthetic, and that is another story.

When he took his first teaching job in Baton Rouge, and then other assignments in Wales, Romania, and Bulgaria, he lugged the

---

[104]Stylistic faults of which, the reader will no doubt notice, he never quite cured himself.

[105]The term "enlighten" is used advisedly to suggest that art puts a spotlight on life, illuminates it for what it is, with all its beauties and blemishes; that this leads to a kind of satori in recognition of what is real rather than what in our fear and desire we would like to be real; and that such epiphanies of the actual lift the heavy burden, lighten the load of our everyday dissatisfaction and allow us to embrace the here and now as hungrily as Salmacis embraced Hermaphroditus, yet without that enervating attachment.

archives of memory with him for decades, metaphorically and sometimes physically in the form of the eight or so bound journals he had filled. He rarely looked into them. Someday, though, he would find the time and discipline—and the courage—to descend into their depths to commune with his ghosts honestly. Odysseus in the underworld began with the young searcher Elpenor, whose body was left behind in Circe's house—"unwept, unburied"—before Odysseus was able to conduct the prolonged interview with the dual-sexed prophet Tiresias, blind, but whose vision extended mercilessly both forwards and backwards.

Carin was his young Elpenor.

She came to him in a dream to fling open the gates of memory. She was still nineteen and they still read each other's minds. They were in a hotel in San Francisco, and Carin was changing clothes to go out, pulling up her fawn jodhpurs, still stylish as ever but now brimming with confidence and self-possession. He introduced her to his nineteen-year-old daughter. "This is Carin," he said. "She was nineteen. I was twenty-eight. It was in London. We fell in love. It was magic. A little tragic, too." But it didn't register. Daughters have dreams of their own.

It took forty years, but finally going back to that annus mirabilis, those lonely and lovely months, those indelible days and nights, was for him a labor both troubling and rewarding. Researching the year of research, he discovered how memory glosses and elides events, how documents can prove recollections and reconstructions false, and how sometimes recollections still veto the proofs in the documents, in spite of all evidence to the contrary. The extant evidence, after all, was sketchy and *besmear'd with sluttish time*. In addition to just a handful of photographs, a few letters with foreign stamps and a single telegram, there were the failed attempts to tell the one story in various character sketches, fragments of fiction, abandoned memoirs, and even a surrealistic fable.

Against these caricatures, though, the journals bore shameless witness. He had kept these jottings doggedly if not meticulously as the year's experience unfolded. Each volume was bound in a different format and size. The last one, pocket-size, 3" x 5", for easy access, was covered in green-and-white marbled paper, handmade by IAN LOGAN ASSOCIATES LONDON, the price penciled in at £1.55, dated in his own hand in bleeding blue ink "Aberdeen/Edinburgh 24 June 1981 to Paris/København/Tirsted, Denmark 13 September 1981," and stuffed with slips of paper, hastily scribbled addresses, receipts for ferries and trains in several languages, and a salmon-pink advertisement for "Le Relais Internationale de la Jeunesse au Cap d'Antibes à 5 minutes de Juan-les-Pins." Even his rather inartistic sketches were included. But no photographs. Somehow he had the acuity to observe things keenly, in some cases minutely, and in any case in real or proximate time, so that these vivid prose sketches stood in for photographs.[106] His powers of observation were, like his sexual adventures, somewhat promiscuous and indiscriminate. He had not the wisdom of selection to know what would be most valuable later on in retrospect. Neither had he the wisdom to know what to do, ultimately, with all of this finely observed phenomena. Yet he gathered it, like a naturalist who might assemble and sort these specimens and identify the unfamiliar species, their patterns and relationships, later in his laboratory.

The tattered covers of the volumes, like his own complexion, had over time become battered and bumped with keratosis from too many California and Mediterranean beaches. They attested to the miles traveled in coat pockets and backpacks, and periods spent in storage and moving vans. The pages were a kind of second skin, stained and scarred with evidence of where they had been together, the bar tops and café tables where he had inked his impressions and depressions, ink that now ran with dirty haloes; the pages even emit-

---

[106] The following piece of doggerel (dis)graces the inside front cover, dated 13 Sept 81. "In London a philosopher stands on a box / Asking 'what are you looking for, what have you lost? / How come you keep searching for things that you're not / When you haven't got round to ask what you've forgotten?'/ Adding, 'why am I standing here talking to you / To make you see that, like you, I haven't a clue. / This oddball life I'm living is nothing so new / But I'm glad I'm not dead and I'm glad I'm not you." It was not exactly Byron's *Don Juan*, but it would have to do.

ted (intimated?) faint aromas of ancient tobacco and booze, sweat, sex and perfume. From these pages, concrete details emerged like melted gems from the volcanic ash of mere emotional spews (or were they better thought of as sarira, the bone fragments found among cremated remains of buddhas, to be treated as relics?). These volumes, nibbled at the edges in attics by small animals and large insects, provided the sometimes very raw material and proof for what had really happened, much of which he had forgotten. The notes and sketches of visits to art museums, the random portraits of people and places, the doodles of high artworks and low humor, the dates and addresses and telephone numbers and names (so many of which remained faceless, anonymous, if perfectly preserved, beneath the volcanic ash of time and forgetfulness)—all of these and more provided the documentary evidence he needed to reconstruct the past, and to correct the tricks of memory that had telescoped time, reordered sequences of events, elided what was uncomfortable, and erased his more egregious acts of cruelty, self-absorption, indulgence, and neglect.

The result was not photorealism, nor was it meant to be. It was not a shadow box to display the dust of the past but an elixir in which to preserve the magic of the moment so that it might be conjured in the future—or, more likely, exorcized so that he might return refreshed to the present and to embrace the here and now.

Revisiting the experience of his year in London turned out to be emotionally perilous. There were days when he felt a kind of "memoir sickness," the past rising up so vividly that he could taste and feel and hear with deceptive clarity, causing him to spend whole hours in an ecstasy of multisensory hallucinations, elated by recovering what he thought had been lost. These flashbacks would be followed by the hangover of heartache. The feeling of loss was real. He wrote with a feverish urgency to preserve what was left, to put it down on paper before it all dissolved before his eyes. He feared he would never finish the story, never get it right. He feared that his reconstructions would not do justice to the fragments, like those Minoan archaeological mistakes that imagined princes where only monkeys played. Then, as the one story took shape page after page, chapter after chapter, he feared that he *would* finish it—it would be a book, an object, dead, subject to critique—and that the living hallucinations would cease. Which would be worse? Losing that part of his life to the forgetfulness of Lethe or to the incapacities of Art? The past was seductive precisely because it was once real and was no longer, that it had happened to him and would never happen again to him—or ever to anyone else. That is what made it all so beautiful, so personal, so precise and so painful, like the phantom pain of a lost limb.[107]

At first, memory seemed much more real than what he was able to write. Then there came a time, a tipping point, when the writing became more substantial than the memories. Whether the writing had captured the historical reality of the events better than memory, or whether the writing had in the end convinced him that it had indeed happened that way, it didn't matter; the writing usurped memory and became reality.

For London itself he felt no nostalgia, oddly enough, even though he understood the sentiment expressed by John Cowper Powys for the city where, in his youth, Psyche and Eros merged: ". . . my quest for the magic that women alone can work endeared London for ever to me! In Paris I found pornography enough, enough to satisfy the trembling knees and the shaking fingers, but in London, always, always, I found poetry and romance!"[108] Although he would return for brief visits as a tourist or pass through on his way to more exotic locales, he never missed the city itself. It was an empty stage-set where other plays—*tragical-historical or tragical-comical-historical-pastoral*, whereas his own were all romantic—were now being performed. Not empty of new players, of course, but empty of the players he had known and therefore empty for him, except for the

---

[107] Of course, the excruciating truth was that the phantom pain of the lost limb of the past could arise whenever he vividly imagined any period—or moment—of his life (the setting didn't have to be London) when love or regret was part of the equation, especially when some concrete sensory detail sent him careening like a dropped camera into a deep pool. These moments and these reactions were not his alone—they are universal.

[108] *Autobiography* (Hamilton, NY: Colgate UP, 1968), 345.

ghosts. He never fetishized places once he left them, only some of the memories enacted there with other actors.

Occasionally, he would happen upon a literary reference that would light up the stage again, as when Gerald Brenan describes his Aunt Tiz's flat at 23 Ashley Place: "Once perhaps comfortable, it now presented the dreariest of aspects."[109] That was when Ashley Gardens was only some thirty or forty years old; another forty or fifty would pass before the hunter of hermaphrodites moved into the even more advanced once-comfortable dreariness of his makeshift student menagerie. Now, in 2024, still another forty or so years hence, the exterior retains its crisp red-and-white Victorian façade, but the interiors have been renovated and their real estate values (location, location) have redoubled into the millions.[110] The faded yellowish tobacco-smoke-stained walls of the shared flat at 214 will have been painted over, the threadbare carpets removed to reveal the intricately inlaid and newly refinished floors, and the barely serviceable kitchen of yore (where servants would have once been expected to *make do*) now updated with all the slick modern conveniences, waterfall stone countertops and stainless steel appliances. In his memory, however, its shabby sepia grandeur, circa 1980, remained timeless, as if preserved in amber.

For the next four decades he would be haunted by the single year he spent haunting Ashley Gardens. It was not the flat, nor the neighborhood, nor even the cityscape of London, that empty world-renowned and sometimes world-weary metropolis, that appeared like a stage-set in his imaginarium, not these so much as the apparitions of the long-gone players, their costumes and their dramas. As these ghosts appeared, beseeching at his desk to drink the revivifying blood of his memory, they told the truth as they had tasted it

---

[109] *Personal Record 1920–1972* (New York: Knopf, 1975), 137.

[110] John and Evelyn Dunwoody sold their two flats soon after I moved on, exchanging their perch in the center of London for a house in Clapham and an estate in the south of France. Each of their former flats is now worth in the neighborhood of £2,000,000.

in all its bittersweetness. Writing down what they dictated to him became an exorcism of sorts. Sometimes the ghosts, for the most part friendly, came to him in dreams, first Carin, then the others, one after another, like an epic catalog of heroines. They returned as they had been, in the freshness of youth, while he continued to age. It was ironic. He had always felt demeaned by the historicity of London. The persistence of things, he felt, rendered him less human as he caromed through its boulevards, mews, squares, and alleyways, mazes of age and agelessness. Now London, renovated and modernized, had become young yet again, while he only grew older, melting in the persistence of memory.

It was Carin, perhaps predictably, who haunted him first and most often. They had been inseparable and had so enmeshed all their senses (*dérangé tous les sens*, they said) that they were deeply etched into each other's sensorium. The result was a whole orchestra of synaesthetic memories not subject to decay over time. The movies they saw, the streets they walked, the foods they ate, the cigarettes they smoked, the alcohol they drank, and the music they listened to could still make him feel as though he were there again: "I'll stop the world and melt with you."[111] The documents reminded him of some important details that he had forgotten but should have remembered: that he was her first love; that in the throes of first love, she had clung to him like Salmacis and he had reacted in fear of losing his precious freedom; that he, thankless and self-absorbed, had treated her miserably.[112]

---

[111] This lyric by Modern English did not come out until 1982. Like his memory of Michael Chabon at Irvine and the Silk Cut ads, the anachronism did not intimidate his memory. It did not keep the song from becoming a belated anthem for their time together. Could it be that they saw Modern English perform it in a London club before it was recorded? Or was it simply a backformation memory? Maybe the woman from Toronto he had met in the shadow of Stirling Castle was right about music being the language of aliens, capable of being plucked from the atmosphere. Or was chronological time an illusion, after all, and only the writing—the reconstruction—real?

[112] Carin survived her first love and thrived in San Francisco and Los Angeles, where she married and had a daughter, took degrees in business and creative

* * *

He had balked at Carin's clinging, yet it only took a single night with Mhairi in the garden of Edinburgh for him to cry out like Salmacis, *Please, ye gods, let us be joined this way forever!* The wiser of the two, Mhairi made sure that they never saw each other again. Mhairi understood instinctively the lesson of Ovid's story. Complete fusion can only lead to disillusion. The myth is defiled by *too much* presence. When Salmacis begs the gods to unite her forever with Hermaphroditus, she loses herself and dooms him to remain a *semivir* (neither boy nor man, but only half-man). And so he was returned to the poem that had launched him on this quest, whose author concluded: "The sad and subtle moral of this myth, which I have desired to indicate in verse, is that perfection once attained on all sides is a thing thenceforward barren of use or fruit; whereas the divided beauty of separate man and woman—a thing inferior and imperfect—can serve all turns of life."[113] By returning to their separate lives, he and Mhairi might retain their individuality, proceed to the next adventure, or lover, reuniting endlessly, if only in their imaginations. He could, in short, grow up.

Yet Mhairi's wisdom was also a myth, based on a misperception and a wish. As soon as she was free from the Dutch Ben, she took up her pen and wrote to him in California again, their correspondence lasting for almost another year. She too dreamed (even if only intermittently in idle moments) of reuniting with him, sending letter after letter, describing her superficial affair with a coffee grower and how she longed to reignite their own more profound connection. A telegram to Balboa Island from Miselind, Zimbabwe, dated April 19, 1982, reads: "J'ATTEND TA VOIX. LOVE Mhairi." The only snap-

---

writing, worked in the fashion industry as a writer and college instructor, all with intermittent trips to her beloved London to treat the symptoms of her chronic case of transatlantica.

[113] A.C. Swinburne, *Notes on Poems and Reviews* (London: John Camden Hotten, 1866). Included in *Swinburne Replies*, edited by C.K. Hyder (Syracuse: Syracuse UP, 1966), 28.

shot he had of her was, aptly, a silhouette of her standing on an anonymous shore, the setting sun behind her, her facial features obscured, one finger pointing in the distance.

She was right, though. Knowing so little about one another allowed them to create each other in the image of what they wanted or needed. Perfect because incomplete. They never had the chance to drag each other from their pedestals or clouds. Their hermaphroditic bliss became sublimated into the "pure myth" that Marie Delcourt insisted was at the bottom of the dual-sexed figure and that inspired *this* young man at least to grope his way toward "his place in the world" and that symbolized "certain of his aspirations."[114] Unable to live out the permanent fusion in Ovid's story, and unable to manage a physical reunion à la Aristophanes, they settled for the spiritual fusion described by Diotima in Plato's *Symposium*, a union that transcended time because it did not rely on space.

Like twins separated at birth but who go on to live parallel lives, both he and Mhairi gravitated later in life to Buddhist practice. He had not remembered a prophetic paragraph in one of her first letters to him until he unearthed it four decades later, a mere speculative aside, which may have planted a seed in them both:

> *But even if I never saw you again (heaven forbid!) or heard from you (please, please write) I would carry something beautiful of you with me forever. I could devote the rest of my life to Buddhism or to saving the sick and dying—because of you.*

In Buddhist terms, their original affair could be described as entire in its *suchness*, the irreproducible here-and-now of it, precious not in spite of being transient but because it was transient. The same principle of *tathātā* could apply to the entire year of the hermaphrodite, and not only to Mhairi but to each of the women and to each of the loves, both those that fizzled and those that flared and caught

---

[114]Marie Delcourt, *Hermaphrodite: Myths and Rites of the Bisexual Figure in Classical Antiquity*, Trans. Jennifer Nicholson (London: Studio Books, 1961), xi.

fire, those that fell flat and those that were "like shining from shook foil."[115]

In his unique encounter with Mhairi, as in the Japanese tea ceremony, i*chi go ichi e:* we have only this one chance, this one meeting. Each moment is perfect in its imperfection. It was not just Mhairi, but it was Mhairi who made him see it. Each of his encounters, seen in this light, did not need to be part of a larger narrative, each shining, transparent, prismatic bead needed no artificial connecting thread. Each encounter made sense in itself, connecting him to the rest of the world, revealing momentarily that everything is interconnected forever. Every act, even every right sexual act, is the action of a buddha.[116] Nothing disappears, nothing perishes. This sense of ineluctable suchness allowed him to keep each love alive in its own being, for what it was in itself. Yet he persisted in framing his experience in some narrative or artistic form, instead of recognizing that its value was in its very ephemerality, its emptiness, what could not be grasped and held onto, represented, possessed or given shape. Thus he kept that July night in Edinburgh as a treasure and an inspiration. A sort of butsudan or personal altar, rarely opened but present nonetheless even in its closure. Perhaps Mhairi kept that night close to her core in some way as well. Not as some illusion or ideal of perfect love, certainly not, but as one experience of love, perfect of its kind.

Mhairi lived on in his heart as a model of grace and beauty, intelligence and idealism, engaged in making the world a better place by alleviating the suffering of others—devoting her life to "saving

---

[115]This line from Hopkins' "God's Grandeur," one of his favorites, suggests that there was always a religious dimension to the young man's quest, however cloaked in conscious atheism and aestheticism, even hedonism. He deeply believed, like Browning's sensualist monk Fra Lippo Lippi, "If you get simple beauty and naught else, / You get about the best thing God invents."

[116]Iharu Saikaku's *Life of an Amorous Woman* (1686) ends with the courtesan of the title seeing five hundred buddha statues in a shrine, and every one of them reminds her of the more than ten thousand men she has been sexually intimate with. This is her grand satori. (Trans. Ivan Morris. New York: New Directions, 1963; viz. 209.)

the sick and dying" in the spirit of Buddhist compassion as she presciently put it—while at the same time making room for her own ecstatic enjoyment of the moment, whether in the arms of a less than holy "holy-man" or a colonial coffee grower or the man who became her husband. In short, she went on to become not just a doctor in Africa, as her father had been, but one who works to save all beings in the world, although her early fugacious literary lover didn't have the word for it at the time, a true bodhisattva.

* * *

He also continued to write to Marianne in Copenhagen, and she to him, after he left her on the dock at Rødbyhavn. His letters, he was sure, were overwritten and romantic, as he tried to stretch the ligaments of language to o'erleap time and distance; he was glad he hadn't kept copies of these tortuous missives of his. Hers, however, were a perpetual delight, as her struggle with the always difficult language of love was compounded by the limitations of her English. She would compose them with dictionaries at her elbow and sometimes a friend more fluent in English by her side.

They made plans for her to visit, although she was conflicted about coming to the United Bluff. She fought against everything the U.S. stood for, but maybe, she rationalized, she could keep an open mind and talk to Americans and convince them there was a better way. ("If Americans are explained to, will they change?" "No, I don't think so." "Then it need something else.") In the end, she couldn't manage to get a visa; a registered communist who had recently been to Cuba: two red flags. The music school also turned out to be more expensive than she had planned, and other commitments to work and family arose. Life, in other words, got in the way, as they in fact suspected it would.

They kept the dream of their love alive for a few years, nurturing the fragile seedling that had taken root in the rich soil of those few weeks together and in those last days in Vester Tirsted. When he lectured at Swansea University in 1984–85, he wrote to Marianne from his sublet house on Terrace Road in the Uplands.[117] They resumed their plans to see each other, but they could never quite close that much narrowed gap in space, even as the gap in time continued to widen. Within a year or so after that, Marianne married another Claus and lived well and happily with her husband in the Danish fashion, dividing each year between Copenhagen in the winter and Dragør in the summer.

* * *

Then one day it struck him. The dreams of love and consummation, whether waking or sleeping dreams, held the key to his desire. But it was not the dreams of past lovers, real or imaginary, that held the key to his quest for the hermaphrodite. Nor was it the bizarre dream of Ann-Margret in the hayloft, although it opened a floodgate, shocking as that dream was to a boy in search of his own sexual identity. Nor was it the traumatic experience of being pursued by the Fifty-Foot Woman that had sent him on his quest to master his memory. No, it was actually the other originary dream, the one that he remembered as the most vivid of his life, when he was sixteen. He was a jester performing his masterpiece for all those women who were not supposed to look too closely lest they see the emptiness inside him when he removed his head for their entertainment—his head that came unscrewed as easily as the Buddha's on the plastic bottle of Jade East aftershave to release its fragrance.[118] (He should not have dismissed the relevance of that second footnote

---

[117] He was two years into his second marriage, already living apart from his wife, who was in her first year of law school in Philadelphia. This marriage too was not destined to last. Each of his three marriages occurred a decade apart: 1972, 1982, and (the charm that lasted) 1992.

[118] It would be another twenty years before he would be able to see the connection between his dream decapitation and the awareness of a profound change in consciousness, a connection coincidentally outlined in a strange little book by D. E. Harding called *On Having No Head: Zen and the Re-Discovery of the Obvious* (London: Routledge and Kegan Paul, 1961).

so cavalierly, as though it were a mere parenthesis, an aside. The dream was not about castration at all, he realized now, although castration could be reflected in its mirror image, genital supplementation. Nor should he have neglected to look into Mencius, not the London soapbox orator but the original one from China, who said, "A man whose mind is set on high ideals never forgets that he may end in a ditch; a man of valour never forgets that he may forfeit his head."[119]) The jester dream was really about the danger—and necessity—of revealing his true self, the empty vessel, the amusing yet terrifying abyss that awaited anyone who would look deeply into the emptiness there, an emptiness sometimes disguised as fullness, an incompleteness disguised as repletion, a silk cut disguised as texture, a wound disguised as a scar. It was also, in the end, about making sense of his experience, no matter how disagreeable the conclusions.[120]

Hadn't he glimpsed this truth sitting for Laury in the studio at the edge of London Fields? Wasn't this precisely what he was doing by writing the story of his year in search of the hermaphrodite, removing the thinking, analytical, scholarly brain so that he could gaze inside to find the body-brain, the unconscious two-fold hermaphroditic coniunctio oppositorum (symbol of all paradox and contradiction, forever unresolved) that can only be found within? Wasn't that his real magic trick, his one story? The road on the way to the dissertation, not the dissertation itself, was his real education, however incomplete; his real masterwork, however flawed, was himself. It was not a unique discovery, since we are all our own masterworks, nor was it particularly profound: but it was *his* discovery, his own. If one was really in search of oneself, whatever that might be, fullness and superfluity were not the answer at all; it was lack

---

[119] *Mencius*, trans. D. C. Lau (London: Penguin, 1970), 157.

[120] "The moment when a man's head drops off is seldom or never, I am inclined to think, precisely the most agreeable of his life. Nevertheless, like the greater part of our misfortunes, even so serious a contingency brings its remedy and consolation with it, if the sufferer will but make the best, rather than the worst, of the accident which has befallen him." Nathaniel Hawthorne, *The Scarlet Letter*.

and absence and vacancy—and emptiness—that held the key, the echo of silence. It was the vast difference between the library and the meditation hall.

18 / Postscript: Epipsychidion

> If day should part us night will mend division
> And if sleep parts us—we will meet in vision
> And if life parts us—we will mix in death.
> —Shelley, "Fragments Connected with Epipsychidion"

At the liminal borders of consciousness just before waking or while falling asleep, Marianne and he sometimes shared a lingering moment of *lysglimt*, communicating without the burden of either physical presence or language.[121] It was always Marianne or Carin in his dreams, it seemed. Mhairi never came to him in dreams, being already a dream unrepeatable.[122] The others—Concha, Stacie, Char-

---

[121] This is not to claim that the communication was literal or mutual, much less simultaneous. It may well be that such communication was not just asynchronous but unilateral and wholly imaginary on his part. A mirage, a hallucination, a fantasy, an illusion that belonged to him only: a reverie, a dream, an arrogation if not an arrogance. He did not flatter himself that his significance for her matched hers for him.

[122] In her own waking life, of course, Mhairi was no dream. She no doubt married and had children and did good bodhisattva work in a place on the other side of the world, far from the northern latitudes of reekie Scotland, until she might reach the age to retire, putting away syringe and stethoscope. She must have looked back once or twice, he felt sure, with amusement on that bold, impulsive, imprudent self, the young medical student throwing herself into bed with a myth and who might still be glimpsed in the mirrored glimmer of her clear blue eyes.

lotte, Roxanne, Eileen, Caroline, Hillarie, Lucias-as-you-like, those with no name that he knew of, and even Mnemosyne, surprisingly —appeared in dreams infrequently or not at all. Posing no dilemma for him to work out in his unconscious, they were uncomplicated and thus un-hermaphroditic in that sense. Tennyson's Ulysses said, "I am a part of all that I have met." It was more true that all whom he had met were a part of *him*.

They took up residence instead as part of his conscious memory, a portrait gallery of his history, a permanent exhibition, each framed in the aura of her own rarity, luminous in her individuality. His late duchesses, if you like, although he had no desire to stop their smiles. Neither had he any desire to improve on them, complete and unique as they were. Nor did he understand the impulse of some men to pick and choose this or that physical or personality trait, since every element was necessary for the whole. God forbid that he deprive Roxanne of her white go-go boots or her dimpled knees, or Eileen of her ennui. Gerald Brenan perceived a gaggle of girls in the Almería paseo as a group portrait from which he selected parts to create a separate Frankenstein beauty: "Although individually few of them, I fancy, were particularly pretty," he writes, "by taking here a nose, there a neck and there a head of glistening, cascading hair, one made up a collective picture that dazzled."[123] No, such dissection and selection was blasphemy, a kind of vivisection indeed. Brenan was wrong: there were no flaws in their design, only in his perception. Herrick's "Delight in Disorder" comes to mind. Although Herrick focuses on the woman's apparel—"erring lace" and "cuff neglectful"—these are only metonymic cover for the moral aesthetic of her mortal dress. In either case, a sweet disorder kindled in him a wantonness "more than when art / Is too precise in every part." Each woman—whether held or beheld, loved or beloved—was *sui generis*, her imperfections, asymmetries, even her neuroses, essential to the design, *sub specie aeternitatis*.

---

[123] *South of Granada: A Sojourn in Southern Spain* (New York: Farrar, Straus, & Cudahy, 1957), 215.

* * *

I did not come here for your amusement. Then why did you come? Some might object that I (or rather "he"—I must keep up the third-person persona to the end, having indulged myself too much already in this fiction of a "first person," a supposed self who pretends to grasp the past) could not possibly have fallen in love—not "real" love—so rapidly with such an array of women in such a short period of time.[124] He himself for many years remained in disbelief at such plenty. It might be supposed that his succession of affairs was only a spate of conquests, superficial dalliances, a serial indulgence. No doubt he was changeable, fickle, disloyal to those he declared he loved—indeed disloyal to himself, simply because he had no idea of who he was, what he was capable of. He was young. He was, to himself, an experiment to see how far he would go. Love, after all, is one test after another that few of us pass with flying colors on our first tests, much less our final exams. These experiences left marks on his character that would scar him like the initials inside hearts carved in the bark of a tree: they would never go away. He did not flatter himself that the women were equally scarred, not believing himself

---

[124] One might also wonder about his relationships with men, who figure conspicuously little in this narrative. Close friendships with men his own age were few and far between both before and after his year in London. Most men his own age were vague acquaintances, like his roommate Eric, or Mike who was passing through London, or Jarod from Mill Valley whom he met in Cap d'Antibes, or even Francis in Tangier. He gravitated toward those ephemeral elders who had some brief lesson to teach him, mentors, professors, kif-smoking prose stylists, the Mencius of Hyde Park Corner. The exception was Laury, with whom he kept in contact for the remainder of the 1980s before they finally lost touch, with brief encounters in New York, Venice Beach, and New Orleans when one or the other was attending a conference or traveling on museum business. Laury never became a famous painter but worked in several New York art galleries, including Tibor de Nagy on Fifth Avenue before becoming a museum curator, first for the Natural History Museum and then for the Holocaust Museum in Washington DC. Nota bene: Never once did our traveler dream of any of these male friends turning into a woman so that he could suckle at their breast, as Siddhartha did at his friend Govinda's. A pity: it would have suited the theme of the book so well.

capable of leaving an indelible impression. Perhaps he was wrong, though; perhaps that was all false modesty, protection, a pose. *If he wasn't remembered, he wasn't culpable.*

Only his immaturity and romanticism, some will say, could have turned the most random of these sordid couplings into some form of love. But what was "real" love, exactly? Wasn't love, after all, always an experiment, an accident, more or less, a fortunate fall, a slip on a banana peel of fate? One's "destiny" being how one recovered from the slip, improvising with a tragic or comic pratfall? (And what of the kind of love that lasts? The kind that calls for commitment through thick and thin and staying together even after the romance pales? He would come to know that kind of love, too, eventually, but that is yet another "one" story.)

A good therapist might have something to say about his sexual history and the "family friend" with the DayGlo orange lipstick and the insatiable sexual appetite who seduced him at fifteen. Nowadays her "gift" to him (for that's how he thought of it then) would be called sexual assault and she would be arrested and required to register, like Desmond Hogan, as a sex offender. In 1967 (it was after all famously known around the world as the "Summer of Love") her indiscretion would have been seen as something more like contributing to the delinquency of a minor, a misdemeanor, less a crime than a moral weakness, if not the basis for a hit movie (here's to you, Mrs. Robinson), perhaps even a sickness, something to be pitied: addictive arousal, pathological nymphomania, lust. Indeed, a good therapist might well see his sexual history too as pathological if not pathetic, and not unconnected to hers. Is promiscuity a communicable condition? Or is it simply something that goes in and out of fashion, from Pagans to Puritans, from Libertines to Victorians, from the Frustrated Fifties to the Sexual Revolution of the Sixties? He would have liked to have asked the Wilmots and LaVeys throughout history, whether in their opinion their dangerous liaisons had been inspired by natural inclination or supernatural intervention, and whether it had been worth it after all. It can hardly be denied that pleasure is addictive, and once tasted can be a powerful drug, as Mhairi confessed. When the biological urgencies awaken with a magic touch and the neurotransmitter dopamine kicks in at an impressionable age, especially when mixed with bubbly romantic notions from centuries of poetry and prose (oxytocin), and stiffened with intellectual pretensions (vasopressin), it can result in a heady, even lethal cocktail. (*Madame Bovary, c'est moi.*) But we leave these questions of mental illness and chemical cocktails, morality and lovemaking, to the therapists and biochemists, philosophers and novelists. Our task here has been merely to tell this young man's "one story."

Still, the question remains, what drove him to this brief but intense spree of entanglements? It would depend on whom you ask. Was it an unresolved homosexual restlessness (according to Concha), an immature and decadent cerebral lechery (according to old A. J. L. Busst), an incapacity to commit (according to Stacie), an extraordinary ability to give of himself (according to Mhairi), perhaps just a typical capitalist acquisitiveness (according to Marianne), an aporia not as deep as it was wide, both bottomless and shallow (according to Mnemosyne), or an insatiable desire to rack up conquests, exploring new stars in his constellation (according to Evelyn)? Or, more likely, would they all just register shock at the shamelessness of his indiscretions and outrage at the extent of his infidelities?

He only knew that this constellation of Hesperides was not exactly a Milky Way, composed as it was of only those few who in some way once entered into him and inhabited him still, not simply in memory but in his very being. Not as imaginary lovers, like Herrick's Julias, Corinnas and Lucias, but as in some way his living complements, his other halves, the true twin siblings of Hypnos, Oneirei, and Thanatos. Just as all lovers, when exiled to the underworld of memory, are the inhabitants of Sleep, Dreams, and Death. In spite of an abundance of theories, the fundamental questions remained.

I did not come here for your amusement. Then why did you come?

* * *

As for Mnemosyne, he and she lived in the same Southern city for over twenty years and never ran into each other, nor attempted to make contact. Hadn't Plato's half-hermaphrodites, once severed, never ceased trying to reunite? Such desire might have an expiration date. Or maybe their union, so perfect for a time (so imperfect over time), was all an illusion. She would no doubt have some credible interpretation to offer, having become a successful literary theorist and psychoanalyst, and thus he could be pinned and tagged with some precise terminology like *erotic displacement*. He never got the chance to ask.[125]

Illusions are endless; I vow to drop them all.[126]

Why was it that he wondered less about Mnemosyne, who had been such a vital part of his life, than about some of the others, those decadent interludes, Roxanne and Eileen, for example, whom he had known in only the most superficial way, or the sex worker with the precision-tool hands in Trompetter Straat, or the short-haired blonde in Haarlem who was so sure they would meet again (and never did)? Did Roxanne ever take up the "secretarial" duties for that businessman in the City in exchange for a maisonette? Or did she go back to modeling for toady little men and lucrative weekends in Lagos or Abuja? And what about Eileen of Éire with her profound ennui? Assuming she did not succumb to the brutal embraces of some Aussie beastie, did she ever manage to overcome her existential crises among her tribe of birds? Or the other women he met in Rumours or Maxwell's or Oliver's or Tutton's or the Venue or Evelyn's mansion flat that year? Which of them survived these forty years?

Then he remembered, glancing in the candid mirror, that no

---

[125] A word about his mother, which might assist in any psychoanalytical reading. He suspected that his mother's womb had been a comfortable waiting room in which to be unconscious before the *trauma of birth*. When he read Otto Rank's book of that title in high school (the American edition was published in 1952, the year of his own birth trauma), it made sense to him, although of course he had no memory of the event. Rank itemizes the outcomes of the shock of that first, unfair separation; the resulting anxiety due to the smothering confinement in the birth canal; even the refusal to admit differences between the sexes; infantile erethism; oedipal scenarios; and fear of castration.

[126] The second of the four bodhisattva vows.

one survives time and age, the great levelers that level some more quickly, completely, and cruelly than others.[127]
Beings are innumerable, I vow to save them all.[128]

*   *   *

Soon after he lost touch with her, Stacie worked as a stylist on cruise ships to the Caribbean and saw a bit of the world, no doubt dropping more quickly than he would have liked—no one likes being a mere means to an end—the idea of marrying a poor American graduate student into the azure waters of the islands where it belonged. Eventually she opened a business with her mother, who moved to the Bahamas, although Bahamian residency evaded the daughter of the ex-beauty queen. Their London shop specialized in antique and collectible dolls and teddy bears. He could envision her at sixty, her trendy days as a West End hair stylist behind her, all her gay colleagues from Hebe, the salon, dead of AIDS. Still attractive in a matronly, pillowy way, the bright but not too intellectual girl waves hello from inside the Halloween fancy dress of age, that bloated and wrinkled costume, trapped by time and the faded glamor of her still oppressive and overbearing mother.[129]

---

[127] I am struck now, writing in a time of pestilence and war (2020-24), how insulated from mortality he was during the years depicted here (1980-82), when he hardly recognized that the Fauré "Elegy" he heard with such pleasure in the Holywell Music Room at Oxford was about death at all! Everything was—to him at this period—all about the *in medias res* of life here and now, hedonistic in the best and worst senses of the word, not recollected or reflected. Even though his grandfather Jesse Tannehill died during this time, he did not return for the funeral. This might account for his superstitious attachment to his grandfather's Stetson, and, in another sense of grieving, to the North Face backpack that Mnemosyne had bequeathed to him.

[128] The first of the four bodhisattva vows.

[129] In a YouTube video interview at their booth in an international doll fair, Stacie and her mother appear together with all of the ambivalent mother-daughter dynamic still in play. Stacie: "I love my Mum but I love dolls more." Her mother: "Ha ha, not true. In fact, when she was a little girl, she didn't like my dolls; she said I gave them too much time."

He resisted the temptation to look them all up on the Internet. Yet all he had to work with for most of them was a first name and a hair color, a nationality, an attitude, a scent or an accent, a turn of phrase or a toss of the head, and the memory of the curve of a waist that would be no longer slim. (Imagine looking for that needle Eileen in the haystack of Ireland!) Not the sort of keywords or phrases you can feed into a search engine, which did not exist in the year of the hermaphrodite. What if it had? If it had, he would have hunted hermaphrodites online instead of in the flesh and might never have left his study, much less the country. He would have been much more efficient professionally and much less enriched personally.[130]

The dawn of the 1980s saw the twilight of the pre-digital era. But it was not just the coming omnipresence of the worldwide web that loomed on the horizon. This was before AIDS, before twenty-four-hour news cycles, before the European Union and Brexit, and before the advent of perpetual international terrorism and perpetual social media taunting. There were more borders then, but they were also more porous. The occasional IRA bomb never leveled a pair of skyscrapers. Pesetas and francs and drachmas and guilders had not yet become euros. Casual sex was not such a high-risk venture. Sex and cigarettes were less demonized. Those who might be alarmed by the erotic spontaneity of the time, what may seem now to be insouciant promiscuity and risky coupling, should recall that the first cases of AIDS were reported in San Francisco on 5 June 1981, the night he met Stacie, as his year in London was beginning to wind down. There was less information but more privacy. Less universal connection but perhaps also more intimacy. Fewer options but more freedom. Less fear and intolerance. People wrote letters on paper as transparent as moth wings and sent them by airmail, with the resultant lag in matters of business and romance providing everyone with an interval of time to ponder what they had or had not said or done,

---

[130] On the other hand, the existence of the Internet now allows the reader to find almost every work of art and literature mentioned in this memoir, putting the riches of the world's museums and libraries are at everyone's fingertips.

what they might or might not say or do. Nor was there a hint of the great coronavirus pandemic to come, during which this memoir was largely written. And the much-needed #MeToo movement had yet to make strides to differentiate between equal sexual freedom and male sexual predation.[131]

It was, in short, a time of relative innocence and security, however brief, tenuous and illusory. The past of forty years ago was not just another country; it was another world.

* * *

And what became of his search for the hermaphrodite?

The question itself was faulty because there was not one hermaphrodite to be discovered in the art and literature of the past but many. And in all of these he found his own reflection.

It all began with the Metaphysical Hermaphrodite of countless origin myths and the religions that blossomed from them, personifications of primal forces in the form of titans and gods, eventually devolving into the effeminate demigods of the Hellenistic sculptors and their revival by the Renaissance sculptors who rediscovered the Plato of the *Symposium*. This is the hermaphrodite not only of the alchemists but of Blake and Shelley and all those who made a distinction between hermaphroditic conflict and androgynous harmony.

Then there was the Ironic Hermaphrodite, a rhetorical figure, that said two things at once, self-contradictory, often humorous, always paradoxical, the hermaphrodite of Beardsley and Wilde and their descendants, like Allen Jones and Pauline Boty and other British Pop Artists, as well as that late discovery in Amsterdam, like a revelation, the disturbing painter Melle, whose hallucinatory land-

---

[131] A not entirely irrelevant aside: it was widely reported in 2020 that Jessica Mann, one of convicted rapist Harvey Weinstein's victims, testified in his trial: "The first time I saw him fully naked, I felt, I thought he was deformed and intersex. He has extreme scarring that I didn't know if maybe he was a burn victim. He does not have testicles and it appears like he has a vagina."

scapes were reminiscent of Bosch, populated with an apocalypse of biological confusion.

And finally the Erotic Hermaphrodite of Ovid, whose rapes and transformations translated the myths of the past in ways that could be taken up again and again in the future, as shown by Bataille and the better surrealists, Breton and Cocteau, as well as the Pre-Raphaelites, a dream-marriage of opposites that spurred the imagination of Gautier and the French Decadents, a symbol of fertility excavated from the subconscious of the past, as well as a warning about the perfection of "the waste wedlock of a sterile kiss," as Swinburne put it.

But these were mere academic distinctions, somewhat satisfying intellectually, yet lacking in terms of some deeper personal meaning.

The answer was perhaps more simple in the end. The hermaphrodite wasn't like some lost manuscript or Maltese Falcon. Nor even like a misplaced memory which might be brought back to mind, data retrieved. It wasn't an object at all; it was an *obscure object of desire*. What he had been looking for was not to be found in the world. Numberless representations in art and literature could point to it but not capture it because desire-and-its-fulfillment cannot be represented. (Of course, heaven and nirvana are two attempts to represent this impossibility, just as God, according to some, is an attempt to represent the impossible conjunction of pure objectivity and pure subjectivity, of fathomless past and endless future, of omnipresence and absolute emptiness.) To be sure, there had been in literature, art, philosophy, and religion abundant attempts to express this concept, to evoke it, but none wholly satisfied. The hermaphrodite, it turned out, with all its contradictions and paradoxes, could only be glimpsed within. It had in fact, in the end, surprisingly little to do with gender, or even sex, which functioned only as clumsy metaphors for something more fundamental, a longing for the end of a congenital estrangement. In his foreword to MacDonald Harris's *Herma*, Michael Chabon tried to put his finger on the secret of his mentor's writing, saying that "isolation and yearning

[. . .] make freaks not just of minotaurs, writers and hermaphrodites, but of us all."[132]

Perhaps it is all much simpler than that and devolves on that old romantic impulse to make sense of one's life, especially as it manifests itself in oppositions and contradictions; to make sense of one's unique, integral, historical self, with all of its fragments and figmentations. Emmanuel Levinas described Aristophanes' myth simply as "a return to self. The enjoyment justifies this interpretation. It brings into relief the ambiguity of an event situated at the limit of immanence and transcendence." The erotic equivocation is its own argument, where "this simultaneity of need and desire, of concupiscence and transcendence, tangency of the avowable and the unavowable, constitutes the originality of the erotic, which, in this sense, is the equivocal par excellence."[133] What else is the hermaphrodite but the *equivocal par excellence*? What began in ambiguity ended in uncertainty, a variety of interpretations *equally voiced*, an enigmatic lifting of the peplos, a simultaneous erotic come-hither-and-begone. Not a promising start for a thesis, much less a satisfactory conclusion for a dissertation.

He had found in Dante Gabriel Rossetti's poetry and painting intimations of immortality, erotic moments that touch the eternal. Bereavement at the loss of the loved one, thus entombed, causes her to become part of oneself, enshrined there and unaging, even as the host withers in decline. He had written in his dissertation about how Rossetti was always in search of "a transcendent union, an hermaphroditic hierogamy capable of outlasting worldly couplings of man and woman." But in the end, somewhat prophetically, he had to conclude: "the poet is left with the obdurate silence of nature and irrevocable Time which leaves only the remnants of memory, desperate attempts at recovery, hallucinations of sights and sounds [and all the other sensory impressions: above all, *touch*] he once

---

[132] Foreword to *Herma* (New York: Overlook, 2015), xiv.
[133] Emmanuel Levinas, *Totality and Infinity: An Essay on Exteriority*. Trans. Alphonso Lingus (Pittsburgh: Duquesne UP, 1969), 254, 255.

knew."[134] He had himself glimpsed this erotic intersection of "immanence and transcendence," both in the psychic union that takes root in one another's consciousness and which can last a lifetime (or forty years, at least), and in the brief speeding up and slowing down of eternity when the sexual union of two beings merge completely for a moment in time, as in the imagined coitus of angels. Once joined in the eternal now, such a coupling can never really be separated.

The result was not immortality but rather what Georges Bataille called vice: a profound experience of mortality as erotic erasure. "The basis of sexual effusion is the negation of the isolation of the ego which only experiences ecstasy by exceeding itself, by surpassing itself in the embrace in which the being loses its solitude. Whether it is a matter of pure eroticism (love-passion) or of bodily sensuality, the intensity increases to the point where destruction, the death of the being, becomes apparent. What we call vice is based on this profound implication of death."[135] Immortality was what the medieval alchemists had fruitlessly hoped to find in the philosopher's stone, the coniunctio oppositorum, symbolized by the hermaphrodite. But the paradox could not be embraced, as Salmacis embraced Hermaphroditus; it was too slippery, it could not be sustained except in the shadows of myth and submerged in the pool of memory. But isn't this the tragedy and yet also the saving grace of love? That it can't last and yet that it does. Mutability itself, mortality itself, makes it all worthwhile. Love and all that messy, fleshy desire. But not desire alone, not the eternal Keatsian deferral depicted on some funereal urn, which can indeed last forever, but rather the desire that is consummated so that one's essence spills out not just in whimpers and whispers but in spit and semen, shared oils and sometimes traces of blood, so that all the senses are engaged—and deranged—indeed.

His obsession with sexual union continued for many years,

---

[134] Richard Collins, *"A Toy of Double Shape": The Hermaphrodite as Art and Literature*. University of California Irvine. PhD dissertation. 1984. 193, 192.

[135] Georges Bataille, *Literature and Evil*. Trans. Alastair Hamilton. (London: Calder & Boyars, 1973), 4.

taking on an almost religious character, he posing as its priest and proselytizer. It could be that he envied Saint Teresa's religious ecstasy. Her total abandonment of self, penetrated by a shaft of God's light, was the closest thing to the abandonment he felt in those rare moments when the sexual act emptied the self into all existences, or, as with Teresa, into God.[136] Then, he felt, once the self was emptied, all existences entered the self like a shaft of light. Like all religious experiences and movements, however, after its first flourishing his devotion devolved into decadence and doubt, mere preaching and posturing.[137] Even sexual union, once a sacred rite, became a coarse caricature—*caritas* devolved into *cupiditas*, gentle *agape* into raging *eros*—a literalization, a degradation, just as the literal hermaphrodite caricatured the androgynous ideal.

The myth of the hermaphrodite, too, was defiled by his presence.

> *The Twofold form Hermaphroditic: and the Double-sexed:*
> *The Female-male & the Male-female, self-dividing stood*
> *Before him in their beauty, & in cruelties of holiness.*
> —Blake, *Milton: a Poem*, Plate 19

Or it might be better to say that he had, from familiarity, exorcized that chimera of an idealistic youth and seen it mature into the paradox of a still optimistic skepticism. The search for the hermaphrodite, that perfect fusion of male and female, may have been illusory, but the imperfect permutations and combinations of male and female in an effort to achieve that perfection were justification enough for the pursuit of a paradoxical and, in the end, elusive unholy grail.

Don Juan turned out, after all, to be just another Don Quixote.

---

[136] It is not surprising, perhaps, that it was the same artist, Bernini, who sculpted the divine *Ecstasy or Transverberation of Saint Teresa* in the Cornaro Chapel, Santa Maria della Vittoria, Rome, and the decadent buttoned mattress on which the Borghese *Hermaphrodite endormi* lies in the Louvre.

[137] "... a new age had come, laughter scarcer, ... and pleasure in the hands of glutton, not artist." Desmond Hogan, *The Leaves on Gray* (London: Hamish Hamilton, 1980), 73.

* * *

He eventually finished the dissertation and abandoned his search for the hermaphrodite, although perhaps he really just exchanged the search for one paradox for the search for others in endless displacements of duality.

His first wife and he never reconciled but divorced amicably after a brief period of confidences shared in friendship. Their daughter grew up beautifully to become a college professor and researcher. A second marriage followed, with additional travels and infidelities that took him to Wales and Mexico. Then a third marriage, the charm, that has lasted for more than three decades instead of just one like the others. After wandering for several years in Greece, Romania, and Bulgaria, they settled for a time in New Orleans, where he went on to discover other, more profound enigmas than those to be found in the excesses of love and the ecstasies of sex.

Dharma gates are endless; I vow to penetrate them all.
The Buddha Way is unfathomable; I vow to follow through.[138]

These new territories of duplicity (in both its modern and its archaic sense) were indeed endless; he vowed to explore them all, like so many peakless mountains and shoreless rivers:[139] the love of family, the pleasures of balance, the realm of memory, the paradox of no self, the being of time, and the texture of emptiness.

---

[138] The third and fourth of the four bodhisattva vows.

[139] A reference to the name of the New Orleans Zen Temple—Muhozan Kozenji, Peakless Mountain Shoreless River Temple, where he became a monk and then abbot.

About the Author

Richard Collins was born in Oregon and grew up in Southern California, earning degrees from the University of Oregon and the University of California, Irvine. He has taught at universities in the U.S., Wales, Romania, and Bulgaria, and is Dean Emeritus of Arts and Humanities at California State University, Bakersfield. His critical essays cover a range of authors from Wilkie Collins and Ronald Firbank to Yannis Ritsos and Lafcadio Hearn, James Merrill and Andrei Codrescu. His poetry and creative nonfiction appear in dozens of literary magazines. His books include translations from the French, as well as *John Fante: A Literary Portrait* (Guernica Editions) and *No Fear Zen: Discovering Balance in an Unbalanced World* (Hohm Press). An ordained Zen monk, he is abbot of the New Orleans Zen Temple and Stone Nest Dojo in Sewanee, Tennessee, where he lives with his wife and two dogs.

Acknowledgments

Thanks to the following for their generous financial support, which helped to defray some of this publication's production costs:

Matthew A, Dominic Ambrose (domnul X),
American Zen Association, David Andrews,
Thomas Young Barmore Jr, Nick Barry, Melissa Beck,
Sam Bertram, Brian R. Boisvert, Bonriguez, Megan Bottorff,
Rose Bratcher, Lee Broadmore, Michael Broder, C M Capolongo,
Andrew B Carper, Scott Chiddister, Greg Cobb, Seth Coblentz,
Eric L. Collette, Henry M. Cook, April Coupel,
Parker & Malcolm Curtis, Robert Dallas, James Denestan,
Joshua Doughty, Craig Duckett, Tim Duning, Echo, R. Eggleton,
Isaac Ehrlich, Frederick Filios, Sinnaka Elena Fitzgerald,
Davidson Garrett, E Gaustad, GMarkC, Nicholas J Godi,
B F Gordon Jr, Jason Gray, Kate Gundersen, David Guy,
Everett Haagsma, Bill Harper, Barbara Hart, Michael Harville,
J. Holmes, Karla Huebner, Conor Hultman, Brian Jagodzinski,
Fred W Johnson, Jacob H Joseph, P Kinahan, Sergey Kochergan,
Douglas Lang, Les Deux Helenes, J.Ed. Marston, Jack Mearns,
Jim McElroy, Donald McGowan, Ken McLaughlin,
Kelly McMahon, Ardell Miller, Jason H Miller,
Spencer F Montgomery, Scott Murphy, Clyde Nads,
Melinda R. Nelson, Alexander Nirenberg, Richard Novak,

Leonid Okneanski, Michael O'Shaughnessy, Trevor Owens,
Ivan Pančić, Luis Panini, Andrew Pearson, Judith Redding,
Hobbie Koban Regan, Regina Sara Ryan, Lana Matthews Sain,
Frank V Saltarelli, David W. Sanderson, Robert Savage,
Florian Schiffmann, K. Seifried, Skye Sisk, Yvonne Solomon,
K. L. Stokes, David Streitfeld, Michelle Thibodeaux,
Ted Travelstead, John Verlenden, Jing Jing Wang,
Margaret Waring, Elizabeth Weitzman, Isaiah Whisner,
Charles Wilkins, T.R. Wolfe, Jalan Woodward, Dale Worsley,
the Zemenides Family, and Anonymous

www.ingramcontent.com/pod-product-compliance
Lightning Source LLC
LaVergne TN
LVHW061540070526
838199LV00077B/6855